CAMBRIDGE LIBRARY COLLECTION

Books of enduring scholarly value

Polar Exploration

This series includes accounts, by eye-witnesses and contemporaries, of early expeditions to the Arctic and the Antarctic. Huge resources were invested in such endeavours, particularly the search for the North-West Passage, which, if successful, promised enormous strategic and commercial rewards. Cartographers and scientists travelled with many of the expeditions, and their work made important contributions to earth sciences, climatology, botany and zoology. They also brought back anthropological information about the indigenous peoples of the Arctic region and the southern fringes of the American continent. The series further includes dramatic and poignant accounts of the harsh realities of working in extreme conditions and utter isolation in bygone centuries.

The Life of Sir Albert Hastings Markham

This biography of the naval officer and explorer Sir Albert Hastings Markham (1841–1918) was published in 1927 by two relatives (both professional authors), using the detailed journals which he kept from 1862. Markham was the cousin of Sir Clements Markham, the historian and geographer, and was greatly influenced by him. Having volunteered for Arctic service, he was rejected by the Admiralty, but took a period of leave in which he went to Baffin Bay as second mate on a whaler. (His account of this voyage, and several other works, are also reissued in this series.) Though best remembered for his Arctic exploration, Markham was involved in active service in China, the Mediterranean and Australian waters, and in the training of naval recruits. He continued in the Royal Navy until 1906, and in his retirement continued to encourage polar exploration, serving for many years on the Council of the Royal Geographical Society.

T0370610

Cambridge University Press has long been a pioneer in the reissuing of out-of-print titles from its own backlist, producing digital reprints of books that are still sought after by scholars and students but could not be reprinted economically using traditional technology. The Cambridge Library Collection extends this activity to a wider range of books which are still of importance to researchers and professionals, either for the source material they contain, or as landmarks in the history of their academic discipline.

Drawing from the world-renowned collections in the Cambridge University Library and other partner libraries, and guided by the advice of experts in each subject area, Cambridge University Press is using state-of-the-art scanning machines in its own Printing House to capture the content of each book selected for inclusion. The files are processed to give a consistently clear, crisp image, and the books finished to the high quality standard for which the Press is recognised around the world. The latest print-on-demand technology ensures that the books will remain available indefinitely, and that orders for single or multiple copies can quickly be supplied.

The Cambridge Library Collection brings back to life books of enduring scholarly value (including out-of-copyright works originally issued by other publishers) across a wide range of disciplines in the humanities and social sciences and in science and technology.

The Life of
Sir Albert Hastings Markham

M.E. MARKHAM
F.A. MARKHAM

CAMBRIDGE
UNIVERSITY PRESS

CAMBRIDGE
UNIVERSITY PRESS

University Printing House, Cambridge, CB2 8BS, United Kingdom

Cambridge University Press is part of the University of Cambridge.

It furthers the University's mission by disseminating knowledge in the pursuit of
education, learning and research at the highest international levels of excellence.

www.cambridge.org
Information on this title: www.cambridge.org/9781108071673

This edition first published 1927
This digitally printed version 2014

ISBN 978-1-108-07167-3 Paperback

THE LIFE OF
SIR ALBERT HASTINGS MARKHAM

CAMBRIDGE

UNIVERSITY PRESS

LONDON : Fetter Lane

NEW YORK
The Macmillan Co.

BOMBAY, CALCUTTA and MADRAS
Macmillan and Co., Ltd.

TORONTO
The Macmillan Co. of Canada, Ltd.

TOKYO
Maruzen-Kabushiki-Kaisha

SIR ALBERT HASTINGS MARKHAM
(*From a portrait by* George Henry)

THE LIFE OF
SIR ALBERT HASTINGS MARKHAM

by

M. E. AND F. A. MARKHAM

CAMBRIDGE
AT THE UNIVERSITY PRESS
1927

AUTHORS' PREFACE

It was with extreme diffidence, almost amounting to reluctance, that we consented to write this biography of Sir Albert Markham—reluctance, not because we were in any way averse from the task which has been throughout a labour of love, but because we felt that it should have been undertaken by more competent hands, perhaps by a brother officer in the great Service to which he was devoted.

But since there appeared to be no one at the time to do it, for the aftermath of the War was still hanging as a cloud over the country, we could only accede, feeling at least there were not many living who had known him so long or so intimately as ourselves, or who could have written with such a close knowledge and deep personal love. While the outside world recognised the charm of his courtesy and bright personality and saw in him a keen officer and an intrepid explorer, we, who knew him well, have an abiding memory of his unselfish sympathy and great tenderness of heart.

His early life was not altogether easy to piece together. We had at our disposal only some letters, none of his own; the recollections of his cousin Mrs Clements; and the remembrance of a few incidents related to us by himself.

For the first years of his Naval career there were only his neatly kept log-books, in no sense a journal, and some notes made a good many years ago at his daughter's request.

From the time he was a lieutenant he always kept a voluminous journal, not only when on active service, but during the various expeditions made when on leave. It was no easy matter amid a mass of such interesting material to make such a selection as to bring it within the limits of the present volume, and much has had, perforce, to be omitted.

We are greatly indebted to Admiral Sir Edward Inglefield, K.C.B., for his kindness in reading through the MS. and for his invaluable assistance in the technicalities of Ch. XVI.

We are also most grateful for the help given to us by Dr Guillemard of Cambridge, without whose warm and practical interest this book might never have appeared, and to whom we are also indebted for the admirable Index.

M. E. AND F. A. MARKHAM

REIGATE
October, 1926

CONTENTS

ILLUSTRATIONS

PLATES

TEXT-FIGURES

MAPS

Chapter I

1841–1856

EARLY YEARS

ALBERT HASTINGS, the fifth son of Lieutenant John Markham, was born at Bagnères de Bigorre, in the Pyrenees, on November 11th, 1841, two days after the birth of the late King Edward, to whom he was considered in later life to bear a remarkable likeness. His father John, who had been obliged to leave the Navy owing to ill-health contracted whilst serving in the *Doris*, in the West Indies, was the second son of William Markham of Becca, near Aberford in Yorkshire, and Elizabeth Bowles; and grandson of Dr William Markham, Archbishop of York. Ten years after his retirement he had married Marianne Wood, and their eldest son, John, was born at Leghorn, in 1835. On their return to England they settled for a short time in Yorkshire, where their second son, George Henry, was born in 1837. In the next year they went back to the Continent, and at Bagnères de Bigorre four more sons were born: Frederick, who was drowned when he was about three years old; Arthur Augustus, born in 1840; Albert Hastings; and William Jervis, who died in infancy.

While Albert was still a child the family moved to Guernsey, and "Ronceval," a low white house, perched on a wooded hill with beautiful views over country and sea, was always the home to which he and his brothers looked back with affectionate remembrance.

The first break in the family circle was caused by the departure of John, the eldest son, for China, on his appointment, in 1852, by Lord Malmesbury, as student-interpreter in the Consular Service.

Three years later the youngest son was sent to England, at the age of thirteen, to prepare for the Navy. This decision does not appear to have been the result of any expressed desire on Albert's own part, but it was evidently thought fitting that one of the sons should follow their father's profession, and there were already naval traditions in the family. Lieutenant Markham's uncle, John Markham, second son of the Archbishop, had risen to the rank of Admiral, and had been at one time First Sea Lord of the Admiralty.

Albert appears to have acquiesced very willingly in the wishes of his parents, and the event proved that they were fully justified in their choice of a profession for him, for he threw himself whole-heartedly into it. He left Guernsey in the spring of 1855, and was confided to the care of the widow of his father's brother, the Rev. David Markham, Canon of Windsor. Mrs Markham, who was at this time living in London, at 4 Onslow Square, was a second mother to Albert. Her only surviving son, afterwards Sir Clements Markham, the well-known geographer and author, became a very close friend of Albert, in spite of his eleven years' seniority; indeed the two cousins grew to be like brothers and the tie between them was a lifelong one. Sixty years later there devolved upon the younger the task of undertaking his cousin's biography.

There were also three sisters. The eldest, married to Captain, afterwards Admiral, Quin, lived in the same Square. The other two, one older, the other younger than himself, were his playmates and confidants; and in later years, when the elder had married and gone to Australia, the Irish home of the younger, after her marriage with Colonel Henry Clements, was often the scene of happy reunions during his periods of leave.

Albert was now full of enthusiasm for a seafaring life. Not far from No. 4 lived Admiral Fitzroy, a well-known naval scientist, also Thackeray, the novelist, who used to pass the window every morning while the family were at breakfast. In these early days Albert made the acquaintance of Captain, afterwards Commodore, Goodenough, and the friendship was maintained until the tragic death of the latter in 1875.

The boy's education was at first entrusted to Mr Neville,

an elderly man, curate of Holy Trinity, Brompton, for whom he had the greatest respect and affection; but in the summer of 1855 Albert was sent to a private tutor, the Rev. John Benthall, at Newport Pagnell, Bucks. This was his first experience of life among strangers, and the discipline was strict. Any lapse on the part of the scholar was treated with scant patience by the teacher, and Albert was at first a good deal discouraged. But it is evident that Mr Benthall really took a kindly interest in the boy; his reports of his conduct and progress were very satisfactory, and Albert in later years always spoke warmly of the months spent at Newport Pagnell, and especially of the admiration inspired in him by Mr Benthall's cricketer son.

But now it seemed as if the boy would be disappointed of entering the profession on which his heart was set. October had come, and he would be fourteen in November, at which age the Navy must be closed to him, and all the strenuous efforts of his family failed to obtain a nomination. This was a great blow, both to himself and his friends, who now began to turn their thoughts to an alternative course. His aunt, writing to him at this time says:

I need not tell you, my dear boy, how much I feel for your disappointment, as I know how great it will be, but you must try and feel that we do not direct any of the events of this life ourselves. God has not thought it good for you that you should succeed in what you wish, but you may rely upon His goodness ...and you may be sure it will not eventually turn out to your disadvantage, though at present you cannot help feeling grieved, having for so many months turned your mind to this profession.

However, just at this time the unexpected experiment of admitting candidates over the age of fourteen was started by the Admiralty. This lasted for a short time only, but just enabled Albert to enter the Service. Three nominations were secured for him, the one accepted being that of his uncle, Mr W. R. Crompton Stansfield, and he was at once sent to Mr Eastman's Naval Academy at Portsmouth for special preparation for the examination for his cadetship. He evidently worked hard at his studies, for he passed out fourth on a list of thirty, to the gratification of all his friends, not least of his father, who wrote with paternal pride:

Everybody that hears of you pronounces you to have done most nobly in passing such a famous examination.

His first act on donning the uniform of a naval cadet was to have his daguerreotype taken as a present for his mother, a picture in which his likeness to his sailor father, always noticeable, is very marked. He was extremely proud of the sword worn in those days by naval cadets. In after years he used to tell the story of how he went in all the glory of his new uniform and sword to visit his great-aunt, the Countess of Mansfield, whose house stood on the site now occupied by the Langham Hotel. The unaccustomed sword tripped him up and the budding naval officer came down full length upon the floor!

On gaining his cadetship, he was given fourteen days' leave, which he spent with his family in France. "Ronceval" had been sold in the previous August, and his parents were now living at Dinan. His brother George was preparing to enter the Army, but considerations of expense decided him to sacrifice the profession he had hoped to follow, and, as the father's affairs were not in a very satisfactory state, Mr and Mrs Markham yielded to the persuasions of certain friends and in spite of protests from relatives made up their minds to emigrate. In July, 1856, they sailed for America, and from that date the house of his aunt, Mrs David Markham, became Albert's home.

His first experience of naval life was on board H.M.S. *Victory*, Nelson's old flagship, lying in Portsmouth Harbour, and flying the flag of the Commander-in-Chief, Admiral Sir George Seymour. Captain Gordon was then in command, and was succeeded in March by the Hon. James Drummond. Albert made many friendships, the greatest of these being with the big Master's assistant, Phillips, regarded by him during those early days as his "sea-daddy, the most kind, unselfish, generous, and best friend it is

possible to conceive." His impression of those first days in
the Navy was of interminable courts martial, carbine and
musket drill, hours of school under the Naval Instructor,
the excitement of going aloft, and the painful spectacle of
flogging, not then abolished in the Navy. He loved keeping
watch on the same boards which Nelson had many times
paced, and his hammock was slung in the cockpit, near the
spot where Nelson breathed his last.

The Russian war was just over, and on April 23rd, 1856,
Queen Victoria reviewed the Fleet at Spithead, the ships
having recently returned to England from the Baltic and
Black Sea at the termination of the war. On May 4th the
proclamation of peace with Russia was publicly read to
the officers and ship's company on board the *Victory*.

On June 17th young Markham was appointed to H.M.S.
Tribune, carrying 31 guns, just commissioned for the Pacific
Station by Captain Edgell, C.B. On learning of his appointment, Phillips succeeded in getting transferred to the same
ship, but their delight was soon changed to bitter disappointment. Before three weeks had elapsed, Albert, for
some unknown reason, was sent round to Plymouth to join
the *St Jean d'Acre*, a steam line-of-battle ship, a two-decker,
carrying 101 guns, fitting out at Devonport to convey
Lord Granville and his staff to Cronstadt, for the purpose
of ratifying our treaty of peace with Russia. She was
commanded by Captain George St Vincent King. This
did not at all suit the young cadet; what he wanted
was to join some ship fitting out for foreign service. He
knew that the trip to the Baltic would be more or less of
a yachting function; the ship would be crowded with
diplomatic officers and their wives and other ladies, and
would be paid off immediately on her return to England.
Moreover, he was informed that the gun room mess was
more than £1000 in debt, and at the end of the ship's commission he would be expected to contribute towards the
liquidation of this debt, for which he was, legally, in no way
responsible. The mess does not appear to have been particularly well managed—there were silver dish-covers to go

over the food, but, as the hungry boy remarked, "There was precious little under them!" On guest nights they were expected to wear expensive fancy waistcoats, which were certainly not uniform, and entailed an unnecessary outlay to a boy whose pay amounted to 11*d.* a day, out of which 3*d.* was deducted for payment to the Naval Instructor.

In this dilemma he wrote to his cousin, Clements Markham, who would, he knew, do all in his power for him, drawing his attention to the fact that there was a small brig named the *Camilla*, about to be commissioned for service on the China station, to which he would much like to be appointed. Clements Markham took up the matter very warmly, as he himself felt strongly that the appointment to the *St Jean d'Acre* would be of no value to his young cousin in his naval career, and he was so successful in his efforts that, less than a fortnight later, when the *Camilla* was put in commission at Devonport, Albert was transferred to her books as a naval cadet.

Chapter II

1856–1858

FIRST FOREIGN SERVICE

THE *Camilla* was a brig of 450 tons, only 120 ft. in length, and her complement was 120 officers and men. She carried sixteen guns (24 prs.), eight on each broadside. She was, as was the custom in those days, a complete shell; she had no masts, no guns, and no tanks; all these had to be taken on board and fitted by the ship's company. She was lying alongside a dockyard jetty, officers and men being quartered on board an old hulk, the *Egeria*.

The *Camilla* was commanded by George Twiselton Colvile, a smart seaman, an excellent gunnery officer, but something of a martinet. In spite, however, of his severity, he had always a warm place in Markham's affections, for he shewed himself most kind and thoughtful for the lad's true welfare.

Young Markham appears to have had a very high opinion of his superiors and messmates on board the *Camilla*. He describes the First Lieutenant, Henry Hawkes, as "a kind, hard-working man, intent on carrying out his duties to the satisfaction of his superior, a more good and kind-hearted man it was impossible to find." The Second Lieutenant, C. M. Andrews, was "a good and loyal officer who knew his work and did it well." The Master, Tom B. Read, was "an excellent navigator, and a good and trustworthy seaman." The mate appears to have been a character. He was a somewhat discontented man, due perhaps to the fact that he had held the rank of mate for a period of eight years, and saw no immediate prospect of promotion. Whenever he came into conflict with the Captain, as he often did, he would go down into the midshipmen's berth and vow he would not remain another day in the Service, that he would smear treacle over his commission, and send it in to the Captain! The occupants of the Gun Room, or midshipmen's berth, as it was then called, were the mate, four midshipmen, the clerk, and the Master's assistant, Markham being the only naval cadet.

It took a month to fit out the ship, and to receive all the stores and provisions, and on August 21st, 1856, the preparations being complete, the *Camilla* was towed out by a tug to the Sound, where she took in her powder and was inspected by Captain Hewlett, of H.M.S. *Cambridge,* and on Monday the 25th the little ship weighed, made sail, and proceeded to work down Channel.

The sea was rather unkind to the keen young sailor. For the first few days after leaving Plymouth he was badly sea-sick, but was allowed by the First Lieutenant to spend the greater part of the day in his hammock. Nor were his spirits raised by the fact that a young seaman who had fallen from aloft was placed under his hammock for examination by the doctor and died a few minutes later. The voyage was a stormy one, and the ship was in the Bay of Biscay for a week. Markham's *mal de mer* passed off in a few days, though he always continued to suffer from it for some days after starting on a cruise.

The accommodation on board the *Camilla* was extremely limited; the midshipmen's berth was a small compartment of about 8 ft. square, and had, as we have seen, eight occupants. There was no room for chairs, and they had to sit on lockers built round the table for the stowage of stores and wine. The only other place to stow anything was a great box, called the "jolly boat," fitted under the table. They had no store-room below, but used to keep salt stock-fish in a box under the main-top. The occupants of the midshipmen's berth had a steward, a cook, and a second class boy to wait upon them.

On September 7th they passed Madeira and the Salvage Islands, the first land they had seen since leaving England, and at 2 a.m. the next morning they anchored at Tenerife, off the town of Santa Cruz, the passage having taken just a fortnight, which was considered a very long one. When daylight appeared Albert's relief and pleasure knew no bounds. There lay the land, almost within a stone's throw of the ship, the quaint and picturesque buildings dotted around, the whole surmounted by the glorious Peak of Tenerife. It was an enchanting scene, but even more delightful after the boisterous voyage was the absolute quietness and stillness of the ship.

Here provisions were taken on board and also water. On a sailing-ship of that period no water for washing was issued to officers and men after leaving port. In harbour a small amount was allowed, provided a supply could be taken in before sailing.

Everything on shore was new to Markham. He was chosen to accompany the Captain on a visit to the Consul and later joined some of his messmates in hiring horses and riding inland. After a meal of peaches, pears, and beer at a hotel, the young men rode back to Santa Cruz. On this red letter day Markham appears to have made up for his enforced abstinence, due to *mal de mer*, by eating three dinners—one in the midshipmen's berth before he went on shore, one in the hotel at Santa Cruz, and one with the Captain at 6.30 on their return!

After a couple of days at Santa Cruz the *Camilla* started on her long voyage to the Cape of Good Hope. Five weeks after leaving Tenerife they crossed the line, and went through the customary ceremonies connected with the visit of Neptune. Young Markham was very kindly dealt with, being passed gently from one Triton to another; the "doctor" did not prescribe any noxious mixture for him, and the "barber" only used his smooth-bladed razor in the process of shaving.

When the wind was light the *Camilla* invariably hove-to, so as to allow the officers and men to bathe in a sail put out for the purpose, but a boat was always lowered and a good look out was kept for sharks. Constant drill was the order of the day, and they soon had their little ship not only efficient, but a smart man-of-war.

During this voyage they suffered much from scarcity of water, and were reduced to a pint per man per day for drinking purposes. Even the pea-soup which was served out twice a week had to be made with a large proportion of sea-water. The complement of the ship was 120 officers and men, and the provision of water stowed in the tanks on leaving port was only sufficient for that number. But, in addition to the crew, there were on board twenty supernumeraries for the China Station, and the voyage between Tenerife and the Cape of Good Hope took fifty-three days, though it was hardly expected to occupy more than six weeks. When they reached the Cape on October 31st they had only 200 gallons of water in their tanks, which would only have lasted another two, or at the most, three days. The officers of the night watches had strict orders to keep the ship under press of sail, and not to shorten on any account until the ship heeled over to 40 degrees!

Although on their arrival at Simon's Bay there was much to be done on board in the way of refitting and the provision of stores, the services of all were dispensed with as much as possible, and plenty of leave was granted. This was invariably spent by the officers in riding up to Cape Town, a distance of about twenty miles.

Young Markham had always to be on duty in the Dock-yard from 6 a.m. to 5.30 p.m., returning to the ship for a short break for dinner at noon. But after a little while he was given four days' leave to go up to Cape Town with the doctor and one of the midshipmen. They travelled by the mail coach, which impressed him as "more like an old baker's cart than anything else," the journey taking about four hours. On the road a little inn, known as Farmer Peck's, was passed, a board over which bore an amusing old inscription, one verse of which ran somewhat as follows:

> To the Gentle Shepherd on Salisbury Plain.
> Multum in parvo: pro bono publico—
> Very good entertainment all of a row.
> Lekker kost[1] as much as you please,
> Very good beds without any fleas.

There were only two hotels in Cape Town at that time,

[1] "Excellent food."

Parke's Hotel and the Masonic; as the Captains invariably put up at the former the young officers naturally patronised the latter, and revelled in its luxury after the discomforts of the little *Camilla*. It was a novel sight to the young cadet to see waggons drawn by teams of sixteen or more oxen in the streets of Cape Town.

The ship remained for a fortnight in Simon's Bay and then put to sea again, beating out of False Bay in a strong breeze. During this cruise, with the wind on their quarter, they logged ninety miles in eight hours, not a bad record, and they looked upon their little ship as a regular clipper.

On January 5th, 1857, land was sighted, and for the next two days they were engaged in beating through the Straits of Sunda, eventually anchoring off Anjer Point, the north-west extremity of the island of Java, where they remained for forty-eight hours, completing with water, and taking in provisions. The Captain and First Lieutenant went on shore, taking Markham with them, and landed close to a little village, consisting of bamboo huts not more than six feet square. Here they bought chickens and eggs from the natives, at marvellously low prices, the chickens being only 6d. each. Pineapples and coconuts provided a delicious supper after many weeks at sea.

The appearance of the land from the ship was most refreshing. Coconut trees in great profusion waved their graceful branches as far as the eye could see; the valleys and hills were covered with profuse tropical vegetation. But this charm was rudely broken on landing, when native women were discovered standing in the water which flowed down from the hills, busily engaged in washing the soiled linen of the ship's company, while at the same time the boats were being loaded, at the mouth of the stream, with the water in which the clothes had been washed, to be taken off to the ship for drinking purposes. It is little wonder that this resulted in a severe epidemic of dysentery, which caused the death of three of the ship's company.

The Captain decided to make the voyage to Hong Kong by the Molucca Passage instead of Macassar Strait, hoping by this means to get a more favourable wind. They accordingly left the anchorage off Anjer Point on January 9th, proceeding through the Straits of Saleyer, a very narrow channel. Night was closing in when they entered the passage; a strong gale had sprung up, and they were nearly driven ashore. Indeed, it was only by consummate seamanship and quick decision that a terrible disaster was averted.

The remaining weeks of the voyage were uneventful. On February 9th a large fleet of Chinese junks, with which Markham was to become very familiar, was sighted; on the next afternoon they anchored off Hong Kong, and found themselves in the midst of a large fleet of English men-of-war and mercantile shipping flying the flags of all nations. The voyage from England had occupied 169 days, including those spent at the various anchorages; the actual number of days at sea was 156, during which time they had sailed 17,830 miles.

No sooner was the anchor down than young Markham was sent on shore to the post office to fetch the mails. On his return to the ship he was greeted with the news—"Your brother has come." This information he regarded as a joke, believing his brother to be at Foochow at the time. But being at last prevailed upon to go below, he discovered his brother comfortably seated at dinner in the ward room mess. This meeting with his eldest brother, after a separation of about eight years, was a great delight. John Markham was a general favourite, and his young brother basked in the light of his popularity.

The whole town of Victoria was at this time in a state of great excitement owing to the attempt of the Chinese to poison the European community, especially the English portion of it, by the introduction of a large quantity of arsenic into the flour of which the bread was being made. This was done under instructions from Pekin and Canton, for we were practically at war with China at the time. But, in the baker's eagerness to carry out his diabolical work, he used too large a portion of the poison, causing those who partook of it to be violently sick before it had time to take fatal effect. In consequence of this no one died, but a great number were very seriously ill, and John Markham was only just recovering from its evil effects.

Sir John Bowring was Governor at that time, and both he and Lady Bowring were most kind to the young naval cadet, and he was frequently at Government House.

The *Calcutta*, bearing the flag of Admiral Sir Michael Seymour, was in the harbour, and the officers of both ships soon became acquainted. Commander Goodenough, already a friend of Markham, shewed him much kindness, generously placing his library at his disposal.

Their stay in the harbour was not wanting in excitement. From time to time Chinese pirates, in their junks and lorchas, would suddenly make their appearance amongst the shipping, the first intimation of their presence being the firing of guns actually in the harbour. Sometimes boats were sent away armed to drive the pirates off, and on one occasion the *Bittern*, a 12-gun brig, somewhat smaller than the *Camilla*, was despatched under sail to protect the boats. For the present the *Camilla* could do nothing, as she was busy refitting, and the breechings of her guns had all been landed.

After twenty-five days at Hong Kong, they proceeded on February 17th to Amoy, to act as Senior Officer at that port. Although the distance from port to port was under 300 miles, it took them nearly a fortnight to work up against the monsoon, and very bad weather was encountered during the voyage.

Amoy was a typical Chinese town, with very narrow and crowded streets. The usual mode of conveyance was by palanquin, a structure made of bamboo and wicker-work, carried by a couple of Chinamen, who went along at a fairly fast trot, singing most lugubriously a rhythmical song to which they kept step.

Markham enjoyed to the full the hospitality of the English officials and merchants resident at the Treaty ports. On one occasion he had a most delightful cruise from Amoy to a port named Sin-chu, about sixty miles up the

coast, in a beautiful little schooner called the *Mazeppa*,
belonging to the great firm of Jardine, Matheson & Co. These
vessels were commanded by gentlemen of great energy, and
excellent sailors. With the exception of the officers they
were manned entirely by lascars. They were well armed
against pirates, and perfect discipline reigned on board;
they were scrupulously clean and in perfect order, and could
compete, in discipline and cleanliness, with any man-of-
war on the station.

The *Camilla* made several expeditions after pirates. Once
she sailed into a small fleet of these piratical junks; after
sinking two or three of them, the order was given to man
all the boats and to attack, and Markham was coolly told
by the First Lieutenant to proceed in the jolly boat with
his six boys and two marines and capture a junk which
was pointed out to him. It was a great moment for the
fifteen-year-old cadet. This was wearing a sword to some
purpose! The junk had apparently a crew of about forty or
fifty men, who were all armed, and beating their gongs and
tomtoms with the intention, no doubt, of scaring the Englishmen away. Nothing daunted, they dashed alongside, only
to find, as they sprang on board, the piratical crew disappearing on the opposite side. They had captured the junk.
It was Markham's first prize, and he was much elated.
About thirty of the pirates were rescued, to be beheaded
by the mandarin when they were handed over to the
Chinese authorities. This engagement took place in Hu-i-tau
Bay, a few miles north of Amoy. There were many similar
encounters with pirates during the short stay at this port.

The *Camilla* was reinforced by H.M.S. *Sampson*, sent up
from Hong Kong for the purpose, and, with the two ships
acting in concert, a good many junks were boarded and
sunk. An important piratical stronghold in the neighbourhood of Hu-i-tau Bay was attacked and destroyed by a
landing-party from the two ships, under the command of
Captain Colvile, consisting of about eighty men. The pirates,
although over 500 strong, made but a feeble resistance, and
the attacking force suffered no casualties. On this occasion

Markham was acting as A.D.C. to the Captain, and was consequently in the first boat. The next day, proceeding to the northward, they again came into contact with the piratical fleet, many of which were destroyed or taken. They had also the satisfaction of capturing a large lorcha, which was sent with a prize crew to Amoy, where she was sold, and the purchase money distributed amongst her captors. Young Markham's share amounted to about $15 or $20—not much actually, but it was prize-money.

While still at Amoy he made great friends with a student-interpreter attached to the British Consulate, Mr Swinhoe, the well-known ornithologist, with whom he made many enjoyable expeditions up the river. These excursions into natural history opened up a fresh source of pleasure and one which Markham pursued with great interest throughout his life.

In May the *Camilla* left Amoy, and proceeded in tow of the *Sampson* to the mouth of the river Min, where is situated the large city of Foochow, the capital of one of the most important tea districts in China. They went up this beautiful river under sail and anchored off a small island called Pagoda Island, which contained only a few little houses and a store; a prominent feature was the pagoda, some 130 ft. high, whence the island derives its name. The store was their only resort when they went on shore. The sole attractions it offered were a miserable bowling-alley, a billiard-table without any cushions, covered with dilapidated cloth, well chipped balls, and broken cues without tips.

At this spot they were compelled to remain for the next ten months, the water further up the river being too shallow to allow of good anchorage nearer the city of Foochow. However, their time passed pleasantly enough, for they were able to make frequent trips up to the city, and the hospitality of the European community was unbounded, especially to naval officers. Markham thoroughly enjoyed his leave whenever he could get it. The Captain was very good to him, occasionally making him his companion when he went on shore, and always taking a keen interest in his welfare.

One of his favourite pastimes was snipe-shooting in the rice-fields, either alone or with one of his messmates. The Captain, seeing that he was fond of shooting, and that he had no gun of his own, sent for him one day and asked him if he would like to have one. The boy naturally replied in the affirmative. The Captain, who had charge of the allowance which he received from home of £40 per annum, in addition to his pay, then suggested that for the next six months he should keep back the monthly payment of £3. 6s. 6d., and write home to Westley Richards (the best gunmaker in London at that time) to send out a gun to him. When it arrived a few months later Markham was the happiest and proudest person in the ship! Every afternoon that he could get leave to go on shore he used to wander over the country and through the paddy-fields, intent only on shooting the wily snipe or any bird that would allow him to get within shot of it. He found the Chinese very kind and hospitable, and never experienced any rudeness from them. A quarter of a dollar, judiciously laid out, invariably made matters smooth.

Stoppage of leave, a very common form of punishment, was naturally a serious matter to a young cadet: it sometimes extended over a period of two months, confining him for that time entirely to the ship. Another form of discipline was "watch and watch." This consisted in his being kept on deck for twelve hours out of the twenty-four, not of course, twelve consecutive hours, but in accordance with the watches, four hours at a time, and even permission to go down to meals was withheld if meal times occurred during those hours. Off duty, the Captain was always extremely kind to Markham; but he kept a strict hand over him to ensure the proper carrying out of his duties, and punished him severely for any neglect of them.

Chapter III

1858–1859

PIRATES IN THE CHINA SEA

O N July 21st, 1858, Markham passed his examination for midshipman. This was no mere formality, and lasted three days. On the first day he was examined by the Captain and First Lieutenant in seamanship; on the next day the Captain examined him in French, and the boatswain reported on his capabilities in knotting and splicing; and on the third day the Master reported on his knowledge of navigation. When it was all over the Captain gave him his certificate and congratulated him and told him he had done very well. Shortly afterwards the First Lieutenant made him "mate of the upper deck"; in this capacity his chief duties were to see that the upper deck was always clean and tidy, and that the brass work was kept bright. In fact, as he afterwards said, he was a sort of "head housemaid" to the First Lieutenant!

In the month of September he had his first experience of what a typhoon in China is really like. It came on to blow very hard in the forenoon, gradually increasing in force until about 3 p.m., when the gale was at its height. But the *Camilla*, having made all preparations, rode through it in safety, though she was tossed about as if at sea in a heavy gale of wind. Many of the ships drifted, but were brought up by letting go a third anchor, and no serious casualties occurred. The wind gradually blew itself out during the night, but there was no communication with the shore for at least twenty-four hours. The store in which they used to play bowls, etc., was completely demolished, and many houses were blown down.

A few days after, a very curious and unfortunate incident occurred. The American river pilots had their headquarters at Pagoda Island, so as to be in readiness for taking the

M   2

tea-clippers down the river on their homeward journeys. Two of these men, being the worse for liquor, became very quarrelsome and a great nuisance to those who had come on shore for a quiet afternoon. Their violent wrangling at last reached such a pitch that one of the officers of the *Camilla* who was present jumped up and said, "Why don't you end this dispute by fighting a duel? There are a couple of duelling pistols in the store, and I shall be very glad to act as one of the seconds." This proposal met with universal approval, and Mr Welch, the proprietor of the store, offered his services as the other second. The two principals somewhat reluctantly agreed. The two seconds went for the pistols, which they loaded, but substituted flour for bullets; this was rammed home tightly. All was made ready, but at the last moment the courage of the combatants oozed, and they refused to fight. The officer of the *Camilla* professed to be highly indignant at their lamentable display of cowardice, and exclaimed, knowing how the pistols were loaded, "If the principals are afraid to fight, the seconds will have to exchange shots." Mr Welch agreed and the signal was given to fire. The pistols went off simultaneously, and, to the officer's horror, he saw his opponent drop his pistol, clap his hand to his arm and spin round, while his white jacket was dyed with blood. Rushing up to his assistance he found that the flour with which the pistol had been loaded was rammed home so hard as to become a veritable bullet, and had gone clean through his arm. Everything possible was done, a doctor was sent for and Mr Welch was put to bed. But he never recovered, and died about three weeks after the mock duel. His death, it should be stated, was not caused by the actual wound, though it was no doubt accelerated by the treatment to which he had to submit afterwards. The event cast a gloom over the little settlement where he was universally liked and respected.

The regular delivery of letters was very uncertain in China during the middle of the nineteenth century, and they invariably took many months in reaching their destination.

It once happened that the vessel bringing mails from Hong Kong was wrecked off the entrance to the river Min, and the *Camilla* received the unwelcome intelligence with the additional information that the Chinese had looted the wreck, opened a number of the letters, and pasted up the contents in the windows of their houses. Four armed boats were at once sent to verify this report and to endeavour to retrieve the letters. They were away for three days, but were unsuccessful; the wreck had been completely gutted and everything of value carried away into the interior.

Discipline on board the *Camilla* was very strict; the Captain had the reputation of being an extremely severe officer, and his ship was always in a high state of efficiency and good order, in fact she was always spoken of as "the line-of-battle brig." Corporal punishment was much in vogue in those days, and men were flogged for offences that would now be treated far more leniently—by stoppage of leave or deductions from pay. At the same time it may be noted that seventy years ago it was the exception to find a man in a ship's company who could read and write.

Young Markham himself had a very unpleasant experience of the Captain's severity. He had been keeping the middle watch (i.e. from midnight until 4 a.m.). The Captain sent for him the following day and asked him very abruptly if he was the officer of the middle watch the previous night. He replied in the affirmative. The Captain then wished to know why the sentry on the forecastle did not call "All's well," as is the custom in the Navy after the bell is struck at every half hour. Markham answered that to the best of his remembrance he did call, and brought forward the sentry himself and the corporal of the watch to corroborate his statement. The Captain, in a towering rage, refused to accept the evidence, disrated him on the spot to a naval cadet, prohibited him from keeping officer's watch, disrated the corporal and otherwise punished the sentry. The poor young midshipman deeply felt the indignity of the punishment, the want of trust, and disbelief of his word, and he could not refrain from crying bitterly when he went below.

If his Captain mistrusted him, and put no reliance on his statements, although he had pledged his honour to the truth of them, there was nothing further to live for, and the sooner he left the Navy the better for that great and glorious profession.

Thus he brooded over the treatment he had received for some days, until, in discussing the affair with the clerk, a brighter view of the case began to present itself; for he was told that the Captain's orders had been only to note in *pencil* in the ship's books the fact of his having been disrated, and that he could again "mount his patch." No words can describe the relief and pleasure this announcement caused to the reinstated midshipman. His discontent vanished. He had lost no "time" in the Service, there was nothing on record against him, and it would never be officially known that he had been disrated from a midshipman to a naval cadet. Everything was bright again, and he became as zealous and as keen in the discharge of his duties as he had ever been before. The officers all congratulated him, and the Captain treated him with even greater kindness than formerly.

Another unpleasant event in Markham's career as a midshipman occurred a little later. It was the custom in the Navy to exercise in preparing for battle once every three months, at night time. The exact time was known only to the Captain who, when he had decided on the date, sent for the sentry to wake the drummer and told him to beat off to night-quarters. He was not supposed to communicate this order to anyone else.

On one of these occasions the sentry in the steerage, where all the midshipmen slept, was ordered by the Captain, shortly before midnight, to call the drummer. Now the sentry happened to be Markham's servant, and in the goodness of his heart, when calling the drummer, apprised his master also. While Markham was hurriedly putting on his clothes, the sentry, having put the authorised turns of lashing round his master's hammock, unhooked it, and ran up the hatchway with it, throwing it, as he thought, into the hammock netting. Instead of which, he was so energetic and anxious to return to his post, that he must have thrown it overboard, for it was never seen again. On this coming to the Captain's knowledge, the unfortunate owner was sent for and asked to explain the loss. He told the truth, and, because he had not taken his own hammock on deck, as under the circumstances he ought to have done, he had his leave stopped for a fortnight, had to pay the value of the missing article, and was ordered to lash up and stow his hammock for a week; the well-meaning servant was also punished.

After eight months in the river Min the *Camilla* was ordered down to Hong Kong, and then, in the early part of 1858, proceeded up river to Canton where they remained rather more than ten months. However, the time did not hang heavily, for there was always something to do. Expeditions against the Chinese were constantly being carried out, for large bodies of Chinese soldiers being in the immediate neighbourhood, the *Camilla's* boats were frequently engaged against them. Canton had been captured by the English, and was garrisoned by soldiers and marines, while several British ships and gunboats were lying off the town. All the men-of-war in the river were compelled to protect themselves with long booms projecting from the bows in order to ward off the fire-ships and fire-rafts that were sent down by the Chinese with the tide, and close vigilance had to be exercised at night by the placing of extra look-outs, and by boats incessantly pulling round the ships during the dark hours. As a reward of $500 was publicly offered by the Chinese Government for the head of every English or French officer, and $100 for that of a bluejacket or private, great caution was necessary in landing, which was only allowed in small armed parties of three or four. But the midshipmen were not slow to avail themselves of the permission to go on shore, even under these conditions. The most dangerous part of the city was the western suburbs, and these they were prohibited from visiting.

The forts on the Honam side of the river were in our possession and were strongly fortified, and Markham was employed in charge of a party of men from the ship in destroying the guns, which were of no use to us. The work was done by dropping heavy shot on the trunnions, or using a sledgehammer to knock them off. The small brass guns, being of some value, were brought on board the ship and sold by the First Lieutenant, the proceeds being devoted to the purchase of paint for the ship.

The young midshipman's general education, apart from the regular professional instruction, was not altogether neglected. The chaplain on shore, the Rev. Dr, afterwards Archdeacon, Gray, conducted Divine Service on board every Sunday. At the Captain's suggestion he offered to come off once or twice during the week and give Markham lessons in Latin, Greek, and arithmetic. The boy was only too glad to avail himself of this kindness and much of his spare time was spent upon Latin and Greek, of which he had always been fond. He also seems to have gone through a systematic course of standard reading at this time—Livingstone's *Travels*, the *Life of Lord Metcalfe*, Scott's novels, etc.

But he had time also for lighter pursuits. One day he and two friends, being on shore in Canton city, made up their minds to call upon the Pikwei, as the Chinese Governor of the province was designated. This desire did not spring from any wish to make the acquaintance of the official in question: what they really wanted was to see the interior of his Yamen. Arriving at the gates and demanding admission, they were requested to send in their cards. Thinking that if they sent in the names of illustrious Englishmen they would be sure of a reception, they wrote on the cards "The Prince of Wales," "The Marquis of Westminster," and "The Duke of Wellington." The ruse, however, did not have the effect of bringing them into the presence of the mandarin, but at least they gained their main object, for they were shewn all over the Yamen, the reception-rooms, courts of justice, gardens, etc. They took their departure with a great deal of chin-chinning on the

part of the household, though Markham afterwards confessed to feeling a little mean in having practised such a
deception.

The heat of Canton during the summer was intense, and
there was a good deal of fever and ague on board. In
consequence of this, orders were given that, if possible, the
men should not be exposed to the sun between the hours
of 7.30 a.m. and 5.30 p.m. Markham had always good
reason to remember this, for he had the unpleasant
experience of being put in "watch and watch" for forty-
eight hours because, in carrying out the usual routine, he
sent a man aloft a few minutes after half-past seven to take
a tackle off the main-yard. He always insisted that, had
he not done so, he would certainly have been punished for
a dereliction of duty!

When not away on boat duty he was responsible for the
signals, and had to be on deck, except at meal times, a good
deal from 5 a.m. until dark, by the Captain's order. He
suffered considerably from the heat, and had frequently to
go on the sick list. It was a real refreshment when he was
allowed to accept the invitations of his friends at Hong
Kong to spend a few days with them. It was, as a rule,
only an eight hours' run in the steamer, and Hong Kong
was a paradise to him. He lived well, slept in a comfortable
bed, was his own master, had no watches to keep, no signals
to look after, no "watch and watch," no Captain or First
Lieutenant to worry him. Instead, everyone was intent on
giving him pleasure and the best of everything, including
a pony which was always placed at his disposal.

Early in June a very strong Naval Brigade, under the
immediate command of Captain Colvile, was landed in
Canton to co-operate with the military in an attack on a
Chinese camp which had been formed in the neighbourhood
of the White Cloud Mountains. In this and all other operations young Markham took part. The expedition was away
three days, but effected very little. As the English force
advanced, the Chinese fell back, and it was not thought
politic to follow them further into the interior. They had,

however, a few skirmishes with the enemy, their losses being three men killed and many wounded. One of the ship's doctors was caught by the Chinese and beheaded. The heat was intense and some of the men even died from the effects of the sun.

In the early part of 1859 an expedition on a larger scale than usual was undertaken against the Chinese on shore. Sir Michael Seymour was Commander-in-Chief at the time. A Naval Brigade of about 700 men was landed from the squadron of British war vessels; the boats were towed by seven gunboats. They left the ship at 5 o'clock in the morning, steaming up the river for about eighteen miles. Orders were then given to land, each officer and man carrying, besides his arms and ammunition, three days' provisions for himself in a haversack, a water-bottle containing about a quart of fresh water, and a rolled blanket. Markham was chosen to carry the colours, so that in addition to his other equipment he bore a white ensign attached to a boarding-pike. This was altogether a pretty heavy load, over execrable country, under a burning sun. All wore a curtain on their caps to protect the backs of their heads and necks. Acting in co-operation with our troops, which had marched out from Canton, a force of about 3000, they advanced on some Chinese forts. But when the defenders saw them coming they deserted the fortifications, and ran off into the country as fast as their legs could carry them, only occasionally pausing to fire. It was impossible to come up with them, but their baggage, guns, and munitions of war, abandoned in their rapid flight, were all captured, and the attacking force, hot and exhausted after their chase uphill in the broiling sun, were glad to halt and pipe to dinner. There were several cases of sunstroke, Markham having a slight one himself. He was very sick, faint, and giddy; he had been without food since the early breakfast at 4.30, and in addition to the ordinary equipment he had the heavy staff of the colours to carry. However, after a short rest, he felt well enough to proceed.

In conjunction with the troops they advanced on the

village of Chuk-sing which they soon cleared and occupied, making themselves fairly comfortable for the night. The foraging parties had brought in some pigs and fowls, and they enjoyed an excellent dinner. Markham made his bed on the floor of a doctor's shop and slept soundly. The casualties for the day were four men wounded.

They were up early the next morning and, leaving a small force to defend Chuk-sing in the event of its being attacked, they started at 7 o'clock, about 2500 strong, and marched along the road taken by the retreating army until about 1 o'clock, when they halted for dinner, at which time, after consultation among the senior officers, it was decided to return to Chuk-sing, which was not reached until past 7 p.m., after a trying and wearisome march of more than twenty miles. They were all terribly disappointed at their inability to come to close grips with the enemy. The next morning they set fire to the village, marched down to their boats, reaching their ships about noon, very tired, very sunburnt, and very dirty. Markham had a sharp attack of fever and ague, but was otherwise none the worse.

On January 27th, 1859, three years after entering the Navy, he passed his intermediate examination. The officers who examined him were Commander Lord Gillford, Mr Brown, First Lieutenant, and Mr Fox, the Master, all of the *Hornet*, and Mr Moore, the Master of the *Camilla*. The examination was held in the cabin of the Captain of the *Hornet*, his own Captain being present the whole time— very disconcerting for his young officer, and to this fact he always attributed his disappointment in obtaining a second, instead of a first, class certificate.

In February the *Camilla* left Canton, and proceeded down the river to Hong Kong. On the way they grounded on the bar off Macao Fort, and did not get off until high tide the following morning. Although the ship was drawing fifteen feet of water there was only nine feet on the bar at low tide!

The time off Hong Kong proved a very delightful one for Markham. A good deal of leave was granted him as, being a light weight, he had been asked to ride a pony at the races.

These races were conducted merely for the sake of the sport; no betting was allowed, and the riders were all gentlemen. Markham afterwards described this as the time of his life.

Now occurred an important event in Markham's life— his first real change of ship. Captain Colvile, having been appointed temporarily to the *Niger*, to relieve her Captain, who was invalided home from Hong Kong, asked Markham if he would go with him, or if he would prefer joining any other ship on the station. Markham was delighted to accompany his old Captain, though he was sorry to leave "the old *Camilla*," in which he had spent two and a half happy years, if not always of unmixed happiness. But a further inducement lay in the fact that, the *Camilla* being a sailing brig, he had had no opportunity of learning steam, which would be essential for the sub-lieutenant's examination. The *Niger* was a full-powered barque-rigged steamer of 1170 tons. She carried thirteen guns (twelve 32 prs. mounted six on each broadside and one large 68 pr. 95 cwt. gun mounted on the forecastle). She had a complement of 130 officers and men, only ten more than were carried in the *Camilla*, which was less than half her size in tonnage.

Markham joined the *Niger* on March 3rd, 1859, and the first duty was on the following morning to tow the *Camilla* to sea and cast her off outside the Ly-ee-mun Channel, *en route* for the north, while they returned to Hong Kong.

No sooner had the *Niger* reached Hong Kong than operations against various piratical strongholds began, and three separate expeditions were made, the first to the northward and the other two in the neighbourhood of Macao. In each case the desired object was obtained, with a freedom from casualties that was astonishing, considering the forces with which they had to contend. Markham acted throughout as A.D.C. to the Captain. These dangerous bands of sea-robbers, who had been in the habit of lying in wait for and attacking all ships entering or leaving Hong Kong which they thought would be an easy prey, were now completely broken up and scattered, and the work done won the full approval of the Commander-in-Chief.

For his services on these occasions, as also in the expedition to Chuk-sing, Markham's name was mentioned in despatches. Although, while commanding one of the boats in the attack and capture of the stronghold near Macao, he was not returned in the list of casualties, he received a contusion on the left shoulder from a spent ball while in pursuit of the enemy, after the works had been carried.

On March 19th the *Niger* started on a cruise to India, touching at the quaint old floating town of Bangkok. They received a visit from the second king of Siam and accorded him royal honours; the king in his turn gave the officers permission to see his beautiful white elephant.

Markham had expected to meet his brother at Bangkok, and to make the acquaintance of his young wife, but he found, to his disappointment, that they had just left for Hong Kong, and the two ships must have passed one another on the way.

They next proceeded to Singapore, where the new Commander-in-Chief, Sir James Hope, arrived to relieve Sir Michael Seymour in command of the China Station. From this place the *Niger* proceeded to Ceylon, carrying the returning Admiral and his staff to Point de Galle, where he embarked for England. As the *Niger* was steaming into the harbour of Trincomalee she struck a rock, and the damage sustained caused her to leak considerably. As the necessary repairs could not be effected at Trincomalee they proceeded to Bombay, where she was docked. Here they spent three pleasant weeks, and then returned to Trincomalee, where they found the *Retribution* flying the broad pennant of Commodore Edgell, senior officer in India. At this time the Indian Navy was in existence, but their duties did not in any way clash with those of the Royal Navy.

On arrival at Trincomalee the Captain sent for Markham and suggested that he should leave the *Niger* and join the *Retribution*, as Commodore Edgell, his old Captain in the *Tribune*, had expressed a wish to have him with him again. Captain Colvile advised this step, as it would give him the benefit of a Naval Instructor, which he had been without for the past three years. Captain Colvile would himself be returning to the *Camilla*, as a captain was being sent out to the *Niger* from England. Markham felt that the reasons for this change of ship were good and sound, and accepted the advice, though with sentiments of deep regret at parting with his old Captain, to whom he was much attached. They never met again, nor did he ever again see the *Camilla*. Two years after he left her she sailed from Hakodate to Yokohama, Captain Colvile being in command, and, it is supposed, foundered in a typhoon a few days after leaving port, for she was never seen again. The loss of his old ship with all hands was a great grief to Markham, who wrote of the Captain in later years:

I have always regarded him as one of the best officers I have ever served with, and, had he lived, he would without doubt have climbed to the very top of the Naval tree, and have made a great name for himself in the Service to which he was so devoted.

Markham was transferred to the *Retribution*, which was a much larger ship than the *Niger*, on June 17th, 1859. The *Retribution* was at this time employed in superintending the laying of the cables between Karachi and Aden, by which India was, for the first time, connected by telegraph with England.

Chapter IV

1859–1867

During the latter part of 1859 news reached India of the defeat sustained by Sir James Hope in his attempt to capture the Taku Forts, at the entrance of the Peiho, and a call was made for volunteers to fill the vacancies caused in the Fleet by the large number of casualties. Markham immediately sent in his name, and, in May, 1860, was despatched from Bombay in a P. & O. steamer, in charge of forty men, to join the *Chesapeake* at Hong Kong.

Sir James Hope at once appointed him to his own flag-ship, and took him on his personal staff as signal mate. This gave him the opportunity of active service for which he longed. After accompanying the Allied forces to Tientsin, where he served in the flag-ship's tender, *Coromandel*, he was put in command of a flotilla of thirty-five boats to convey provisions for the troops from Tientsin to Tongchau. He was present at the capture both of the Taku Forts and of Pekin. At the conclusion of hostilities he commanded the flotilla of boats that conveyed Lord Elgin and Mr Bruce from Tongchau to Tientsin. The cold was so severe that it became necessary to break the ice on the river in order to make progress. The sudden change from the intense heat of summer to the great cold of early winter, combined with hard work and exposure, brought on a serious attack of fever, and Markham arrived on board his ship in a high state of delirium. He was sent to a hospital ship and taken down to Hong Kong, where, for three weeks, his life was despaired of. However, he had a good and strong constitution, and made a complete recovery.

Sir James Hope, having transferred his flag to the *Imperieuse*, took his favourite midshipman with him, and kept him on his personal staff. In consequence of his clear handwriting, he employed him to copy out all his private correspondence. Markham always wrote a very clear neat hand, and his log books were beautifully kept. He wrote black letter, and any kind of ornamental writing, with the utmost ease and accuracy.

After visiting Japan, at that time practically a *terra incognita*, the *Imperieuse* proceeded to Shanghai, and began that series of operations against the Taiping rebels which resulted in their being driven from the neighbourhood of the city.

On January 23rd, 1862, Markham passed his examination for sub-lieutenant and obtained a first-class certificate, and on February 1st Sir James Hope promoted him, and appointed him Second Lieutenant of the *Centaur* (Captain Montgomerie), a vacancy having been caused by the invaliding of one of the younger officers. Thus Markham never wore sub-lieutenant's uniform, but passed straight from midshipman to lieutenant.

During the early part of 1862 the officers and crew of the *Centaur* were actively engaged in the suppression of the Taiping rebellion, in which they played a very important part, garrisoning the town of Sunkung and holding it successfully against a very large force of the enemy, besides being instrumental in the capture of Ming Hong and other fortified cities in possession of the Taipings.

Pirates were still making it unsafe for merchant vessels to enter the river, besides making great depredations on the coast round about Ningpo. Accordingly, on the evening of April 2nd, 1862, while the *Centaur* was at anchor off that town, Markham was sent on board a Chinese lorcha in our possession—the *Vivid*—with an assistant surgeon, twenty bluejackets and marines, and a 12 pr. howitzer. The Captain, whose name was Barclay, was described as "a nice, quiet, civil man." At 9 p.m. they dropped down the river as quietly as possible to prevent the numerous spies of the pirates from learning anything of their intentions, and anchored off Chinhae. At 8 o'clock next morning they sculled in the direction of Friendly Island, to the north of

Chinhae, there being no wind. About 11 o'clock two lorchas were observed alongside of each other, about three miles off. This looked suspicious, and Markham immediately ordered all the men below to dinner, remaining on deck himself, wrapped in a Chinese fur, to avoid all appearance of having men on board. The howitzer was covered with a sail, and they pulled steadily in the direction of the pirate craft. The bait took, for when they were about 500 yards off, one of the junks shoved off, and stood toward them, hoisting the pirate flag (red, triangular, with a black jagged border) and fired upon them from three or four heavy guns (12 and 7 prs.), the shot passing through their sail. Markham immediately ordered up his men and opened fire from the howitzer, an unpleasant surprise for the pirates, who instantly turned and sculled in the direction of the mainland, about four miles off. As the pirate had sweeps and the *Vivid* only one steer oar abaft, the distance between them was rapidly increasing, when a shot struck the fugitive forward, between wind and water, and it could plainly be seen that she was filling. This, however, had only the effect of causing her to go down a little by the head and of lessening her speed, as she was built in compartments, and she still continued to keep up a heavy fire upon her pursuers.

The advantage gained by the *Vivid* was neutralised by her Chinese crew refusing to work as they came to close quarters, and the bluejackets were not able to use the steer oars. Nothing daunted, Markham determined to board the pirate, and, ordering a small sampan, which would hold three men, to be lowered, jumped into it, and managed to crowd in five men besides. They sculled towards the enemy vessel, which allowed them to come within forty yards of her, and then opened a heavy fire upon them from all her guns and small arms. Two men were wounded, one of them severely, and the Chinaman dropped his oar and refused to scull any further, which necessitated the return to the *Vivid*. The other lorcha had, in the meantime, hoisted the American flag and a house flag, but did not offer any assistance. The ammunition for the howitzer was expended, with the exception of one round, but the last shot proved a very successful one, for it shot away the pirate's steer oar, and they were now able to get within twenty yards of her.

The Chinamen still refused to go alongside, and Markham had to put sentries over them and force them to work. At this point Barclay, Captain of the *Vivid*, was dangerously wounded, and had to be carried below, and two seamen were also incapacitated by wounds. Nevertheless the *Vivid* at length succeeded in running alongside the enemy junk, whose deck presented a frightful spectacle, upwards of thirty men lying stretched upon it terribly mangled by shot. Markham gave the order to board, and was in the act of springing on board when the pirates, determined to resist to the last, blew themselves up, and it was necessary to shove off in order to avoid the fragments which were falling in all directions. Thirteen of her men who had thrown themselves overboard were picked up, two of them dying the same day from the effects of the explosion and from wounds. Thus, after a running fight of three and a half hours, the object of the expedition was accomplished. The *Vivid* remained by the disabled junk until she sank.

The other vessel was found to be the American lorcha, *Spec*, and the reason for her offering no assistance to the *Vivid* was soon discovered. She had been captured by the pirate that morning, and her Captain, a Scotchman, and a European passenger had been put to a terrible death, being crucified on board the pirate vessel. Markham put a prize crew on board and proceeded with her in company to Chinhae, where they arrived at 9 p.m. At 2 a.m. the following day he reached the *Centaur* at Ningpo, and transferred the men and guns before daylight. Only eleven of the prisoners proved to be *bonâ fide* pirates, and were consequently handed over to the Chinese authorities, who beheaded them; the rest were found to be fishermen who had been taken out of their boats and made to work.

Captain Montgomerie expressed himself as very much pleased with Markham's promptitude and efficiency in carrying out his orders. The loss incurred was five men killed and wounded out of a force of twenty.

For his services on this occasion Markham was confirmed by the Admiralty in the rank of lieutenant, his commission being dated to the day of action, and orders were given that the following letter should be read on the quarter deck in the presence of the officers and ship's company:

Admiralty,
16th June, 1862.

Sir,
Referring to Sir James Hope's letter of the 19th of April last No. 153, reporting the gallant conduct of Mr Albert H. Markham acting Lieutenant of H.M. Ship *Centaur* in capturing a Pirate with a Party under his command, detached from the ship. I am commanded by my Lords Commissioners of the Admiralty to acquaint you that their Lordships have been pleased to promote Mr Markham to the rank of Acting Lieutenant in Her Majesty's Fleet, with seniority from the 3rd of April last, and he will be confirmed provided he shall pass the several examinations on his arrival in England, according to the Regulations.

The Commission is enclosed herewith.
I am,
Sir,
Your very obedient servant,
(Signed) C. PAGET.

The only drawback to this appointment, from Markham's point of view, was that it meant another eighteen months or two years on the China Station, where he had already spent, with the exception of a short time off India, about five years. Indeed, one of his naval friends, writing to him, enquired whether he intended to pass the rest of his life in China, and whether he had taken to a pigtail! But he considered himself very fortunate to have had such quick promotion; he liked his Captain and messmates very much, and felt that he had a true friend in the Admiral.

In May he was ordered to go with a prize crew of ten men and take charge of the English barque *Paragon* which had been seized in consequence of having on board contraband of war, destined for sale to the rebels. According to instructions he dropped down the river with her, clear of the shipping, and anchored to await the *Centaur*. The Master of the ship had clearly shewn that the proceeding was much against his will, and, at midnight, Lieutenant Markham awoke to hear a great noise. overhead. He instantly went on deck, and found the Master surrounded by his crew of about thirty Malays, urging them, at a given signal, to attack the prize crew and throw them overboard. Markham immediately interfered, when the Master threatened to shoot him and the Malays began to handle their knives. Markham, ordering his own men aft, told the Master to dismiss his crew and go below himself under arrest, failing which he should be put in irons. The prompt exercise of lawful authority prevailed; the Master, who was the worse for drink, obeyed, and the following morning made a humble apology for his conduct, begging that it should not be reported. As he appeared to be very penitent, and had apologised publicly before all hands, the matter was allowed to drop. Markham proceeded with the *Paragon*, in tow of the *Centaur*, and was in charge of her about a fortnight.

To the disappointment of her crew, the *Centaur* was out of most of the fighting. Ningpo had been taken, with rather severe losses, the day before their arrival there. It was about this time that Markham became acquainted with General Gordon, who, as a Major in the Royal Engineers, took a passage in the *Centaur* from the Peiho to Shanghai, and the *Centaur* subsequently co-operated with him when he was in command of his "Ever-Victorious Army." John Markham was a great friend of Gordon and belonged to his volunteer force, known as the "Rangers." During the time the *Centaur* was stationed at Ming Hong, Albert Markham had charge of a small Chinese army, consisting of 80 infantry and 20 cavalry. He took a keen interest in them and used to go on shore two or three times a day to drill them and march them out for ball practice.

The crew of the *Centaur*, having suffered very severely from cholera, smallpox, and fever, were ordered to Japan to recuperate, and here they remained for about eighteen months, with an occasional visit to China.

A very hostile feeling was at that time entertained by the Japanese officials against Europeans, culminating in an attack on the high road upon a party of Englishmen, one of whom was barbarously murdered. This outrage took place on the afternoon of Sunday, September 14th, 1862, about seven miles from Yokohama. The party consisted of three gentlemen, Messrs. Richardson, Marshall, and Clarke, and a lady, Mrs Borradaile, who were riding out to Kawasaki. They had passed several processions of Daimios on the high road, and had always taken the precaution of avoiding any collision with them by pulling up on one side of the road. When they had ridden a mile beyond Kanagawa they met another larger procession than before, and a man of gigantic stature stepped up and waved them with his hand to go back. They instantly turned their horses, but the man drew his sword and rushed at Mr Richardson, the last of the party, dealing him a ferocious blow which cut him all along the left side, and then aiming another at Mrs Borradaile's head. This was averted by Mr Richardson, who, although mortally wounded, guarded her with his arm, which was nearly severed. The other two men were severely wounded by others of the party, but managed to retain their seats on their horses until they reached the American Consulate at Kanagawa. Mrs Borradaile arrived at the British Legation at Yokohama covered with blood, stating that she had seen the three gentlemen cut down, but thought only one was killed. One of the attachés immediately went off to the *Centaur*, which was then lying off the town, with the terrible news. He found Markham in command, as the Captain and First Lieutenant were both on shore. Markham immediately landed with a small party of men, all he could muster on board the ship, and, finding the wounded men had come safely in, marched out to Kanagawa to pick up the dead body. After proceeding for about four miles he met a detachment of military bringing it in. Apart from the horror of the outrage, it was a personal

sorrow to Markham, to whom Mr Richardson was well
known, being a great friend of his brother's. He had just
made his fortune in China, and was paying a visit to Japan
before returning to England. As the *Euryalus* and *Ringdove*
had just arrived, all on board the *Centaur* expected that
instant punishment would be inflicted on the Japanese, but
the British Chargé d'Affaires would not permit any demonstration at the time, to the indignation of the young officers,
though later the squadron bombarded and destroyed the
stronghold of Satsuma at Kagoshima. To the chagrin of those
on board, the *Centaur* did not accompany the Fleet, but
remained behind to protect British interests at Yokohama
and Yeddo.

At last the long period of service on the China Station
came to an end, and in February, 1864, the *Centaur* began
her homeward voyage. The passage was uneventful, save
for a severe hurricane off the coast of Mauritius, which
Markham describes as the worst he had ever known. The
following June the *Centaur* reached home and was paid off
at Plymouth. Thus, after an absence of over eight years,
Markham once more set foot on English soil, and four
months on half-pay were pleasantly spent in visiting his
relations and friends. For his services in China he received
the China medal and one clasp.

Towards the close of July he went up to the Royal Naval
College at Portsmouth for his lieutenant's examination;
this he passed well, and in the following November he
was appointed to the *Victoria*, the last three-decker ever
commissioned. The *Victoria* was the flag-ship on the
Mediterranean Station, and during the period of nearly
three years which he served in her she flew the flags of
Sir Robert Smart and Lord Clarence Paget. In Sir Robert
Smart's time the Captain was his old and steadfast friend
James G. Goodenough. The Commander was William Cod-
rington, to whom Markham always averred he owed all his
professional knowledge of the details connected with the
internal administration of a perfect man-of-war.

This was a singularly happy commission. The *Victoria*

had a very warm place in his heart, and he always alluded to her affectionately as "the old *Victoria*." These early days in the Navy were fruitful in the formation of friendships that proved lifelong. Markham himself—a man of many-sided but by no means complex nature—was a universal favourite.

During the time he was in the Mediterranean he visited nearly every port of Spain, Italy, and the western coast of Greece; besides this, a few days' leave from time to time afforded him the opportunity of making excursions farther afield.

He was also attached to the suite of Lord Clarence Paget, and accompanied that officer when he was sent to Cairo to invest the Khedive, Ismail Pacha, with the Grand Cross of the Bath. It was at this time, too, that a system of naval tactics was introduced into the Navy, and was worked out in the Mediterranean Squadron, then the only Fleet that could be considered as a "tactical" one.

On the return of the *Victoria* to England, in the summer of 1867, she was selected as the flag-ship at the grand Naval Review at Spithead on July 17th of the same year, in honour of the visit of the Sultan of Turkey and the Khedive of Egypt. On August 7th the ship was paid off.

It was during this commission that a seed was sown which was destined to bear fruit in the chief work of Markham's life. His cousin, Clements Markham, and his old shipmate Sherard Osborn, were beginning to urge the renewal of Arctic exploration. Captain Goodenough, realising the importance of such enterprises both to the Navy itself and in the interests of science generally, took up the idea warmly. Influenced both by his cousin and the Captain, Albert Markham turned his thoughts in that direction, and Captain Goodenough advised him to volunteer for Arctic service. But for the time the Government was slow to act; it was not until ten years later that these ardent spirits saw the accomplishment of their desire in the despatch of an expedition to the Polar regions. Owing, doubtless, to the same influence, two other young officers of the *Victoria*,

Lieutenants May and Parr, were fired with the same enthusiasm.

From this time Markham seems to have made Arctic exploration one of his studies, not only reading up the history of previous expeditions, but mastering, as far as possible, all the details necessary to successful enterprise in the future.

Chapter V

1867–1872

Markham had only five months on half pay, two of which were spent in carrying out the long-cherished dream of visiting his family in America. He left England on September 12th, 1867, and after a somewhat tedious and uncomfortable journey landed at New York on the 25th.

After a trip to Niagara, he turned his face towards his parents' home in Wisconsin, viâ Detroit and Chicago. The latter city struck him as very bustling and prosperous. This was, of course, four years before the great fire. The streets were very much lower than the footpaths (which were nearly all made of wood) on account of all the houses having been raised by means of screw jacks under their foundations!

Markham's progress after leaving Chicago was not easy. He describes the trains as "very slow," adding, "I have now travelled over a thousand miles and have seldom done more than twenty-four miles per hour." His luggage had gone astray, and someone had stolen his stick, which he greatly prized, having had it in the *Victoria*. His difficulties were increased by not knowing how to proceed from La Crosse to Elk Creek, the nearest point from home, and, unfortunately, no one seemed able to enlighten him. He left Chicago at 5 p.m. on September 28th, his luggage having happily turned up at the last moment. Travelling through the southern part of Michigan, he reached La Crosse at 8.30 a.m. on the 29th. As they steamed up the Mississippi he was delighted with the grandeur and beauty of the scenery. He had not the slightest idea which was his best way, or where he was to get out, but seeing a village named Trempeleau (his parents living in Trempeleau Co.) he took his ticket for that place, which was reached at noon. Here he found, to his disappointment, that he was still forty-two miles from his home without a chance of procuring a conveyance to take him on. Nothing daunted, he started off, having left his luggage at Trempeleau, first hiring a team with a man who said he knew his brother George very well, then proceeding a stage on foot, carrying his carpet-bag, then getting a lift in a cart for about nine miles. It was now getting very late, and having by these means travelled a long distance he fancied himself about seven miles from home; so, hailing a man on a haystack, he asked him if he were on the right road to Markham's Farm.

"Guess you won't get there to-night," was the answer.

"Why not? How far is it?"

"Guess it's a matter of four-and-twenty miles."

This was rather disquieting; still he was determined to press on. After walking a couple of miles further he stopped to enquire at a house and was told he was fourteen miles from the farm, and thankfully closed with the offer to drive him there for four dollars.

He reached his destination at 10 o'clock at night, to find the whole household in bed and fast asleep. Great was their surprise when they found out who the visitor was.

Twenty-five very happy days followed. Albert thoroughly enjoyed the free, open-air life on the farm, lending a hand in the farm work, driving about the country, and shooting prairie chicken. The only shadow on that happy time was the increasing ill-health of his father, and the leave-taking was a very painful one. Three years later Captain John Markham died at the age of seventy-three. The news only reached his youngest son, then on the Australian Station, about three months after the event.

On January 7th, 1868, although a lieutenant of only five and a half years' standing, Albert Markham was appointed First Lieutenant of H.M.S. *Blanche,* fitting out at Chatham for the Australian Station. They left England in February, on what was to prove an eventful commission in the southern hemisphere, extending over three and a half years. On several occasions the ship was very nearly lost.

Once she grounded on a coral reef in Torres Straits, and the situation looked so serious that a raft was constructed to carry the ship's company, in the very probable event of her going to pieces. Happily this precaution proved unnecessary, for, by throwing all heavy weights overboard, they succeeded in lightening the vessel sufficiently to float her. On another occasion the ship was barely saved from destruction, some forty miles to the eastward of Sydney; in fact, her deliverance was largely due to Markham's sagacity and forethought. Anticipating the danger, he had urged the Captain the night before to have her two anchors unlashed and prepared to be let go.

"The beautiful *Blanche*" was described by Markham as "a perfect success as a steamer, besides sailing very well." She made the voyage from the Cape to King George's Sound in thirty-two days, under sail all the time, in spite of unpropitious weather, sometimes calms, at others gales of wind, with a very heavy south-west swell the whole way. His pride in the *Blanche* was amply justified, for she was always well reported on by the Senior Officer of the Station during this commission, and was invariably regarded as a perfectly efficient and happy man-of-war.

She was employed in several punitive expeditions in the Solomon Islands, in Torres Strait, in New Zealand, and elsewhere. Markham was always in charge of the landing-parties or boats, as the case might be. In Tauranga, in New Zealand, during the hostilities against Te-Koo-ti, the Maori chief, the men were landed as a Naval Brigade under his command for a period of about three weeks.

Twice Markham was instrumental in saving lives at sea. Once he jumped overboard to the assistance of a boy, when the ship was steaming about ten knots—a fair speed in those days. Not long afterwards, during a gale of wind and in a heavy sea, off the east coast of New Zealand, the jib-boom was carried away, taking with it one of the crew. It was hardly a sea in which to lower a boat with safety, and, seeing a hesitancy on the part of the men to go to the rescue of their unfortunate comrade, he jumped into a boat himself and called for volunteers. They only needed a leader, and immediately responded to the call. They succeeded in picking up the man in an exhausted condition, but had the greatest difficulty in getting back to the ship in safety; indeed, in getting alongside, their boat was stove in in several places.

During his term of service on the Australian Station an incident occurred which had an interesting development, and is not generally known. It was the time of the beginning of the New Zealand Marine, which then consisted of a single ship! In quite an informal way Markham was asked if he could suggest a distinctive flag.

"You have already- the right," he replied, "to fly the Blue Ensign, why not add to it the stars of the Southern Cross?"

The suggestion was received with delight. A drawing was made on board the *Blanche*, and duly despatched. After a short interval it was returned with an appreciative note, asking that the design might be enlarged, as the stars would hardly shew sufficiently, and accompanied by a parody on Lewis Carroll's lines: "Will you walk a little faster?" with the refrain—"Will you, won't you, will you, won't you, magnify the star?"

The star was accordingly "magnified," and the flag now proudly floats over the shipping of New Zealand.

When, in October, 1871, the *Blanche* was re-commissioned by a new crew at Sydney, Markham was appointed as Acting Commander of the *Rosario*, a wooden sloop of 673 tons (old measurement), carrying an armament of three revolving guns, all of which worked on one or both broadsides, and a complement of 145 officers and men.

A new and onerous duty was now laid upon him, demanding the qualities of tact, firmness, and courage. In consequence of the enormous success of the cotton plantations, first started in 1860 in the Fiji Islands, and later, in 1863, in Queensland, not far from Brisbane, the demand for labour had grown extraordinarily, and natives were pressed into the service of the plantations. As the demand for labour increased and the traffic proved highly lucrative, the practice of visiting the various islands and carrying away the islanders, frequently without their own consent, prevailed to a deplorable degree, and was often attended by shocking cruelty. It is small wonder that the unfortunate natives, whenever they had an opportunity, retaliated on the white men, enticing boat-loads to their shores with every appearance of friendliness, and then treacherously murdering them: in many cases, since they exercised no discrimination, innocent missionaries and others often suffered for the guilty traders.

Both of these evils the Home Government felt must be dealt with, and later, in 1872, a Bill to prevent kidnapping in the South Seas was passed, and schooners, commanded and manned by officers and men of the Royal Navy, were equipped in order to cruise among the islands for the suppression of this iniquitous traffic. In 1868 the Polynesian Labourers' Act had come into being, but unfortunately the employers, for the most part, appear to have paid little regard to its enactments, and, in any case, it had no power in those places unconnected with the Queensland Government.

Towards the latter part of 1871 Commodore Stirling, Senior Naval Officer on the Australian Station, felt compelled to send a man-of-war to cruise among the New Hebrides and Santa Cruz groups in order to deal with the complicated state of affairs. The vessel chosen was the *Rosario*, and Markham's orders were to visit, as far as time would permit, each one of these islands, putting himself into communication with missionaries, planters, and other persons from whom he might obtain reliable information. He was to board all vessels carrying English colours, and to satisfy himself that they were acting strictly in accordance with the Merchant Shipping Act. Further, he was to give the subject of deportation of natives from their homes to other South Sea Islands his earnest attention, and fully to report the conclusions at which he arrived. Finally, he was informed that, although it was the desire of the

British Government to prevent any irregularities connected with the so-called labour traffic in these islands, yet in all he did he was to act in accordance with law. He was to carry a mail to Norfolk Island, where he was to put himself into communication with Bishop Patteson, tidings of whose murder had not then reached Sydney.

As Markham carefully read these instructions, he was impressed with the difficulty and responsibility of his task. He knew too well that the labour traffic was closely associated with the cotton-planting interests of the Colonies, and that the ships engaged in the so-called labour trade were practically owned by large and influential houses in Sydney, Melbourne, Brisbane, and Auckland. Moreover, he was aware that, until then the commanders of men-of-war, in their efforts to stop the iniquitous practice of kidnapping natives, had lacked the support of the Colonial law-courts; indeed, on two occasions, when slavers had been seized and sent to Sydney to be dealt with, they were acquitted, and the officers who had captured them had been compelled to pay heavy damages for detention and injury done to the slave vessels. Bearing these facts in mind, he realised that he must act with extreme caution, since, apart from any personal annoyance, it would surely be detrimental to the prestige of the British Navy to be continually put in the wrong while discharging their obvious duties. He therefore determined that, unless he caught any of these vessels actually red-handed, he would simply warn them and leave them alone, since the rules laid down in the Merchant Shipping Act were utterly inadequate to deal with this thorny question. On the other hand, the men-of-war employed in the past on punitive expeditions against the natives had adopted such severe measures as had often led to open hostilities. After long and careful consideration of the problem, Markham decided to try the effect of a more conciliatory policy, and to this determination he invariably adhered. Punishment had to be meted out, but it was never accompanied by loss of life among the natives.

On the arrival of the *Rosario* at Norfolk Island they

heard, for the first time, the sad intelligence of the murder of Bishop Patteson and his fellow-worker, Mr Atkin, and two natives, at the island of Nukapu, one of the Swallow group, about thirty miles to the northward of Santa Cruz. Anxious to obtain particulars, Markham landed with a party from the ship, and rode to the headquarters of the Melanesian Mission.

It is now a matter of history that the sole reason for the murder of the beloved Bishop was the visit of one of the iniquitous labour vessels to the island some time previously, which led to the determination of the natives to take the lives of the next white men who should come to their shores, so that, when the Bishop arrived on his mission of peace, his fate was sealed. The whole sad story is too well known to need repetition here. Later, Markham visited the island of Nukapu, both for the purpose of obtaining further information and, if possible, of finding some relic of the Bishop and his companions.

This island, two miles in circumference, was found to be situated on a coral reef extending one and a half miles from its south-western shore, and was covered with a dense bush to within a few feet of the water's edge. Numerous stone breastworks were thrown up along the beach in front of the village, which was situated on the south-west side of the island. This description must be borne in mind in view of subsequent adverse criticism. In a speech made in the House of Lords on May 4th, 1872, the island was described as no larger in area than the site occupied by both Houses of Parliament, and affording no shelter for the unfortunate natives fired upon by a man-of-war. In point of fact the island covered ten times the space indicated above, and the facts of the case are these. As the ship steamed up to the western edge of the reef several native canoes paddled out into the lagoon. The Second Lieutenant was sent in the gig to open friendly communications, but with stringent orders to avoid any chance of a collision with the natives, and on no account to use fire-arms, except in actual self-defence. The occupants of the sixteen canoes made signs to

the crew to come on shore, the islanders on the beach
waving green branches as signs of peace and goodwill, but
the state of the tide rendering this impracticable, they
returned to the ship, which then steamed up to the north
end of the island. By this time most of the natives had
landed, and it was plainly seen that they were all armed
with bows and arrows, spears and clubs. Hoping to be able
to effect a landing at this spot the Second Lieutenant was
again sent away with the same orders, and instructions to
call out for the two chiefs, Taula and Motu, who had acted
as decoys in connection with the murder of the Bishop.
The officer was bidden to approach cautiously, holding up
his hands, unarmed, and shewing white handkerchiefs. As
they drew near to the shore, the natives began yelling and
dancing a kind of war dance, and when the boat was within
a hundred yards it was assailed by a flight of arrows,
fortunately without success. The boat was then recalled
without having fired a single shot, and when it was again
sent to attempt to establish friendly relations, a fierce
attack was again made on her. It was then necessary, both
for the protection of the boat and for the upholding of
lawful authority, that the ship should be cleared for action,
and three shells were fired. This dispersed the natives, who
sought refuge in the bush, though some more audacious
spirits occasionally came down and shouted defiance, shooting
their arrows towards the ship. It must be borne in mind that
the natives had acted with their wonted treachery, deluding
the boat's crew with signs of friendship. Markham felt that
to leave now, without landing, would be an unwise act, as
the natives would undoubtedly say they had driven off a
man-of-war, and would in future have little respect for the
courage of the white men. He therefore brought round the
vessel, and opened fire upon the village, using six rounds of
shot and shell, at an elevation of 2400 yards, *which all fell
short.* Later, when the tide served, two cutters and both
gigs pulled about a mile up the lagoon towards the village.
Markham's gig was some distance in advance, and he again
attempted friendly communications, repeatedly asking for

the two chiefs, Taula and Motu. The only answer was a
flight of arrows, many striking his boat, the natives dancing
on the beach, freely exposing themselves, though they all
retired under cover when a shot was fired. When the other
boats approached the order was given to open fire into the
bush. They were so well protected by their stone breastworks that it was impossible to dislodge them, except by
landing and driving them out. This was accordingly done,
but so good was their protection that they were able to
retire without, as far as could be seen, the loss of a single
man. The village of huts was then set on fire, and several
canoes were destroyed, but the original object in visiting
the island, that of obtaining information as to the motives
for the murder of Bishop Patteson, was not effected. Two
of the landing party were wounded by poisoned arrows,
one, Markham's orderly, eventually dying of tetanus.
Markham himself had a narrow escape, one of the arrows
piercing his pith hat.

Had the islanders not been punished for their dastardly
attack on the boat's crew they would have been left with
the impression that such things could be done with im-
punity. Further, it was Markham's duty in his magisterial
capacity to investigate and punish the outrages perpetrated
by the natives.

Another deed of violence, committed this time by the
natives of Nguna, in the New Hebrides, had caused wide-
spread feelings of horror and indignation. The story, briefly,
is as follows: On July 9th, 1871, the schooner *Fanny*
anchored in the bay off the Mission house. Mr and Mrs Milne,
the resident missionaries, were absent at the time, and the
house was left in charge of three Rarotongan teachers. The
crew of the *Fanny* consisted of the Master, two other white
men, and four natives. She had brought back some five or
six islanders who had been for some years in Fiji as labourers.
They were paid, and landed on the 10th, and the Captain
asked for more men to go back with him to Fiji. The following day a number consented to go, and seven presented
themselves on board. They then told the Captain to send

his boat, as there were some more who wished to come. It was accordingly despatched in charge of a white man and two natives. No foul play was suspected until the Captain requested those who had come off to the ship to give up the tomahawks they had brought with them. With signs of indignation they refused, and at the sound of a yell from the shore set upon the crew, exclaiming, "You come here to steal men, do you?"

The Captain hurried below to load his revolver, and the mate, coming up on hearing the noise, was struck with a tomahawk, which cut off his chin and wounded him on the shoulder, directly his head appeared above the companion-hatch. The natives then fastened down the scuttle, imprisoning the Captain and the mate. The cable was then cut, and the vessel allowed to drift on shore. For two days the Captain and mate held the ship against the natives, but on the second night they effected their escape, having first thrown overboard all the ammunition. On reaching shore they proceeded first to the Mission house, but, finding it closed, they went to that of the Rarotongan teachers. It would have been as much as these men's lives were worth to have been seen helping them, but they did all in their power, concealing them sometimes in their own house, sometimes in the cellar of the Mission house, and sometimes in the bush, feeding the unfortunate mate like a child. However, poor fellow, being probably in delirium, he would not remain in hiding, and was discovered and tomahawked by the hostile natives. The vessel was plundered of her stores and articles of trade, but left uninjured. The fate of the boat which, as already related, had in the first instance been sent on shore was sad in the extreme. On reaching the island, the three men were immediately attacked, one native was killed, the other, being recognised as belonging to the neighbouring island of Mau, was suffered to escape. The white man, severely wounded, by a desperate effort shoved off from the beach, and, as neither he nor the boat were ever heard of again, it was supposed he must have drifted out to sea before the trade wind and perished.

After seven days' concealment, the Captain was rescued by Mr Thurston, the ex-Acting British Consul at Fiji. With some difficulty the remains of the unhappy mate were recovered from the hands of the cannibals, and accorded Christian burial.

As soon as the outrage on the *Fanny* became known everyone was clamorous that Markham should at once proceed to the island and punish the natives, but he delayed taking any steps until he had communicated with Mr Milne, the missionary. He never forgot that when the natives received injuries from the white men they very naturally retaliated upon the first that came within their reach.

Having invited the Rev. Peter Milne and the Rev. William Watt to come on board and confer with him, he left the ship on the following morning with a force consisting of his own boat and the two cutters, numbering in all seven officers and thirty-three seamen and marines. He made several attempts to obtain an interview with the chiefs, for he was anxious to make it clear to them that a man-of-war was as much for the protection of the natives as for that of the white men. He even offered to meet the chiefs alone and unarmed at any place they might like to appoint, giving them two hours in which to decide—but all in vain. Not only did he receive no answer, but they were frequently fired upon from the bush, fortunately without any harm being done. Their fire was not returned. In consequence of this persistent refusal to come to terms it became necessary to inflict punishment by burning two villages, which he did with great reluctance. Before leaving, he entrusted Mr Milne with a message to the chiefs telling them that all this might have been avoided had they not refused his overtures to bring about a friendly discussion.

In compliance with a suggestion of Mr Milne's, the *Rosario* was brought round in order to demonstrate the size and power of a man-of-war, and a few rounds were fired, due notice being given to the natives, so as to guard against any injury being done to them.

On the return of the ship to the island in six weeks' time,

Mr Milne reported that the steps taken had had an excellent effect, and some of the natives were persuaded to meet Commander Markham at the Mission house. They listened attentively to all he had to say, acknowledging the justice of their punishment, and promised in future not to take the law into their own hands, and to pay heed to the missionary's admonitions. They pleaded, in extenuation of their conduct, that they had received great provocation in the kidnapping of an albino woman, the wife of a chief named Marewatta, who had been taken by a white man to Tanna, and there sold for labour. They were much pleased at the assurance of Commander Markham that he was going to Tanna, and would enquire into the matter. This he did, and with some trouble at last learned from a white man named Bill that she was somewhere in the vicinity of the village near which he had landed. Accompanied by the First Lieutenant he instituted a diligent search, which was eventually crowned with success. He describes her recovery as follows:

Seeing a pair of white feet near the doorway of one of the huts I determined upon looking in, and was rewarded by discovering the very woman I was in search of. I called her out, and through the medium of Bill, who acted as interpreter, asked her whether she would remain where she was, or come on board the *Rosario* with me and be taken back to her husband; informing her at the same time that I had recently come from Nguna, where I had seen her sorrowing and heart-broken spouse. Without hesitation she decided upon accompanying me, and, picking up her bundle, containing her entire wardrobe, followed me. She seemed delighted at getting away, but shewed a little concern at parting with one man, a native of Sandwich Island, with whom she had been living for the past two or three months, and during the time she was on board the ship she would never part with a large knife which this man had given her on leaving, nor suffer it to be out of her hand or mouth, in which latter it might invariably be seen.

He describes her thus: "Her skin was as fair as any man's on board the ship, but covered with large red blotches all over the exposed parts. Her wool was coarse and of a yellowish hue. She had an enormous mouth with thick lips, a flat nose, and small receding eyes of a pinkish colour."

When the Commander's intention to take the *Rosario* back to Nguna, a distance of 200 miles, with this not very desirable passenger, instead of proceeding to Sydney, was made known to those on board there was considerable disappointment, but, on their realising the good effect likely to be produced on the natives by the kindly intervention of a man-of-war on their behalf, their spirits rose, for they were all greatly interested in the efforts to establish friendly relations with the islanders. The satisfaction of the people on the return of the "fair" Nepolow to her husband knew no bounds, and on the departure of her rescuers they would have loaded the boat up to the thwarts with pigs, coconuts, and bananas had they been permitted to do so. As it was they ran along the beach as the boat shoved off, cheering repeatedly, thus manifesting their goodwill.

The *Rosario* eventually met with the *Donald Maclean*, the schooner which had carried off the albino woman from Nguna. On her being boarded it was found she had no papers whatever; her Master was therefore made to sign a paper acknowledging the illegality of his proceedings. This, in view of the attitude already alluded to of the courts at Sydney, was all that could be done in this and similar cases, for every suspicious vessel was boarded and her papers demanded for examination. It was a remarkable circumstance that even those whose papers appeared to be in order invariably sought to evade the *Rosario* when she came in sight. A shot across their bows was sufficient to pull them up, and they always had numberless excuses ready. On one occasion the *Rosario* was taken first for a "rock," then for a "whaler." "Complimentary," adds Markham in his record!

Amid the serious work of the cruise Markham found time to interest himself in the natural attractions of his surroundings—the formation of the islands, the distribution of races, the character and customs of the natives, and to enjoy the varied and beautiful scenery. On one occasion,

H.M.S. *ROSARIO* OVERHAULING A SLAVER

when visiting Tanna in company with Mr Neilson, the resident missionary, he made the ascent of Mt Yasowa, the most powerful and active volcano in this group of islands.

In connection with one of the islands visited he used to tell the following story. When home on leave after his first commission, an old uncle, who was fond of putting posers to his young nephews and nieces, suddenly startled him at a dinner-table full of people with the question: "Albert, where's Tongataboo?" Not to appear nonplussed, the young lieutenant instantly hazarded an answer which proved wide of the mark, and elicited the jeering comment—"Oo-o, you a sailor, and don't know where Tongataboo is!" During this voyage he learned to some purpose where Tongataboo is, for it was one of the islands he had to visit in the course of the cruise.

Throughout the whole time sickness was prevalent amongst the ship's company, attributable, among other causes, to the fact that the *Rosario's* cruise was made during the hottest and most unhealthy months of the year, and to the lack of fresh provisions. On one occasion, after hearing Markham's report of the condition of things on board, Mrs Paton, wife of the veteran missionary to the New Hebrides, insisted on making them a present of one of their small bullocks, and this gift was sufficient to supply them with fresh meat for two days.

It was with feelings of great satisfaction that they at last reached Sydney, arriving on February 8th, 1872, exactly sixteen weeks from the day on which they had left, and conscious that their expedition had not been fruitless.

Here sad news awaited Markham. Many months had passed since he had received any letters, and during the four months' cruise no papers had reached the *Rosario*. He had no sooner set foot on land than he was accosted by an acquaintance who asked him if he were any relation of the Consul Markham who had died suddenly at the age of thirty-six in China, adding that the intelligence was in all the papers. The news was confirmed by a letter from his cousin in New Zealand which he found awaiting him. Consul John Markham had been deservedly popular, and the day of his death was called "black Monday" by the community in Shanghai.

Markham left the *Rosario* in March, 1872, and travelled home across America. He found on reaching England that his actions in the South Seas were the subject of adverse criticism, and had been discussed in both Houses of Parliament. He was not greatly moved by it, for his own conscience was clear. A very different view was taken by the missionaries on the spot, who, in letters written to the Foreign Mission Committee of the Reformed Church of Scotland, laid great stress on the moderation and forbearance with which Markham had acted. This Committee even went so far as to draw up and forward to Members of Parliament and others a statement in which they spoke in terms of approbation of the course taken by Commander Markham who "although repeatedly fired upon...evinced a rare self-control and moderation in forbidding his men to return the fire; and certainly if punishment was to be inflicted at all, it assumed the mildest form in the destruction of a few canoes and some native huts." They added that it would be a matter of regret to them if his conduct were met by Parliament otherwise than with the commendation it merited. Markham's relations with the missionaries were always of the happiest, and he thoroughly appreciated their good work and brave self-denying lives[1].

It is noteworthy that, when four years after, Captain Goodenough, then Commodore on the Australian Station, visited the same islands in the *Pearl*, he adopted a similar line of conduct to that taken by Markham. It was here that this brilliant officer, respected by all for his remarkable talents and his fine Christian life, met his death by poisoned arrows when seeking to enter into friendly negotiations with the natives.

The view taken by the Admiralty of the work of the

---

[1] For a full account of his work in the South Seas see *The Cruise of the "Rosario,"* by A. H. Markham. Sampson Low and Co., 1873.

Rosario, when the main facts became known to them, was shewn not only in their expressing approval of all that Markham had done, but also by promoting him to the rank of Commander, after he had served for three months as First Lieutenant of the *Ariadne*. In this training-ship he had forty-eight naval cadets under his immediate charge, and visited Bermuda, Halifax, Lisbon, and Gibraltar.

Chapter VI

1872–1874

THE CALL OF THE NORTH

ON Markham's return to England in December, 1872, he found that the question of an Arctic expedition was being discussed. He was, as we have seen, already deeply interested in the subject, and so, as it was deemed essential that a report concerning the state of the ice in Davis Strait and Baffin's Bay should be obtained from personal observation, he sought seven months' leave from the Admiralty to devote himself to this purpose, backed up by Sherard Osborn and Clements Markham. This request being granted, he made terms with the owners and shipped as second mate on board a Dundee whaler, the *Arctic*, which sailed for Greenland on May 3rd, 1873. He had selected this particular vessel on account of the reputation of her skipper, Captain Adams, for dash and enterprise. The whalers were not licensed to carry passengers, therefore anyone wishing to make a voyage in one was obliged to sign articles as one of the crew; that done, he was at liberty to do as he liked, and to enjoy himself in his own way.

The terms under which he sailed were as follows: "To serve on board the good ship *Arctic* on a voyage from Dundee to Greenland and Davis Straits and seas adjacent for whale and other fishing and back to Dundee." Moreover, he agreed to conduct himself in an orderly, faithful, honest, and sober manner, and to be at all times diligent in his respective duties, and to be obedient to the lawful commands of his master! The daily allowance of butter, cheese, oatmeal, bread, beef, pork, flour, tea, sugar, lemon-juice, water, and other stores were previously read to him and the whole crew at the shipping office. His wages were to be a shilling per month and he was to receive in addition a penny for every ton of oil brought home in the ship and a farthing for every ton of whalebone!

He was thoroughly pleased with the Captain and ship's company. The former he described as "kind, jovial, and good-tempered," while, as to the crew, "a fine sturdy set of fellows," he was agreeably surprised to find they were not such a drunken set as the ordinary crew of a whaler had been represented to him. This comment throws a side-light on Markham's persistent habit of seeing the best in everyone, for it was some days before they could benefit by the services of their cook, who took that time to recover from his last day on shore; also, one of their number had a slight attack of *delirium tremens* in the early part of their cruise. One member of the crew was deaf and dumb, but in spite of this proved an excellent seaman; he went by the *sobriquet* of "Dummy." The doctor was a medical student at Edinburgh University and an ardent naturalist.

The life on board was rough, but Markham soon shook down into it, and he was treated by all with the utmost civility and attention; he was always addressed as "Captain." The hours for meals were—breakfast at 8, dinner at 12, and tea at 5. In consequence of the limited accommodation in the cabin these had always to be served in relays. The aphorism that "fingers were made before forks" was in full force on board the whaler, and it was with keen wonder and interest that he watched the dexterous manner in which some of his messmates performed the extraordinary feat of eating eggs with a large knife! When a joint shewed the least portion of bone protruding, this was seized by the carver as he cut off large junks of meat to be handed to the rest—certainly a simple, if not appetising, mode of carving. Whelks were a delicacy to which he had to be introduced, and following the advice of the skipper to smother them well with vinegar, mushroom ketchup, and pepper, found them palatable enough. This was at the 10 o'clock supper with which the skipper, doctor and himself often supple-mented the recognised meals of the day. When the whelks came to an end their place was taken by lobsters, or cheese and grog, and on one occasion he describes the *pièce de résistance* as "a villainous compound of cheese, pepper,

and mustard, called a 'crab'"! This time of recreation
was enlivened by the skipper's jokes, endless yarns, recitations from Shakespeare, etc., etc., interspersed with conversation over the events of the day. The daily routine was
sufficiently monotonous, and the ship was certainly not
built for comfort, particularly in wet weather. Her decks
leaked "like a sieve" from the continual straining, and both
the main cabin and Markham's received perpetual drips.
The upper deck, even in moderate weather, was always wet,
as the ship had open waterways running fore and aft which
seemed to admit more water than they drained off. However, as they were running well, he looked forward hopefully
to reaching, before long, the smooth waters of Davis Straits.

But, before this, they had to pass through a period of no
small anxiety as, not having obtained sights for three days,
they were uncertain as to their position. On the morning
of May 12th which, after a miserably uncomfortable night,
dawned fine and clear, at 2 p.m. land was discovered on
the starboard bow. This proved to be Cape Farewell, and
Markham was able to make a rough sketch of it, though
it was about thirty miles distant. The land "appeared bold,
bleak, and rugged, and seemed to consist of a number of
sharp, conical-shaped black hills, covered where the summits
were not too peaked with snow. The strong contrast of
the black and white gave the land a most sublime and
picturesque appearance."

Favoured by beautiful weather they were unusually
fortunate in rounding the Cape under a bright sun and
clear sky, though the temperature had fallen several degrees.
They were now fairly in Davis Straits, and the day was spent
in preparations for the real object of their cruise. All hands
were busy "spanning on," i.e. attaching the lines to the
harpoons and coiling them away in the boats, which were
got out in readiness to go away at a moment's notice.

In the course of the day one of the crew remarked that
the greyish appearance of the sky "denounced" the
proximity of ice. This proved to be a true prediction, and
when at midnight the same man reported to the skipper

that they were actually passing ice, the little supper-party was immediately broken up, and as they were hastily donning their coats a heavy crash and the tumbling of the ship proclaimed that they were already in it. They had struck a huge piece and as they hurried on deck they could see large broken fragments rising to the surface, and found themselves surrounded by innumerable masses. All was now excitement on the whaler, extra look-outs were stationed, with another man at the helm: orders rang out on the misty night. But, in spite of the utmost care, the ship from time to time came into contact with the ice, the impact causing the bell to toll out in mournful cadence. By 7 a.m. they were clear and made sail to a light northerly wind. To Markham the scene was entrancing, the masses of ice taking on all kinds of fantastic forms, many of them a bright, shimmering blue.

Their first capture was a huge seal, which, according to the Captain's decree, fell to Markham's gun. Several bottle-nose whales were seen, but the skipper being anxious to press on to the south-western fishing-ground they were left unmolested.

In a day or two they began to encounter large icebergs, for the presence of which they had been prepared by the light, whitish tint along the horizon, known as the "ice blink." One of these, of huge dimensions, which they judged to be at least a mile in length, and its height between 200 and 300 feet, was at first mistaken for land about 70 miles distant by Markham's unpractised eye. Soon, as they pushed forward, the ice proving heavier than they had anticipated, the ship became completely hemmed in, and in spite of having every stitch of sail set and the engines going full speed ahead, they were held fast for at least twenty-five or thirty minutes, even the wake of the vessel being closed up. However, after persistent screwing and boring, they at last got through safely into the clear water, or *polynia*, having sustained collisions in the passage sufficient to damage an ordinarily built ship, but the whalers are specially constructed to withstand the pressure of heavy ice.

They now began to look out for whales, or "fish," as they are technically called, in good earnest, but at first they met with no luck. For days, in spite of the bustle and excitement, lowering of boats, and long and tedious chases, they were always unsuccessful. Sometimes a boat would get almost within striking distance only to see the prey escape under the ice as soon as the harpooner prepared to launch his weapon. To add to their exasperation one of the other whalers, which had now joined them, caught, under their very eyes, a fine "fish" which one of their own men had been the first to sight. The men are extremely superstitious, and ridiculous reasons were advanced for their want of success. Sometimes it was the presence of a comb in common requisition by all in the cabin, and with the services of which, as a result, they nearly dispensed. Again, it was a small pig whose life was for a time in imminent danger. Markham hoped they would not regard his presence on board in the same light!

Success came at last, on May 23rd. At 7.30 a.m., after an earlier chase ending in disappointment, the welcome cry "A fall, a fall,"[1] rang out, announcing that a boat was at length "fast" to a fish, the harpooner having succeeded in striking his quarry. Hastily throwing on his coat, Markham joined the rest on deck and watched all the operations with the keenest interest. The boats of the whalers are distinctively painted so that it shall be known to which ship they belong, those of the *Arctic* being in longitudinal lines of blue, white, blue, with black gunwales; their fishing flag being white with a blue five-pointed star. It is customary, when ships are fishing in company, to hoist the fishing-jack at the mizen top-gallant masthead of the one to which the first boat that gets "fast" belongs.

The whale having received six harpoons in its body, the *coup de grâce* was administered with lances, upon which the

---

[1] The word "fall" is thought by some to be derived from the Dutch, and various explanations are advanced, the most likely being that it comes from the Dutch *walvisch* or *wal* (pronounced "vall") signifying "whale."

monster turned over on its back and expired, amid much cheering. Markham was next initiated into the mysteries of "flensing" or "flinching"—taking in the blubber, extracting the "whalebone" from the mouth, and separating the tail from the carcase, or "kreng," all of which is done in the water, after which the huge body is let go, disappearing into the depths amid more cheering. The men were so quick about their work that it was completed in exactly two hours. They attributed their good fortune to the fact that they had the previous night burned in effigy two of the crew who were thought to have brought ill-luck owing to their having for a few years past served in vessels which either had returned "clean," or having met with very small success!

While the operation of "flinching" was in progress, a bear was noticed upon an iceberg about 200 yards off. Markham at once ran for his rifle, and, accompanied by the doctor and two hands, pulled off in the dinghy. A couple of shots from Markham's rifle secured him the prize of the fine young bear, which measured nearly seven feet.

The following day was devoted to the task of "making off," which consists in cutting up and stowing the blubber. This, as well as the flinching, is a very methodical operation, each man being told off to special work. The skins of the whales are usually thrown overboard, but the kind and considerate Captain of the *Arctic* used to reserve them and place them in a tank, for distribution among the Eskimo inhabitants of Lively, or Godhavn, who esteem them highly as an article of diet; they are also prized as an anti-scorbutic. But, so far as Markham was able to make out, these and other kind gifts were received with scant thanks; the Eskimos struck him as an ungrateful people, who take any kindness as their due.

During the operation of flinching, large numbers of the fulmar petrel, commonly called "mollies," gather round the carcase, fighting for the titbits, and gorging themselves to such a horrible extent as often to be unable to fly.

The ship was now once more surrounded by ice, and Markham was to experience what ice-navigation really means. Viewed from the crow's nest by his unaccustomed eyes, the ship seemed to be hopelessly jammed, and even the Captain expected to get through only with great difficulty. In fact they were sixteen hours before they got free, having made their way through at least fifty miles of pack ice, boring and pushing, under steam and sail, through fields upon fields of it, now wedged between heavy floes, now dashing forward, the broken fragments flying before them. Sometimes the ship would recoil several yards, and then gather way for a fresh onslaught against the mighty barrier. Nothing but ice could be seen as far as eye could reach; it was a gloomy and desolate scene, in which the only break in the monotony was the countless icebergs to be descried on the horizon. Snow fell heavily, and deck and rigging were shrouded in a thick white mantle. Markham now realised to the full the importance of steam for ice-navigation; a vessel depending upon sail alone would have required as many days as they did hours for the passage. This part of Davis Straits, known among whalers as the south-west fishing-ground, has, from earliest days, been regarded as a particularly dangerous locality. Markham felt convinced from his own experience, even though they were favoured with exceptionally fine weather, that it should be avoided as much as possible by vessels not having steam power. Shaping their course for Disco, as the whales had now left for the north, they pushed on through heavy snowstorms, against a head wind, an adverse current, and a choppy sea.

Another new experience of this voyage was the absence of real darkness, and it was a great interest to remain up and watch the sun sink in slow majesty below the north-west horizon; and even when it was out of sight there was sufficient light in the cabin to read at midnight.

On May 31st they crossed the Arctic Circle. This was formerly attended on board whalers with ceremonies akin to those still observed on most ships in crossing the equator, but the introduction of steamers in the whale trade has rendered obsolete this and certain other old customs.

The following day Disco was reached, and in the evening they anchored in the snug harbour of Lively. Here Markham, landing with the Captain and doctor, was received by his Excellency the Inspector, an officer who holds his commission direct from the King of Denmark. At this place they were hospitably entertained during their short stay.

The evening of June 3rd saw them again northward bound; and threading their way through islands of ice in Baffin's Bay, they reached the island of Upernavik two days later. No news from Europe had been received at this place for nearly twelve months, and they were the first to bring intelligence of the finding of Livingstone, the death of Napoleon III, and the abdication of the King of Spain. A Danish blacksmith, who was an enthusiastic admirer of the ex-emperor, was so overcome on hearing the news of his death that he burst into tears and ran out of the room.

Markham had a conversation with Dr Rudolph, the Governor, who entertained them hospitably during their stay, on the subject of securing some of the dogs from this settlement in the event of an Arctic Expedition from England.

Here they left the confines of civilisation, the last opportunity of leaving letters for home. The difficult and dangerous navigation of Melville Bay now lay before them, with the untiring look-out for a "lead," or open stream of water, between those terrible floes, which have proved a veritable death-trap for hundreds of ships, though attended, curiously enough, with little loss of human life. On Friday, June 6th, preparations were made in the event of the ship being nipped. Provisions were brought from below and stacked on the upper deck, in readiness to be put in the boats, or thrown on the ice, should she have to be abandoned. Each man was ordered to have a shift of clothing packed in a small bag. But the *Arctic* made an extraordinarily rapid passage across this, "the whaler's bugbear," into the North Water. Markham confessed to a sense of disappointment at the freedom from the dangers and adventures usually ex-

perienced in this locality. He also regretted the impossibility
of a nearer inspection of the glaciers extending far into the
interior which could be plainly seen from the ship. These
and other attractions, not coming into the scope of a
whaling cruise, had to be passed by. They now were only 850
miles from the North Pole, and, to the ardent explorer
who had come so far, it seemed no distance. Both he and
the Captain were of the opinion that this would have been
the very year for discovery, following, as it did, upon four
extraordinarily open seasons, and Markham felt that with
such a ship as the one he was now in there was no saying
what such men as M'Clintock, Richards, or Osborn might
not accomplish. He comforted himself with the reflection
that, should this summer be followed by a mild winter,
next year's prospects would be brighter still.

On June 11th they reached the fishing-ground, and
preparations were made for beginning work in good earnest.
Other whalers had also arrived, and in the evening a
"mollie" was held on board the *Arctic*. A "mollie" is a
gathering of Captains who meet together for the purpose
of discussing their fishing. Incidentally, it means a night's
carouse, as it is always accompanied by liberal potations
of spirits and beer. It has even been known to last several
days! At 7 p.m. the skipper of the *Arctic* hoisted a bucket
at the mizen top-gallant mast head, a polite invitation to
his fellow-Captains. A season of drinking, smoking, and free
discussion of all things connected with whaling followed.
To a non-smoker and very abstemious man this must have
been something of a trial. Markham made the best of it,
however, and found his conversation with some of the
skippers most interesting in view of Arctic exploration. In
spite of having previously been drawn into signing a paper
advocating the route by Spitsbergen as the best for reaching
the North Pole, they were of unanimous opinion that the
best, and perhaps the only way, was by Smith's Sound.

Just at the time when their hopes of good fishing had
risen, the *Arctic* had to encounter the trying conditions
that are the fate of all who sail in those northern regions—

THE *ARCTIC* AMONG ICE

tantalising "leads," to be followed by swiftly closing ice, so that at times they were hopelessly beset, and were obliged to witness, with what equanimity they could, whales disporting themselves in the open water beyond, and another vessel more fortunately placed than themselves effecting a capture. After this state of things had lasted some days the spirits, even of the jovial skipper, went down to zero, for the capture, or not, of "fish" is the touchstone on board a whaler. However, changes in those regions are rapid, and a few more days saw them again free, with water ahead as far as eye could see, perfectly navigable. Markham's heart turned longingly towards the shore where there was much that was alluring. Moreover, he thought it probable that the Eskimos might be able to throw some light on the all-absorbing subject of the Polar regions. He was also anxious to discover whether any news could be obtained from them of the American exploring ship *Polaris*, tidings of which were being eagerly awaited by all interested in her fate.

On June 15th the crew of the *Arctic* succeeded in securing no less than four whales, which put the whole party, Markham included, into high spirits. His personal objective, however, was not the killing of whales; his one desire was to explore the unknown regions of the North. As to the whaling itself it became almost monotonous in time, the capture and subsequent processes soon palled upon the disinterested spectator when the novelty, its only charm, wore off. In spite of the natural excitement of the chase he owned to a never-failing sense of repugnance in watching the dying struggles of the unfortunate monsters. But, for all this, he took his share in the laborious and hazardous work, and in a little while the steer oar was always entrusted to him, a distinction which he greatly appreciated. In the actual fishing there was really no monotony, for whales have strange vagaries, and there was always more than a spice of adventure. On one occasion, for instance, seeing from the ship that one of the boats was having considerable trouble with a very heavy "fish," he volunteered to go off in the dinghy with the rocket-gun to kill it. The great beast had already three harpoons in its body, and was very wild in consequence. The rocket-gun was fired, and Markham, in charge of the steer oar, swept the dinghy round, but being rather an unmanageable boat and but ill-adapted for that particular work, it was not able to avoid the tail of the monster, which descended with tremendous force on the gunwale, sweeping Markham overboard into the icy water, only a few degrees above freezing point. No loose boats were near, and even those fast to "fish" were at some distance, while it appeared probable that the dinghy was smashed to pieces, and he feared, encumbered as he was with his monkey jacket and heavy sea boots, he would not be able to keep up for long. To his relief, however, on rising to the surface, he saw the dinghy a couple of boats' lengths off. His companion had jumped into the water in anticipation of another blow from the powerful tail. Had the boat been one foot nearer the monster nothing could have saved it from destruction or the occupants from death. As it was, both were soon picked up, none the worse for their immersion though very thankful, when the whale was killed an hour and a half after, to return to the ship and get into dry clothes.

At another time, a whale proved extremely tenacious of life. The boats were over six hours fast to it, and during that time were towed by the "fish" a distance of over fifteen miles. A part of the time the ship and seven boats were drawn after the monster at the rate of three miles an hour. Markham, describing the incident in his journal, remarks that if anyone were to enquire how he entered Barrow Straits he could say he was towed by a whale! But this is anticipating. Sometimes the tables were turned, and once their morning's work consisted in towing a dead whale for eight hours—a more uninteresting and toilsome duty it would be hard to conceive; the only comfort was that it meant the monster was conquered, and every ton of blubber brought them, so to speak, nearer home.

As more and more of this valuable commodity had to be

stored the cleanliness of the ship was not improved. Not only was the deck rendered greasy and slippery, but when the coal tanks had to be requisitioned and tons of coal stacked on each side of the quarter deck from the wheel to the mainmast, the space aft being taken up by large piles of whalebone, the condition of things became indescribable. The coal dust, mixed with the grease, reduced the vessel to a filthy condition, and the scattering of sawdust made walking along the gangways only just possible. When things seemed to have reached their worst the Captain calmly remarked, "If we get another fish or twa we shall be in a fearsome mess." Markham doubted the possibility of anything worse!

On June 20th they were off Cape Walter Bathurst. Here they heard from a passenger on board another whaler of certain Eskimos who had evidently been in contact with white men, and had in their possession a couple of American Government rifles, with the date 1864, which, from their appearance, had only recently come into their hands. Markham at once thought of the *Polaris*, and feared it pointed to the fact that the ship had been abandoned and subsequently plundered, and his mind constantly reverted to the probability of the vessel being found somewhere not far from the entrance to Smith Sound, if only a search could be made. But the exigencies of fishing carried the *Arctic* backwards and forwards in a way most tantalising to the would-be explorer. The skipper had already thrown out a hint of possibly going up Prince Regent Inlet, as far as Fury Beach, and Markham had been overjoyed at the prospect of visiting that historic ground.

On July 3rd, owing to the wind and high sea, the Captain put into Port Leopold to await suitable weather and to complete with water. To the right, as they entered, was Whaler Point, and as they made fast to the land ice they descried the skeleton framework of a house, a boat turned keel up, and a number of casks strewing the ground for some distance. Markham's thoughts at once flew to Sir James Ross's Expedition of 1848–49, when the *Enterprise* and

Investigator wintered in this very spot. The house, composed of spare spars covered with housing cloths, was built by his orders, and the casks of provisions left as a depôt for the crews of the ill-fated *Erebus* and *Terror*. The *Investigator's* steam launch, enlarged so as to be able to convey the whole of Sir John Franklin's party to the whale ship, was also left. As he stood surveying the desolate scene, his heart thrilled with memories, not only of Sir James Ross, the discoverer of the North Magnetic Pole, but of McClure, the discoverer of the North West passage, and M'Clintock, the discoverer of the fate of Franklin—for all three had spent nearly a year in this dreary and barren spot. But more interesting than mere reflections on the past was it to tread in the very footsteps of the explorers, which he presently did when he went on shore in company with the Captain.

The first thing he saw lying on the beach was a tin cylinder, red with rust, which as he suspected contained records. Upon opening the tin when he returned on board, he found first a paper signed by Sir Leopold M'Clintock, dated August 19th, 1858, which was only just legible, being thoroughly saturated with water. Inside were the yet older records of Sir James Ross, under date of August, 1849. These were in such a condition that it was necessary to dry them before they could be read. He decided, after much thought, to take home these interesting relics in order to save them from falling into careless hands. This he did, delivering them, on his return, to the Hydrographer of the Admiralty, and putting a notice as to what he had done in the tin cylinder, which he then caused to be soldered up and secured with wire to the centre support of the house erected by Sir James Ross. The provisions in the casks he found to be still in a wonderful state of preservation. He also saw the graves of the officer and four men who had died during the winter of 1848–49. At the foot of one of the graves a bottle was found containing the following pathetic and somewhat quaint document:

Near this spot lay the remains of Thomas Combs (late belonging to the carpenter's crew of Her Majesty's ship *Investigator*) who died on board that ship on the 27th day of October, 1848, after a lingering illness of three months which he bore with Christian fortitude. And I sincerely hope, should any Christian fall in with *this*, that he will leave his body rest in peace and undisturbed and oblige his late chum and messmate Charles Harris A.B.

In the evening, going on shore again in company with the mate and steward to shoot eider duck, they climbed a hill, a more laborious undertaking than they had anticipated, and had a glorious view up Barrow Strait, which seemed to be blocked with ice. The opposite shore was plainly discernible, and what he conjectured to be Beechey Island and its surrounding land could be clearly seen, for by that time the morning sun (it was 3 a.m.) was shining brightly, and everything stood out in bold relief. After a well-earned rest Markham again went on shore to make closer investigations, and to take sights, using, as he always did, the artificial horizon which he found admirably adapted to these regions.

Two days later, off Admiralty Inlet, Markham had just retired for the night, when the Captain came into his cabin to inform him that the *Ravenscraig*, another whaler, was in sight, steaming up Lancaster Sound. As the news did not greatly interest him, Markham settled down again to sleep, when the words *Polaris* and "survivors" effectually roused him, and, hastily throwing on his clothes, he prepared to go on deck. Before he was ready word was brought to him that the *Ravenscraig* had picked up a portion of the crew of the *Polaris*, and that the Captain of the *Arctic* had gone on board. In a very short time Markham had followed him, and eventually they brought off seven of the fourteen men, Dr Bessels the scientist, Mr Chester the first mate, Mr Schumann the engineer, and four of the crew.

With thrilling interest Markham listened to the story of the ill-fated *Polaris*, realising the value of every detail concerning her voyage, both with respect to all discoveries made and also in view of the very inadequate equipment of the vessel for her task. Her ship's company had been for the most part ill-chosen. Captain Hall himself was a remarkable man and full of enthusiasm, but in no sense a seaman, so that he had been obliged to yield to the advice of his sailing master, an old whaling captain, who had no interest in exploration. The *Polaris* had been singularly favoured by weather conditions, and indeed was stopped by a very insignificant stream of ice which had a clear "lead" through into open water with every indication of continuance. Captain Hall, much against his own wish, was forced to comply with the advice of the old whaler who was not prepared to run any risks. Even under such disadvantages they had attained a higher latitude than any previous expedition, and, it was confidently believed, would have succeeded in reaching the North Pole but for the half-heartedness of the subordinates and the unfortunate death of the leader, Captain Hall, the only casualty that occurred. Eventually the *Polaris* had to be abandoned, being run on shore just inside Smith Sound, and the crew reached safety in two detachments, one of which had been picked up by the *Ravenscraig*. The great achievement of this unfortunate expedition was that it proved the navigability of the strait leading from Smith Sound to the north.

Enthralled by the tale of these more absorbing matters Markham's interest in the fishing decidedly waned, his chief reason for any anxiety for a catch being that they might fill up the required amount of oil and return home, for he was keenly desirous that the *Arctic* should carry the first news of the rescue of these survivors from the *Polaris*.

The presence of Dr Bessels and Mr Chester on board was an acquisition. His conversations with Dr Bessels and yet more their comradeship in various scientific pursuits gave him keen enjoyment. They took turns in making observations, dividing the twenty-four hours between them. They were also able to register the temperature of the sun, as the doctor produced from among his possessions a solar thermometer, and the very best was made of all opportunities of research. Markham was deeply interested in geological investigations, whenever he was able to land, and he brought back a good many specimens. His ornithological and botanical studies also bore good results. Dr Bessels' help was invaluable and moreover he instructed him in the art of skinning birds. Soundings were frequently taken, by means of which he discovered that any theory of a warm current flowing up Davis Straits was untenable, as the temperature at a depth of 200 fathoms was 9° below that of air, and 4° less than the surface.

The one drawback to the new arrivals was that he lost the quiet of the cabin, and even the use of the table for his writing and the working up of his specimens, as the Americans spent the whole day on board, from shortly after breakfast until midnight, in playing euchre, and it was only when they had retired for the night that he was able to secure the peace and stillness required for his studies, for which reason he greatly regretted the prospect, when August came, of losing the benefit of the midnight sun.

Meanwhile the *Arctic* was wandering hither and thither in search of the best fishing ground, sometimes making fast to a floe in consequence of persistent fog, for they had come to the season when a clear day is almost an exception. Such a rare occasion was seized upon by Markham for taking observations. He was surprised at the inaccuracy of the charts in some particulars, and, by careful survey, was able to correct the coast-line. He also named a high headland, hitherto unnoticed on the maps, Cape Sherard Osborn, and a number of glaciers which he counted behind Cape Liverpool he called after Sir Bartle Frere.

When they were off the mouth of Admiralty Inlet several parties of Eskimos paid them a visit. These " dirty, unkempt-looking people " struck him as about the lowest specimens of humanity he had ever seen, not excepting the Solomon Islanders. One man seized upon the carcase of a loom that the doctor had been skinning and devoured the raw flesh, apparently with great enjoyment. Seeing Markham observing him intently, he proffered him a portion of the delicacy.

To Markham's great disappointment Fury Beach had to be passed by, the eager search for whales taking them into Cresswell Bay, at the entrance to the Gulf of Boothia. But, after a weary chase, the whale they were pursuing eluded them, with three or four loud, triumphant blasts; and fearing lest the ice should close them in, they headed the ship to the northward, and, to Markham's great delight, it was possible to land at Fury Beach after all. This is one of the classic spots in Arctic history, and no human foot had touched the shore since March, 1859. The names of Parry, Hoppner, James Ross, Bellot, and others rose before him as he stood looking on the relics of former expeditions.

Perceiving a cairn at the water's edge, and anticipating the discovery of some record, he eagerly went towards it. But what was his horror when, after an hour's hard work with pick and shovel, he discovered a human body sewn up in canvas. He reverently replaced it, re-arranging the stones so as to give the appearance of a grave rather than a cairn. He was able to identify the body as that of Chinham Thomas, carpenter of the *Victory* with Sir John Ross, who died on February 2nd, 1833, being the only man ever interred on Fury Beach.

Markham's keen enthusiasm for Arctic exploration could not fail to communicate itself to those around him. His conversations when away in the whale boats with the men frequently turned upon the subject, and he was much gratified to find that more than a third of the ship's crew were prepared to go with him in the event of a Government Expedition being sent out.

Towards the end of August unmistakable signs of winter determined the skipper to turn homewards, especially as he had on board the best cargo he had ever taken. Even the bread and water tanks between decks were filled with blubber, and there were only a few small tanks still available. Markham had now to learn that "homeward bound" in an *Arctic* whaler is a most tantalising experience. Had they not been returning at once he would have liked, above all things, to have gone further north, but this, being impracticable, his one desire now was to get home. But between alternate storms and dead calms, and heavy ice floes which effectually barred their way, the progress was irritatingly slow, added to which "fish" were sighted, and the skipper, declaring he would be "happy with ane or twa mair," set his heart on further captures.

A slight compensation during this trying time was the delight of witnessing for the first time brilliant and perfect parhelia, or "mock suns," even though old Arctic sailors regard the phenomenon as a presage of bad weather. Hunting bears and walrus helped somewhat to relieve the tedium of the days; indeed, throughout the cruise Markham had had a considerable amount of sport, sometimes of a very exciting nature, in bear-hunting.

The weather conditions at length improved, and favoured by a strong wind they sailed unhindered through Davis Straits; and the whale boats, having been denuded of their whaling gear, were hoisted in-board, and other preparations made for crossing the Atlantic. When Cape Farewell had been passed, cleaning and painting the ship became the order of the day, and on September 19th they anchored off Dundee.

The cruise had been to Markham a most interesting and illuminating one, and, moreover, the best preparation he could possibly have had for the work of Arctic exploration which was the goal of his ambition. His report shewed that steam as the propelling power of a ship had made a complete revolution in ice navigation, and it very materially strengthened the hands of those who were endeavouring to bring pressure to bear on the Government to despatch an expedition to the Arctic regions. In fact, as was asserted at the time, his trip up Baffin's Bay and Lancaster Sound was the trigger that eventually fired off the Arctic Expedition of 1875.

Immediately on his return from this cruise, in September 1873, he was appointed as Commander to the *Sultan*, one of the ships composing the Channel Squadron, and commanded by Captain Hoskins. This ship, when he joined her, was in notoriously bad order, and a great want of discipline prevailed on board. He had always a strong sense of the respect due to lawful authority, whether he commanded or served, and, within the space of a few months, through his tact and firmness, the *Sultan* was brought from a state of chaos to be one of the smartest and happiest ships in the squadron.

In December, 1874, a decision was reached to send out an Arctic Expedition, and Markham was summoned to England to take up his appointment as Commander of the *Alert*.

Chapter VII

May–September 1875

NORTHWARD HO!

On September 1st, 1874, Admiral Sherard Osborn had been granted an interview with the Prime Minister, which resulted in the despatch of the Arctic Expedition of 1875. The Expedition consisted of two ships, the *Alert*, commanded by Captain George S. Nares, F.R.S., and the *Discovery* by Captain H. F. Stephenson. Markham was appointed Commander of the former. Both vessels had been very carefully selected and prepared for their important work. The *Alert* was a 17-gun sloop belonging to the Royal Navy, and had already been used in foreign service. The *Discovery* was originally built and used as a whaler, and was purchased expressly for the Expedition. The alterations needed in the *Alert* were carried out under the supervision of Sir Leopold M'Clintock, Admiral Superintendent of Portsmouth Dockyard, and a more suitable man for the purpose could not have been found. The ship had to be fitted with extra beam power, and specially strengthened with timber and iron to resist the tremendous pressure of the ice. Further, sheets of felt were introduced between the inside planking and the lining for the sake of warmth, and the ship was divided into watertight compartments. The water-supply was provided for in an ingenious manner. A large reservoir was constructed around the galley-funnel pipe to receive either snow or ice which, dissolved by the heat of the fire beneath, could be drawn off by a tap. Each ship had exactly the same figure-head. They were what are called "fiddle-heads," painted with the Union Jack, and under it the word "Ubique."

Equal care was taken in the choice of officers and men. From the numerous offers of service (in one case a whole ship's company, nearly 800 men!) only a very small pro-

portion could be selected, and the slightest defect, even bad
teeth or an old wound, was a disqualification. Temperamental qualities were also taken into consideration. "What
can you do for the amusement of others?" was one of the
questions asked. The ice-quartermasters chosen for the
Alert were all in the whaling trade, and one had been a
shipmate with Markham in his whaling cruise in the *Arctic*.

Every space available on board both ships was requisitioned for the reception of stores and provisions for
a possible absence of three years. But they could hardly
have carried with safety across the stormy Atlantic all that
was required had it not been for the wise provision by the
Admiralty of an extra ship, the *Valorous*, which was to
accompany them carrying all surplus stores as far as Disco.

Gifts of various kinds poured in from all classes, from
the Queen downwards. The ex-Empress Eugénie shewed
a deep interest in the Expedition, and presented a woollen
cap to each member of it. These proved the greatest comfort
during the sledging, and were popularly known as "Eugénies."
Markham's allusion to her late husband in his *Whaling
Cruise to Baffin's Bay* had deeply touched her, and she ever
after evinced a warm interest in him.

Amongst the numerous letters received from unknown
admirers was the following quaint epistle from a little girl:

Dear Capt. Markham,

  I am Captain ——'s niece, and my Aunt Mary says that
you are a kind gentleman and if I ask you you will ask an
Esquimaux woman to give me a little Esquimaux baby about
3 when it will arrive at England a boy if you can find one.
I think an orphan would be best because it will not remember
its mother. Will you find out its last name please I am going
to call it after you. What will its food be, will you ask someone
to give it some bathes when it came near England will you
bring it to Dalarne.

  My little brother wants a *tiny* little bear. Hoping you are
getting on well

I remain always

A— L— S—.

Even before the preparations were complete, visitors

began to flock to Portsmouth to inspect the two ships. Among them were the Prince of Wales, the Duke of Edinburgh, and the ex-Empress Eugénie.

At 4 p.m. on May 29th, 1875, the two ships steamed out of Portsmouth Harbour. At Spithead they were joined by the *Valorous*, and, favoured by a fresh north-easterly wind, the three ships made sail down Channel. How and when would they return? In his journal, written that night, Markham answers—"God only knows. In Him we must place our trust. To Him we must look for support and assistance." When they were off Plymouth the following day, the Commander-in-Chief, Sir Harry Keppel, came out in his yacht to wish them success. On June 1st they put into Bantry Bay, while the *Valorous* was sent to Queenstown for letters; on the next day all three ships were headed for the broad Atlantic.

The ship's company proved to have been well chosen; the men were "a fine willing set of fellows," and the petty officers shewed a true spirit of comradeship by asking to be allowed to take turns with the able seamen in steering the ship. Most of the ward room mess were already well known to Markham, and the First Lieutenant of the *Discovery*, Lieutenant Lewis A. Beaumont (the late Admiral Sir Lewis Beaumont, K.C.B.) was not only an old shipmate in the *Blanche*, but also his greatest friend. Two other members of the Expedition on board the *Alert* must not be forgotten: "Nellie," Markham's black retriever, between whom and her master there was a very close attachment, and a cat. With regard to the latter, he was wont to tell admiring listeners that she came back *white*. This information was invariably received with much surprise and interest, but, as he laughingly remarked in relating this, "They never enquired what colour she was when she started." She was a white cat, named "Blanche"!

The *Alert* had on board a very delightful guest in the person of Clements Markham, to whose zeal and energy the Expedition owed so much. He travelled with them as far as Greenland, and returned in the *Valorous*.

On the first few days of the voyage the whole ship's company, from the Captain downwards, were subjected to strict medical examination, and age, height, weight, girth of chest, temperature, etc., were taken and noted down for comparison on their return, with a view to ascertaining the effect of Arctic life upon each. Lime-juice was served out regularly to every officer and man each day throughout the whole period of the Expedition, and in order to ensure its being duly taken this was done on the quarter deck in the presence of an officer.

The passage across the Atlantic was very stormy, and of one gale Markham declared he had not known such a hurricane since the one he had experienced off Mauritius; one of the whale-boats was carried away and other damage done. Once, owing to constant head winds, they were actually twenty-six miles further off Cape Farewell than they had been the previous day. But Markham's optimistic temperament led him to the reflection that the very gales that were retarding their progress might be blowing the ice down Smith Sound and Baffin's Bay, which would enable them to pass through rapidly and unhindered. The *Discovery* proved to be a very bad sailing ship, and the *Alert* had to go slowly in order to keep her in sight, but, even so, they lost sight of her during a storm and were in some anxiety until she was again sighted off the coast of Greenland. She had not after all suffered more than her consort.

On June 27th the first ice was met with, which caused great excitement among those who were novices in Arctic exploration; to Markham it was like an old friend. Exactly a month after they left Portsmouth they came for the first time seriously into contact with ice. The *Alert*, in consequence of her length, proved herself less manageable than a whaler, striking the floes more heavily. On July 1st the coast of Greenland came into view, and Markham recalled with interest as they passed Godthaab that this was the starting-point of the noble work of the Moravian Mission under Hans Egede at the beginning of the eighteenth century which was the means of eventually bringing Greenland under the influence of Christianity. On July 2nd it was light at midnight; on the 4th, the Arctic Circle was crossed, and two days later the three ships anchored in the little harbour of Lievely. Here the business of taking in stores from the *Valorous* began in good earnest, and twenty-four dogs were purchased for the dog-sledges. The Danish Inspector at Godhavn, Mr Krarup Smith, assisted in procuring the services of an Eskimo dog-driver and interpreter, named Frederic, a cheery, good-tempered man, with the reputation of being a successful hunter. The dogs proved a very noisy and unruly addition to the ship's company, and, worse than all was the atrocious odour they brought with them, which pervaded the whole ship. "Nellie" objected to them strongly, and always maintained her sense of British superiority, refusing to allow them to come near her!

It was a great relief to get on shore after thirty-four days of tumbling about at sea and from the summits of the hills to enjoy the magnificent views of glaciers, fiords, and fantastically-shaped icebergs rising in white majesty out of the calm blue waters. The vegetation, dense in places, was composed mainly of stunted willows.

On July 15th they went on to Rittenbenk, where more dogs were purchased. Here they parted from the *Valorous*, whose Captain and officers had shewn them the utmost kindness. The scenery, as they steamed through the Waigat, the strait separating Disco from the mainland, delighted them with its grandeur and sublimity. To the west, on the Disco side, rose the beautiful, snowclad hills, whilst the opposite shore of Greenland shewed a bold, precipitous coast, the lofty headlands rising in needle-shaped peaks, interspersed with glaciers and fiords, and the magnificent discharging glacier of Itivdliarsuk could be clearly descried as they steamed slowly along. A rapid progress was impossible, as the ships had to be carefully steered through the icebergs that nearly blocked the passage.

On July 19th they anchored in the harbour of Proven and received from the Governor the rather disquieting news that the whalers had been forced to put back

BRITISH TARS AND GREENLAND NAIADS

to Upernavik, owing to their inability to get through the ice in Melville Bay, and, after waiting for eight days, they had made a second attempt, since when they had not been heard of. This either meant success, or else that they had been obliged to abandon Melville Bay and take the middle passage. The following day they heard from the Eskimos that there was very heavy ice as far south as Upernavik, and that portions of a whale-boat had been picked up near that place. Markham's comment in his journal is—"Push on we must, and success will follow."

More dogs for both ships were secured, making a total of sixty-one, also the services of another expert dog-driver and hunter, who had accompanied all the American expeditions; and, on the evening of the 21st, they left Proven. The next morning Upernavik was reached. The Governor here confirmed the news of the return of the whalers; the explanation appeared to be that, owing to the unusual prevalence of northerly winds during the preceding four months, the ice had been blown to the southward, thereby detaining the whalers in Melville Bay. This would, however, prove of use to the discovery ships, as it would mean that the north water was free from ice and navigable for some distance up Smith Sound. The Governor presented Markham with some old flint and bone implements lately found in the graves of Eskimos. The same evening they left Upernavik, and bade farewell to civilisation.

Writing to a cousin about this time, Markham says: "Don't you think it would be rather nice, on certain Sundays, in Ashfield Church, to have the prayers of the congregation for our Expedition? I should like it very much, but I leave it to you. I shall be glad when I can attend Service there again."

In addition to his duties as Commander, Markham was entrusted with the special charge of all the magnetic observations; and his was to be the task, later, of organising and arranging the sledging parties, for which he began drawing up plans early in the voyage.

Guided by an Eskimo pilot, the *Alert*, with the *Discovery* in tow, proceeded through the narrow passages between the islands to the eastward of Upernavik amid magnificent

THE *ALERT* TOWING THE *DISCOVERY*

scenery, soon, however, to be blotted out by a fog, which made it necessary to anchor for a short time. As soon as navigation was again possible they steered a westerly course, Captain Nares deeming it advisable after the reports they had received to avoid Melville Bay and to make for the middle passage.

Preparations were now made for encountering the ice. Provisions were placed in readiness should it become necessary to abandon the ship, the officers and men were told off to the boats, and each individual had issued to him a knapsack, containing two pairs of blanket-wrappers, one pair of boot-hose, one pair of stockings, one pair of mitts, one pair of drawers, a Welsh wig, a jersey, a comforter, a pair of mocassins, a comb, a towel and a piece of soap. To these Markham added in his own knapsack his sledge flag and a few other articles of value. The knapsacks were kept ready in appointed places so as to be handy at a moment's notice. All other necessary preparations, including the formation of crews for cutting docks in the ice, having been made, the whole ship's company awaited the conflict with confidence and impatience. Thirty-four hours through the ice and they reached the north water—an unprecedented passage, taking only seventy hours from Upernavik to Cape York. The weather had been perfect, not a breath of wind stirred the glassy surface of the sea, whilst the ice was so soft and "brashy" and so loosely packed that the ship could easily cut the floes in two. This seemed to point to the fact that they were encountering ice of this year's formation only, the real pack having been blown southward by the recent northerly winds. So far as they could see, it was all clear ahead, and the spirits of all rose high in anticipation of a rapid and successful progress. When the following day's observations shewed the surface temperature of the water to be 40°, the natural inference was that there could be little or no ice about. This, however, may have been due to a warmer current than usual setting from the north, as, after steaming slowly through a dense fog, they found themselves, when it lifted, nearly twenty miles further from the Cary Islands than they had expected to be, the result of a strong south-easterly set. Markham was now further north than he had yet been, and every mile of progress increased the interest of all on board.

All letters for home were to be left at the Cary Islands, and the evening of July 26th was devoted to writing. There was the hope of Sir Allen Young visiting these islands in the *Pandora* for the purpose of collecting their letters; failing this there was the possibility that Captain Adams, of the *Arctic*, might do so in the following summer. Therefore, when at midnight on July 26th they hove-to off the north-easternmost island of the Cary group, Captain Nares went on shore to choose the most suitable place for a depôt.

All were astir early on board the ship preparing the provisions to be left on shore. By 2 a.m., with the help of a watch from the *Discovery*, the whaler and both cutters were laden and despatched, manned by a party of twenty-four, with Markham in command. The landing was very difficult, as the boats had to be run alongside the rocks; but, the water being very smooth, they succeeded in getting everything on shore without mishap. The casks, which weighed over 500 lbs., and the boat which was to be left, had to be dragged up over steep and uneven rocks. But the men worked splendidly, and by 6 a.m. all was completed, and a cairn erected on the highest hill, in which was placed a tin canister containing the letters for England. The whale-boat was lashed keel uppermost, and Markham attached the record, also in a tin case, to the after thwart of the boat, on the bottom of which directions were written as to the position both of the record and the cairn. Returning to the ship, they pursued their northward course through clear water under a bright sun. Passing between Northumberland and Hakluyt Islands, their steep, precipitous cliffs almost overhanging the ship, past Murchison Sound, they entered Smith Sound. Markham would have given much to land, but the north was calling, and with such weather and a sea as smooth as glass, the advantage of these favourable conditions could not be lost.

Bird life abounded. Rotches, or little auks (*Alca alle*), were seen in countless clusters, diving quickly under water as the ship appeared, looms (*Uria brunnichii*), dovekies

(*Uria grylle*), king-ducks (*Somateria spectabilis*), the glaucous gull and the kittiwake (*Larus tridactylus*) soared in the blue sky above, whilst now and then a stray ivory gull (*Larus eburneus*) flapped by on leisurely wing.

As they opened out Murchison Sound they saw the land-ice extending from Tyrconnell to Beaufort Bluff at the mouth of the Inglefield Gulf—the first ice of any importance they had seen since leaving the middle pack—and icebergs larger than any they had hitherto met. At 8 p.m. on July 22nd Capes Alexander and Isabella were sighted. Off Cape Alexander, at 3 o'clock on the morning of July 28th, a fine view could be obtained right up Smith Sound without a vestige of ice to be seen, and four hours and a half later they anchored in Hartstene Bay. Here all hands went on shore, some to take observations, some to collect specimens, others to hunt and shoot. No sign of an inhabitant was to be found. At 11 o'clock Captain Nares and Markham started in one of the whale boats with four hands with provisions for one day, for the purpose of visiting the *Polaris* encampment where the winter of 1872–73 had been spent, also to search for an iron boat on Littleton Island, believed to have been left there by Hayes in 1860. It was an uncomfortable little voyage, lasting about five hours, in the teeth of a fresh northerly wind, the spray almost freezing upon their faces. They had no sooner landed at Lifeboat Cove than they discovered some of the remains of which they were in search—boats, trunks, books, instruments, and stores, but not everything they had expected to find; it was very evident that the various articles had been disturbed, probably by the Eskimos, and some had apparently been removed altogether. Taking everything of any value to be returned to the U.S. Government and possessing themselves of the two native boats, they went on to Littleton Island, but the iron boat was nowhere to be found. A cairn was built on the top of a hill at the south-west end of the island, and a round of angles taken.

The following day Markham, with four men, went off in a whale boat to Cape Isabella. The landing was extremely

difficult, and after reaching the shore they had to lay some
oars over a chasm and cross it with the assistance of long
boathooks; they were encumbered with an empty cask,
150 lbs. of preserved beef, and Markham carried two pickaxes on his shoulders. Having "cached" the cask, which
was for the reception of possible letters, and the provisions,
they built a small cairn, and then proceeded to make the
toilsome and dangerous ascent of the highest peak, where
they erected a large cairn with records and directions as
to the position of the smaller one.

In spite of the clear water which had been seen from the
summit of the hill and had buoyed up their hopes, the ice
soon began to close in around the ship, and they had to bore
their way, in the midst of heavy snowstorms, until they
reached Cape Sabine, and made fast to the land ice until a
passage opened. For this they had to wait five days, but
the expeditions on shore were fruitful in collections of geological and botanical interest; and traces of very ancient
Eskimo life were also found. Captain Nares thought it
would be a good opportunity to gain some experience of
sledge-travelling, and they learned a great deal that would
be useful later, proving what an exceedingly arduous task it
is to drag a heavy sledge with an ice-boat over hummocky ice.

As soon as there was the smallest chance of a move they
made their way westward up Hayes Sound, where a grand
and beautiful sight opened out before them. Two immense
glaciers coming from different directions met, the one
seeming to push and force the other from it. Determined
on a closer inspection, Markham, accompanied by the
doctor and "Nellie," went on shore; a laborious walk of
between four and five miles brought them to the bed of
the glacier. Markham could compare it to nothing but
"Niagara frozen, magnified about twenty times!" The left-
hand glacier was rounded off to its end like a great icy
wave, receding from view in long milky undulations which
lost themselves in the clouds. The pressure of the right-
hand glacier had raised a slight ridge between the two.

On August 5th they attempted to proceed, but before

long the ice packed up so tight as to render further progress
impossible except at the expense of too large a consumption
of fuel, which was disappearing with alarming rapidity.
Means of saving coal were carefully thought out by Markham.
The galley-fire was let out at 4 o'clock, after the supper of
the ship's company had been prepared, and the water for
the Ward Room tea was heated on their own stove. This
saved from 15 to 20 lb. of coal a day.

Another of the rapid changes peculiar to these regions
again set them free, and they had a grand run of three hours
in open water, until they were off Cape Albert, where
again encountering heavy ice they anchored to a floe.
That night was a never-to-be-forgotten one. Markham,
having just written up his journal, was preparing to retire,
when the sound of the engines made him hurry on deck
to find the ship in a terribly perilous position. A heavy
floe was rapidly forcing her towards a huge grounded iceberg, and it seemed inevitable that the vessel would be
crushed. It was now near midnight; all hands were on deck,
working with a will, clearing away the boats, unshipping
the rudder, and raising the screw. There appeared no hope
of saving the ship, since blasting would have been useless,
and there was no time to cut a dock. Crushing and forcing
its way the heavy ice floe was hurrying them towards the
stern, immoveable berg, when suddenly an unexpected
movement of the ice split the floe to which they were
attached into fragments and—they were clear! The *Discovery*, being on the other side of the berg, was comparatively
safe, although, at one time, it was a question which was in
the greater danger, as both were drifting towards the berg.

As Markham was too busy on deck to attend to any
personal matters, one of his shipmates had asked what
valuables he could put together for him. All he could think
of for the moment were his Bible, Prayer Book, a few
photographs, and his journal. To these, he afterwards found,
his kind friend, mindful of his creature comforts, had added
two or three boxes of sardines!

Although the immediate danger was over, they were now

going through a very critical time, along the coast of Grinnell Land, and the Captain "almost lived" in the crow's nest, not even coming down for meals; Markham also spent much time at the mast-head. Every inch of their perilous course had to be contested. On one occasion the ice suddenly opened in a marvellous manner, cracking right across from land to land, as if expressly to admit of the ship's passage, and then closing again so rapidly that the *Discovery*, a little way behind, was caught, and remained beset for a short time, eventually boring her way through. She proved herself a better ship for penetrating the ice than the *Alert*.

Markham records it as a curious fact that at every place they visited, however remote, traces of Eskimo were found, many evidently of ancient date, proving that the natives were once far more numerous than at present. He hoped that, at a higher latitude, they might find something to throw further light on the ethnology of these nomadic tribes. No matter how barren or desolate the surroundings, his eager mind, always athirst for information, found food for study. Whether geological, zoological, ornithological, or botanical, every item was of interest; and, added to all this, was his keen delight in his professional duties. Apart from his enjoyment of the grandeur of the scenery his mind was much exercised on the geographical aspect. From close investigation it was decided that, in some cases, mere headlands had been magnified into capes, and peninsulas mistaken for islands, by some of the later explorers. They were, also, interested to see a small fish, something like a sprat, thrown up on the ice towards the southern coast of Grinnell Land; this they believed to be the highest latitude in which a sea-water fish had been found.

While they were anchored to the land ice in Franklin Pierce Bay, walrus were seen. A whale boat was sent after them, and Markham, who acted as harpooner, succeeded in capturing one, which supplied their dogs with plenty of fresh meat. Walrus steaks were served on the lower deck and much appreciated, and walrus liver was tried and not found amiss in the Ward Room. The tusks Markham presented to the Captain.

Football on the upper deck and on the ice, enjoyed by officers and men in company, served to while away some of the enforced periods of waiting.

At last Dobbin Bay was reached; here the *Discovery* was to establish depôt B, similar to depôt A established by the *Alert* on the Cary Islands. As they rounded Cape Hawks, the water was so calm that Markham and a brother-officer were able to use it as an artificial horizon for the purpose of taking solar observations. The Cape, which has been compared to the Rock of Gibraltar, towered, steep and precipitous, above their heads, deep ravines stretching away for miles into the interior. A large glacier at the head of the bay loomed out prominently, glistening in the light of a brilliant sun. The bay itself was one sheet of ice, only broken by the presence of some long, low icebergs. The few clouds immediately above the sun gleamed with an exquisite iridescence, the reflections in the clear smooth water adding to the beauty of the scene.

After establishing the depôt, they again encountered heavy ice. Blasting had to be resorted to, and by the "lead" thus secured they steamed up the bay. Arriving at the edge of a large floe on the northern side it was determined, for safety's sake, to dock the ships. This, their first dock, took four hours to cut.

The next day was fine and warm, but, in spite of this, new ice formed at an alarming rate, and the following day Markham took out a party of men to make a "lead" by blasting. This proved so successful that the floe split up and cracked in all directions, leaving a splendid channel for the ships which steamed once more in a northerly direction. But about midnight the way was again completely blocked after they had rounded Cape Louis Napoleon. The only course was to return to Dobbin Bay, but they had barely gone a couple of miles when they were again beset, and the order was given to cut a dock. The ice, however, proved too thick for their 12 ft. saws, being from 10 to 20 ft. in thickness. By means of blasting they were able to bring the ship into a small indentation which afforded some slight protection from the floes. The operation was carried out by Markham, who had a narrow escape from one of the explosions. As it was, he was drenched with water, and received a severe bruise on the shoulder from a large piece of ice.

They had no sooner completed this operation than, as the Captain and Markham were talking on the bridge, they suddenly saw that one of the bergs was afloat and, drifting to the southward, had released the enormous floe to which they were made fast, and that they were being borne rapidly down towards another grounded berg. No time was to be lost—five minutes and the ship must be crushed; the noise of the crashing ice was horrible, but in those five minutes the ship was saved. All hands were called, and quickly they responded to the call. Had the Captain and Markham not been on the bridge and seen the danger in time, the vessel would in all probability have been lost.

During this period they had many more hairbreadth escapes, and were only making progress at the rate of four and a half miles a day. On the evening of August 19th they succeeded in rounding Cape Fraser, as the ice was beginning to give, and on the 20th, passing Cape Collinson, they made fast to a large floe. At noon their latitude was 80° 2'.

In the midst of all the perils the photographer on board made rather a gruesome suggestion: he proposed photographing each individual separately, so that when they died their photos might be buried with them, thus enabling their bodies to be identified!

The crow's nest was a matter of great anxiety to poor "Nellie," who hated to see her master go aloft and would remain on the bridge for hours together. With her great aversion to anything Eskimo she invariably chased the dogs off the quarter deck, if they attempted to invade it.

The resolution was now taken to steam to the eastward and endeavour to force a way through the pack, instead of hugging the coast. This brought them out into the open

water of Kennedy Channel, and they had a splendid run
to a latitude of about 80° 45', not more than sixty miles
from the *Polaris* winter quarters. At the northern end of
Kennedy Channel, however, they met an impenetrable
barrier of ice right across Hall Basin. As far as eye could
reach, even from the crow's nest, solid floes stretched northward with no outlet and no indication of open water. There
was Polaris Bay, distant only about twenty miles, and they
could even see the position of Hall's winter quarters, but
with no present hope of reaching it. The Captain and Markham paid a visit to Hannah Island for the purpose of building
a cairn and leaving a record on its highest point.

The *Discovery* had the misfortune to lose several dogs
from rabies; the *Alert's* dogs had therefore to be rigidly
kept away from them, as, coming from different localities,
it was hoped they had not been infected. The coal of both
ships was now diminishing in an alarming manner, and it
became evident that it would have been a wiser plan had
the Government arranged for them to replenish at Upernavik, or some more northern station than Disco. In his
journal Markham observes: "We might fail in accom-
plishing the object of our mission for the sake of 10 tons
of coal!"

On August 24th the Captain, having gone on shore in
order to discover from high ground what were the conditions ahead, descried a magnificent "lead" of open water
along the western coast, extending as far north as Cape
Beechey and perhaps further. Steam was immediately
raised, and after dinner that night they were able to drink
the Queen's health at a higher latitude than it had ever
been drunk before. But alas for the hopes of Arctic
voyagers! As they steamed along with the expectation of
soon outdistancing all previous explorers, an impenetrable
barrier of ice lay before them. The only course was to steam
across Lady Franklin Sound towards Cape Bellot, in the
hope of being able to find some land-floe to which they
could make fast while awaiting a northerly wind which
would clear them a passage. Their latitude was now about

81° 40', a little to the northward of the *Polaris* winter quarters. Their night's rest was disturbed by the exciting news that a herd of musk oxen had been seen browsing on a hill. The prospect of so much fresh meat was too enticing to be resisted. Shooting parties from both ships were organised and a goodly bag was brought back, the largest ox falling to Markham's rifle. The amount of fresh beef thus obtained for the *Alert* was 2124 lb., and for the *Discovery* about 900 lb. Traces of animal life were abundant on shore, and as the place where the two ships were now anchored afforded a snug little land-locked harbour, Captain Nares decided upon the spot, which they named Bellot Harbour, as suitable winter quarters for the *Discovery*.

On the evening of the 25th Markham and some of the others went on board to bid farewell to their friends, who were very downhearted at the prospect of being left behind. Lieutenant Rawson and a sledge party of seven men were taken to strengthen the ship's company of the *Alert*, and it was found necessary, in order to accommodate the additional numbers, to add 15 ft. to the lower deck, taken from the port passage in which fuel had been stored. The much-desired northerly wind having sprung up, the *Alert* steamed slowly out of harbour on August 20th, exchanging hearty cheers with her disconsolate consort. The *Discovery's* parting signal was "May Providence prosper your efforts," to which the *Alert* replied "Happy winter." To Lieutenant Beaumont Markham committed his private instructions in the possible event of the ship not being heard of again.

A duty devolving on the *Discovery* was to visit "Hall's Rest," and to place on the grave of Captain Hall a brass plate made expressly in England bearing the following inscription: "Captain C. F. Hall of the U.S. ship *Polaris*, who sacrificed his life in the advancement of science on November 8th, 1871. This tablet has been erected by the British Polar Expedition of 1875, who, following in his footsteps, have profited by his experience." So long as they were in England this tablet had been kept a profound secret, as they might have failed in reaching the latitude attained by the *Polaris.* Again detained by the ice, the *Alert* was compelled once more to anchor, within only three miles of the *Discovery.* This was the more trying as the navigable season was shortening, and signs of coming winter were upon them, the temperature falling to 24° and the daylight beginning to wane, so that it was difficult to read without candles at 11 p.m. But, whilst feeling disappointments very keenly, Markham's buoyant disposition always seized upon the faintest ray of hope in a dark situation. September 1st was a red-letter day. The *Alert* had now reached a higher northern latitude than had ever before been attained by a ship, and Markham felt the honour of hoisting the British colours where no flag had ever yet been displayed. But greater things were to follow.

The variations of temperature at this time were trying— 20° on deck and 55° in the cabin, which, in comparison, appeared to them almost unbearably hot; and the condensation, causing a continual dripping which saturated everything unprotected, was most disagreeable. Sometimes it froze and hung in icicles overhead.

They were now about 450 miles from the Pole, and it appeared unlikely that they could take the ship any farther. Though the spot was not ideal for winter quarters it seemed the best they could obtain, and at least it was far better than to retire, as they must otherwise do, as far to the southward as Lincoln Bay. It was about one mile farther south than the farthest point the ship had reached, and protection was afforded by a chain of small grounded bergs or, rather, as they discovered, huge hummocks with every appearance of icebergs, close in to a low shore slightly undulating, and completely covered with snow. The spot was merely a small indentation, too insignificant to be called a bay, but one that would, they felt, with the aid of the grounded bergs, form no despicable winter quarters. An effort to bring the ship a trifle farther inside the friendly wall of bergs was all but disastrous. A violent squall striking her, she was blown clean out of the harbour, and they were in imminent peril. Their only hope was to haul the ship inside again, which they succeeded in doing, but not a moment too soon. They had only just succeeded when the whole body of the pack came in contact with the bergs with a hideous, crunching sound that gave them an unpleasant idea of the fate that would have been theirs had the vessel remained between.

From high ground on shore land could be seen to the north-west and north-east, equidistant from the Pole, but none was apparent due north; this made it doubtful which would be the best route for the sledging parties to take, a question to be decided by means of the autumn travelling, the organising of which kept Markham busy, as it was hoped they would be able to start in about three weeks' time. In the meanwhile all preparations were made for finally settling where they were for the winter, and a large depôt, consisting of 2500 rations, was landed so as to be available to recruit the sledges should the ship be blown out from the protecting bergs and be forced to winter farther south.

As the Captain was keen to find out whether there was any harbour up the bay that could be used as winter quarters, if the ice opened sufficiently to enable the ship to be taken farther, Markham volunteered to go on a short exploring expedition. Two sledges, each with a team of eight dogs, commanded respectively by Markham and Lieutenant Aldrich and accompanied by two dog-drivers, left the *Alert* on September 5th. Markham speaks of the dog-sledging as indescribably "exciting and exhilarating." At one moment they were dashing along at the rate of eight or ten miles an hour, "the fine snow flying into your face, as the dogs tear through pell-mell; at another, brought up amongst high hummocks over which the sledge had to be lifted and the dogs coaxed; and at another slowly ascending the side of a deep ravine and then plunging headlong down on the other side." During this little expedition Markham was initiated by the Eskimo in charge of his team in the art of dog-driving. Although the temperature was as low as 12° and 8° Fahr., yet Markham did not feel the cold and was even too warm up to within about half an hour

of their return in the evening at 7.30. But they were un-
pleasantly reminded of the fact that they were in the Arctic
regions when, at lunch, they unthinkingly pulled off their
mittens, and then handled their knives and the preserved
meat-tins; one of the dog-drivers, a Dane, in taking hold of
a tin cup with his unmittened hand, was severely burnt. As
a result of the reconnaissance, the Captain decided to
remain in their present quarters for the winter.

Chapter VIII

September–December 1875

MARKHAM was now to have his first experience, no light one, of real sledging—its hardships and perils. As the Captain wished to take advantage of a channel, some miles in length and opening in a north-westerly direction, for the purpose of advancing a couple of boats for future use, Markham volunteered to go in charge of the expedition. His party consisted of two eight-man sledges and one five-man sledge (i.e. drawn by men instead of dogs), with one 20 ft. and one 10 ft. ice boat and ten men. They left the ship at 12.30 p.m. in the boats on September 11th, Lieutenants Parr and Egerton having started first by land with a five-man sledge and seven men. The two parties were to meet on shore, and with their united forces haul up the boats in readiness for the autumn and spring travelling parties. Markham himself, with the detachment of men and sledges under him, set sail to a light south-westerly wind. That night, joined by the land party, they had to camp on an enormous floe about a mile from the shore, and the spot was only reached by a laborious march of four hours. The two sledges, lashed one above the other and piled with the gear and provisions of the whole party, were dragged over rough and difficult ground, some of the hummocks reaching a height of from 10 to 20 ft.; and when the surface was level the snow was so deep that they sometimes sank into it up to their waists. But the men worked splendidly, "never complaining, always cheerful, the harder the work the more mirth and merriment." While the tents were being pitched, sledges unpacked, and supper being cooked, Markham set himself to write his journal, but, having drawn off his gloves, his hands refused the task, and the gloves, when he tried to put them on again, were frozen so hard that he had to have recourse to his mitts. His stockings were frozen so completely inside his boots that they had to be removed as one, and later he thawed the boots by lying on them in his bag. The water in their bottles froze, also, and was of no use to them on the march. Markham found later that, by placing his bottle inside the band of his trousers, he could keep the water in a liquid state. The temperature in the tent when under a coverlet (they all slept in a row) was 18°, but all slept fairly comfortably, except the two outside ones, the cook, who needed to be astir before the others to prepare breakfast, and Markham himself. He had the curiosity to try the temperature inside his bag during the night, and found that on the side next to which someone was sleeping it was 74°, on the other side it was 30°.

To Markham there was great interest in those evenings when, after a hard day's work, all safely tucked up in their bags regaling themselves with a hot drink and freed by the peculiar circumstances of the position from the usual sense of restraint in the presence of the Commander, the men talked freely, their conversation enlivened by much native wit, and displaying, in many cases, an extensive knowledge of arctic exploration and a thirst to acquire more.

On September 12th the boats were hauled up and deposited on a long spit at the western extremity of a large bay, a laborious undertaking which occupied from 9 a.m. to 5 p.m., with only a halt for lunch. Though the temperature was as low as 7° they could only work in their overalls, so arduous was the task. It was discovered that the overalls supplied were too small for the majority of the men to be able to wear them over their duffel jumpers, so that the driving snow froze on them and thawed most uncomfortably when they got into their bags at night.

The next day the boats were taken on the sledges to a further point eighteen miles distant from the ship, and left there with all the provisions that could be spared, these and all the gear being placed under the boats, which were

A SLEDGE PARTY CAMPING FOR THE NIGHT

turned bottom up. It was a satisfaction to have taken them so far, but Markham was even more pleased at the spirit of the men. He always insisted that, so far as serving one another went, they were all on an equality: they worked together, sharing alike, and were on exactly the same footing with regard to clothing and provision.

The following day they marched on, Lieutenant Egerton delineating the land as they went, as accurately as was possible in a furious gale of wind and blinding snow-drift. Had the temperature not been as high as 24°, progress would have been impossible. They had halted for lunch, pitching their tents on a floe under lee of an iceberg, and had scarcely finished when the floe began to break up, and they had to strike their tents and pack sledges with the utmost rapidity, and move on. Five minutes later their piece of ice was at sea.

They were now making their way back to the ship, but under tremendous difficulties—the wind blowing almost a hurricane and dead against them, beating mercilessly with showers of pebbles and bits of shingle into their faces, and causing acute pain, as they jogged wearily along; no lee under which to encamp; the men growing more and more tired, though still working splendidly. The snow was so thick that they could not see more than five yards ahead; and push on they must, for to pitch their tents was impossible. Then, to add to their difficulties and anxieties, one of the party fell down from sheer exhaustion and had to be placed on the sledge. From time to time during the next half hour they were obliged to halt for a moment's rest and shelter, and then, examining the exhausted man, Markham found that he was rapidly freezing. He instantly ordered the tents to be pitched, but it was blowing so furiously that his could not be got up. Lieutenants Parr and Egerton were happily able to succeed with theirs, but as the sick man was now not only freezing but getting delirious, Markham felt the only thing was to push on at all hazards and make for the ship. After giving the unfortunate man a stimulant and putting him inside his sleeping-bag, covered with the tent robes and coverlet and lashed securely to the sledge, they pursued their weary march, only to find that the ice on which they had to travel had been broken up and blown out by the wind, so that there was no ice-foot to sledge on.

After an hour's toil Markham resolved to push on alone to the ship to procure assistance in bringing in the sledge, bidding the men do their best until help arrived, and to keep carefully to the coast line. That walk was a never-to-be-forgotten one—floundering on through deep snow-drifts, so exhausted that again and again he was blown flat on his face—nothing but the urgent necessity of obtaining help for his men prevented him lying down in the snow where he fell and giving up the unequal struggle. At last, through the dense, drifting snow, he saw the welcome sight of the ship looming through the thick whiteness: an answer, he confessed, to a prayer "offered to Him in Whose hands we all are." Approaching the edge of the beach, for the vessel was surrounded now not by ice but by water, he yelled and hailed until he was hoarse, but for a time in vain. After twenty minutes that seemed interminable to his intense relief he saw the affirmative fluttering up to the peak—then he threw himself down on the snow utterly spent. It was still some time before he was actually rescued, and, wet with perspiration, he was rapidly freezing, and had to put forth every effort to keep himself warm.

Never was sight more delightful than the cheery, comfortable-looking Ward Room, the lamps alight, the fire burning brightly, a white cloth on the table, and supper spread. Friendly hands were ready offering hot coffee, pulling off his jumper and his boots and stockings, in spite of protests that he was able to do all for himself. Masses of ice were taken out of his collar, and his comforter was frozen hard to his shirt. He had already explained the plight of his men, and a party had been sent out to their assistance. They were found trying vainly to pitch their tents, and thoroughly exhausted. Two hours later they arrived safely on board. The sick man, with others who were taken ill afterwards, made satisfactory progress under medical care;

and the doctor thoroughly approved the treatment which had been used for him. He had the curiosity to weigh his patient's clothes before they were thawed, and found the weight to be 38 lbs. As all the party were dressed alike and all their clothing was frozen, they must each have had this weight to carry, while Markham had in addition his instruments, books, etc.

The expedition had been an altogether successful one, and the Captain expressed himself very pleased—a small party, absent little more than three days, had advanced a couple of boats with provisions nearly twenty miles from the ship, an important preparation for the autumn work. They were all novices in the art of sledging, they had over-come all the difficulties, and those of no ordinary nature, that they had encountered, and on their return journey had made the unprecedented march of more than eighteen miles, over very heavy ground, in the face of a hurricane. Markham's own fear throughout was for his men. The following day, to his great relief, Lieutenants Parr and Egerton returned with their parties, having spent a not uncomfortable night. Those on board the *Alert* had been having a by no means easy time owing to the ice beginning to break up, and all had been exerting themselves to the utmost, Captain Nares "working like a horse."

On the following Sunday a special thanksgiving was offered for the late mercies vouchsafed them. The sight of the men mustered for divisions arrayed in box-cloth shirts and Shetland caps was an uncommon one on board a man-of-war.

Markham now gave himself to making what he hoped, from his recent experience, might be improvements in the sledge equipments; the Captain entrusting him with the carrying out of his suggestions. A novel employment was attempted in his leisure time, when, with the aid of a packing-needle and some wool, he embroidered his initials on all his travelling gear, and felt quite proud of the performance when it was completed.

Unfortunately at this time rabies again broke out among

the Eskimo dogs, resulting in the death of five; and five more having died from other causes, the pack of thirty-three was much reduced. It was therefore decided, after consultation with the dog-drivers, to put them on shore with Frederic the Eskimo, which they seemed greatly to appreciate.

In spite of a general desire for better quarters, all efforts to get the ship out had failed, and operations now went forward energetically towards making needful arrangements for the winter. Markham was busy with all hands building a long house in which to stow sails and rope; this was made of casks which were dug out of the snow and rolled further up the hill. The result was an imposing structure, roofed with the mainsail; it was 38 ft. long by 12 ft. wide and about 10 ft. high, with a small room adjoining, about 12 ft. square; and it went by the name of "Markham's Hall." Snow-houses, too, sprang up in all directions.

The condition of the ice was not very favourable to sledging, but, as the time in which any work could be done was rapidly passing and the long Arctic night would be beginning in about three weeks' time, an attempt had to be made. Consequently, on September 22nd, Lieutenant Aldrich started away with two dog teams and four days' provisions for the purpose of pushing on, if possible, to Cape Joseph Henry, there to erect a cairn and place a record containing information regarding the practicability of travelling, for the enlightenment of the main party which was to follow. This main party, under Markham's leadership, left on the 25th, and consisted of his own sledge the "Marco Polo"—with the motto given him by his old chief on the *Sultan*, Captain Hoskins:

> I dare do all that may become a man,
> Who dares do more is none—

manned by the same crew as before, except for one man still on the sick list who had been replaced by another; Lieutenant May's sledge the "Hercules" and Lieutenant Parr's "Victoria." All were eight-man sledges. Each flew its own standard, and Markham's also bore his blue pennant as Commander, with the motto *Luctor et emergo*. Before they started the leader had the difficult task of working out quantities and weights, and decided that, besides twenty days' provisions, they could carry between 1400 and 1500 lb. of pemmican and bacon to lay out as a depôt in readiness for the spring travelling.

The party were absent about three weeks. Autumn sledging is peculiarly trying on account of the brief period of daylight, or rather twilight; the sun's altitude decreases daily and breakfast and supper must be partaken of in total darkness. Besides this, the ice, being of recent formation, is weak and treacherous, whilst its even, snow-covered surface tempts the uninitiated to choose it rather than the rough floes; the result is a soaking in icy water, with consequent frost-bites, and the risk of losing the sledge. Only by exhausting efforts can it be saved, whilst the carefully-rationed biscuits are rendered uneatable. This happened at the outset of this particular journey—one of the experiences dearly and bitterly bought. Further, if tent and sleeping-bags are wetted, their frozen condition brings not only discomfort but an appreciable shrinkage.

The ship's company of the *Alert* had been warned by Captain Nares before leaving England that the sledging duties would be no sinecure; speaking from previous personal experience, he had told them that if they could imagine the hardest work that they had ever been called upon to perform in their lives intensified to the utmost degree, it would only be as child's play in comparison with the work they would have to perform whilst sledging! Markham and his party, like all other Arctic explorers, could heartily endorse this. Yet, in spite of all discomforts, dangers, and acute sufferings, there was no complaining; heavy loads were made light of, and the one aim of each was to do his own job well and faithfully. When they settled down in the dark tents, nestling in their stiff, frozen bags, cheerful conversation and laughter was the order of the night.

During the first three days of marching, in each of which

they did twelve or thirteen miles, they encountered, first, ice as smooth as glass; then, being unable to round a point of land owing to several lanes of water, they were obliged to unload the sledges and carry everything piecemeal across a neck of land about two miles in width and 100 ft. above the level of the sea; finally, on the evening of the third day, the snow began and never ceased for the remainder of the time, that is, for sixteen days out of the twenty! Day by day it grew in depth, so that at times they were obliged to halt the sledges whilst they cleared a pathway.

On October 4th, as only half the allotted provisions remained, and there was every prospect of very heavy travelling on the return journey, they decided to place the depôt on the brow of a ridge above their present encampment and turn their steps homeward. Markham, with Lieutenant May, made an effort to reach Cape Joseph Henry, but the thickness of the weather rendered it impossible to see anything. Lieutenant Aldrich, who had preceded them, had succeeded in ascending a hill 2000 ft. in height, and the day being clear, could see the land from Cape Joseph Henry trending westward, but with no indication of land to the north, only the vast polar pack. Before retracing their steps they had attained the latitude of 80° 50′ north.

The return proved even more arduous than anything they had yet experienced; so deep was the snow that some of the ravines and promontories were almost impassable and they pursued their way knee-deep. Once they were forced to take the sledges up a range of hills 250 ft. above sea level and to lower them down a steep incline on the opposite side, in order to pass a precipitous cliff, off which was a stream of water. These hills were subsequently named by them "Frost-bite Range," as a sudden fall of temperature added to their troubles by producing frost-bites of great severity. Markham had minute directions from the doctor as to the treatment of these, as well as of other forms of sickness, but the frost-bites were often so insidious that they became aggravated before the unfortunate victim realised their presence, and some who were attacked were obliged, after their return to the ship, to suffer the amputation of a toe.

During the last three nights before reaching the ship sleep was impossible owing to the indescribable discomfort, amounting to positive pain, of frozen bags and coverlet. The temperature now stood at 22° below zero, and Markham feared another night under similar conditions would induce more frost-bites; he therefore determined to make a strenuous effort to push on as fast as practicable, in order to get the men a warm meal and a comfortable night in their hammocks. Calling a halt at 5 p.m. (they were then about three and a half miles from the ship) he ordered some tea to be prepared so as to refresh and invigorate them for the final exertion. While this was being got ready he kept the men continually moving about, not allowing anyone to sit down. The last bit of travelling was the best they had known since leaving the ship, over beautiful new ice, the moon shining brightly overhead. At 7.30 he called another short halt, and while they discussed their allowance of grog, he made them a short speech, expressing his approbation and satisfaction at the way they had carried out their duties. He then proposed health, long life, and prosperity to Captain Nares, hoping that in the ensuing spring he would achieve such success as would redound to the honour of the country and the flag, and reflect credit upon himself and those under his command. This was received with three ringing cheers and one cheer more. In drinking, the utmost caution had to be observed, for so great was the cold that the pannikin stuck to the lips unless it had been previously well rubbed with the mittened hand.

It was indeed a pleasing and welcome sight to behold the mast heads of the ship, and, when within a mile of it, to see figures approaching—some of the ship's company coming out to drag the weary travellers in. Captain Nares was among the first, and among other friends not the least welcome to her master was faithful old "Nellie," overjoyed to see him once more. Lieutenant Parr had been sent forward so that, being apprised on board of their coming, hot food should be ready for the men as soon as they arrived. At 9.15 p.m. they reached the ship—"hungry, dirty, and a little tired, but all in capital spirits." The luxury of a warm bath and being able to brush hair and teeth was indescribable.

All the party had lost weight during the expedition, but with the exception of frost-bites, none were any the worse for their hardships. The following day the men were not disturbed but allowed unlimited rest in their hammocks. During those three weeks the ship had been undergoing a regular transformation, preparatory to being made suitable for a winter residence, and the work went on apace throughout October. She was now at last completely frozen in, the ice increasing in thickness daily; but further steps to ensure her safety were taken by burying two of the largest anchors on shore and freezing them into their holes by pouring water over them. Chain cables were attached to these. Large quantities of provisions were landed in case misfortune should make it necessary to abandon the ship. The vessel was housed in with a material called tilt cloth, such as is used to cover waggons in England. Lamps were hung from the spars over the centre of the deck, and kept alight night and day, for they had bidden farewell to the sun on October 11th, and the long dark Arctic night was gradually setting in. A wall composed of solid blocks of snow, in height about 4 ft., was built at a distance of about 6 ft. from the ship, in order to preserve warmth on board. The upper deck was cleared of everything superfluous and covered with snow to a depth of about twelve inches, and a layer of gravel and ashes strewn on the top. It proved, however, a rather precarious promenade, as it was desperately slippery. Winter garments were issued to the ship's company, officers and men being, for the most part, dressed alike. Cloth was replaced by sealskin, not the elegant sealskin of fashion, but that obtained from the ordinary Greenland seal, the skin of which is covered with coarse bristly hairs; but the garments were warm, comfortable and light, their only drawback being the unpleasant smell, to which, however, use made the wearer accustomed after a time. Leather boots had to be discarded, as, with a temperature below zero, they froze so hard that they became perfectly stiff, and actually increased the danger of frost-bites. These were replaced by carpet boots, or moccasins made of moose skin, the former with duffel tops reaching to the knees, and with cork soles over an inch in thickness.

The temperature was extremely low, considerably lower than any experienced by the *Polaris* during the same month; sometimes it dropped to 25° below zero, and Markham found the only way to keep warm in his cabin, where the thermometer registered on occasions 30° below freezing, was to sit in his armchair arrayed in fur coat, the hood over his head, and a sheepskin rug, an acceptable gift before leaving England, wrapped round his legs. "Then indeed," he says, "I was nice and warm." The condensation in the cabin was extremely trying, the drops from the beams falling on his head and face while he tried to sleep and completely soaking the bed. "Nellie" seemed to thrive in spite of the cold, and nothing delighted her so much as a run on the floe or in the snow-drifts.

A wooden observatory for astronomical observations, and various snow houses, one for a powder magazine, some for magnetic observations, others for the storage of salt beef and such like, began to grow up round the ship, giving almost the appearance of a village. The houses went by different names, appropriate to their several uses—"Kew," "Woolwich," "Greenwich," "Deptford," etc. The salt beef was very salt and tough and the days when fresh meat, i.e. the flesh of the musk oxen and sheep that had been killed, was served out were eagerly anticipated. This was issued at the rate of 1 lb. per man on two consecutive days every three weeks, this being considered by the doctor the best plan. Towards the end of October an additional evening allowance of grog was served out to the men, an indulgence of which Markham did not approve.

Regular two hours' exercise on shore was enforced as

essential to health, and, as darkness began to close in earlier, arrangements were proceeded with for making the long and otherwise dreary winter pass as pleasantly as might be. To Markham's hands had been committed the management of the entertainments, which were always given on Thursdays, and went by the name of "Thursday Pops." To these officers and men alike contributed. Lectures by various officers, music, recitations, magic-lantern exhibitions (given by Markham), dramatic entertainments, etc., varied the programme, and all threw themselves into the arrangements with their whole hearts. Markham also added to the general amusement by displaying his conjuring tricks, learnt for this express purpose, his identity being hidden from the men in the printed bills under the pseudonym of "The Wizard of the North," and great delight was expressed by all at his performances, one of the men remarking that he was "quite like an official." Doubtless "professional" was the word intended, and Markham took it as a compliment.

Lieutenant Egerton was stage manager of the "Royal Arctic Theatre," Markham offering to do anything in his power to contribute to the general amusement. On the assignment to him of his first rôle, that of "Grumbleton Griffin," the comment in his journal is "I don't know how I shall get on as I have to sing several songs! And I have as much idea about singing as 'Nellie' has. However, it will all add to the burlesque." The men also contributed to the theatrical performances, getting up plays among themselves, and Markham, who superintended the rehearsals in the stokehole, remarked that they needed a great deal of coaching.

A printing press was set up by Lieutenant Giffard, assisted by an able-bodied seaman, and most creditable work was turned out.

Besides amusement, Markham inaugurated a school for the crew, with himself and certain of the officers as instructors, and the response of those desirous of benefiting by further tuition in the three R's and one or two other

THE ROYAL ARCTIC THEATRE

THEATRICALS ON BOARD THE *ALERT*

subjects was most gratifying, nearly the whole ship's
company assembling on the lower deck evening by evening.

Markham had sketched out a programme for himself for
the winter months, to include the study of French, polarisa-
tion of light, and other subjects. But his multifarious
employments for the amusement and well-being of others, in
the shape of rehearsals, Penny Readings, teaching in the
evening school four nights out of the five, and even having
special classes for the ice-quartermasters, who did not wish
to join the others, besides magnetic observations, and his
ordinary duties as commander, left him very little time to
himself. He ran no risk of the long months of winter hanging
heavily on his hands, and his only fear was lest he should
be unable to compress into them all he had planned. His
days were long; he was always called at 6.45 and was never
in bed before 12 or 1 o'clock, his only time for reading and
his French exercises being in the evening after the school
closed at 9 o'clock, and then there was his journal to be
written. A good deal of his time was taken up in magnetic
observations, in company with Lieutenant Giffard, and the
work was carried on through no common difficulties, with
the temperature inside below zero, while the observations
sometimes took five or six hours to complete; indeed, they
occasionally occupied the best part of the day. The delicate
instruments could scarcely be manipulated by hands en-
cased in thick gloves, but to remove them was to court
frost-bites. Sometimes the cold was so intense that they
were obliged to restore circulation by running about as
quickly as possible outside, no easy matter when arrayed
in heavy boots with a large amount of clothing. On one
occasion they were completely snowed up by the drift
against the entrance, and could only get out by pulling
down the whole framework of the door. Added to all this,
they were furnished with instruments unknown to them.
However, these and other obstacles were successfully over-
come, and they pursued their work with interest and enthusiasm, realising that magnetic observations had never
been taken in such a high latitude before.

A wonderful meteor was observed on August 27th, at noon, passing from south-east to north-west, and apparently falling about a quarter of a mile away. It was of a bright emerald green, and was falling so quietly and slowly that at first they thought the Captain was letting off a rocket or Roman candle. It burst about 40 ft. from the ground, shewing bright red and green colours. Auroras were seen, also paraselenae, or mock moons, one on November 19th being very beautiful; and observations were carefully taken on all occasions. A very curious phenomenon was witnessed a little later—the doctor came in with the report that there was a star behaving in a most eccentric manner, moving about and taking long jumps in the sky. Needless to say there was a general exit on to the ice, and, sure enough, there was Aldebaran doing exactly as had been reported. It was with difficulty that the men watching it could be persuaded that the star was not in motion. The cause was thought to have been a thick mist composed of fine frozen particles passing between them and the star.

On October 31st it was just possible to read the *Times* in the open air for about an hour at midday, and on November 6th, with great difficulty, a few enterprising spirits succeeded in just deciphering it.

To render open-air exercise possible, a walk of half a mile was constructed on the floe near the ship, which the careful doctor had rendered practicable by placing small heaps of empty preserved-meat tins along it to indicate the path. It was the aim of each officer to take as many turns up and down this uninteresting promenade as he could. It went by the name of the "Lady's mile."

Birthdays were duly celebrated, and inviting menus arranged to do honour to the hero of the occasion; also other important anniversaries. But above all, Christmas was observed in great style. The kind thought of friends at home served to add brightness to the day; the ladies of Queenstown had given to each ship a large box containing gifts for everyone on board, and a cousin of Markham's had directed a letter containing a Christmas card to each

MENU

POTAGES
Mulligatawny

POISSONS
Pégouse à la Couverture de Laine*

ENTRÉES
Petits Pâtés d'Homard à la Chasse†
Rognons à la Pain rôti

RELEVÉS
Mouton rôti à l'Anglais.   Tongues en Gimbals

ENTREMETS
Poudin aux Raisins
Blanc-Manger à la Hummock
Petits pâtés d'Hahis à la place d'Eccleston

DESSERT
Poudin glacé à la Hyperborean
Figues   Noce
Gâteau à l'Irlandais
Café et Liqueur à la Jesson

November 11th, 1875

* Blanket wrappers were articles of wearing apparel.
† The name of the cook was Hunt.

individual on board the *Alert*, a used postage stamp having
been affixed to each envelope so as to give it the appearance
of having been delivered through the post. After Service
was over and Markham had taken his usual constitutional
along the "Lady's mile," he found, on returning to his
cabin, that in his absence it had been brightened with twigs
of artificial holly, a delicate and touching attention on the
part of some of his messmates which he greatly appreciated.
The ship itself was decorated, and the table in the Ward
Room was adorned with a magnificent bouquet of artificial
flowers. Special Christmas fare, including the luxury of
an extra supply of fresh meat, was served in both officers'
and men's messes, and, from his private stock, Markham
presented each mess with a contribution consisting of
sardines, biscuits, potted meat, soup, etc. Everyone was
determined to make the day as bright as possible, and the
whole ship's company appear to have enjoyed themselves
thoroughly.

Chapter IX

January–November 1876

THE New Year dawned brightly so far as the health and spirits of the members of the Expedition were concerned, though they suffered a good deal from sleeplessness.

On New Year's Day they gathered the first crop of mustard and cress, grown in a small shallow box kept in a locker near the Ward Room fire. There was just enough for everyone to have a mouthful, and never was mustard and cress so appreciated and praised, even though it was of a decidedly anaemic character, possessing not a particle of colour! Later, the returning light revealed the men as being in much the same condition, the result of long months of darkness.

Faint indications of an increase of light were hailed with rejoicing, though it was not until the end of February that the sun was to cheer them by his re-appearance; and like all Arctic explorers, they proved to the full the truth of the adage that "as the day lengthens the cold strengthens." Hitherto they had recorded some of the highest known temperatures in the Polar regions during the month of December, but in the latter part of January and onwards they learned, far more than they had yet done, what Arctic cold can be. With a temperature of 50° below zero the utmost care had to be taken, when exposed to it, to prevent severe frost-bites, and no one was allowed to go out alone for fear he might be attacked unperceived; and they were obliged, as they walked, to watch each other closely that, at the first signs, they could at once work to restore circulation in the affected part. There were times when it was impossible to go out without face coverings, and frequently the cold was so intense as to cause difficulty in breathing when first emerging from the shelter of the ship, and tears would come to the eyes, which immediately froze and had to be extracted as ice! The breath also froze on beards and moustaches and caused great discomfort.

Markham appears seldom, if ever, to have omitted his constitutional along "the mile," even when the temperature was as low as 59° below zero, and one night, thinking to induce sleep, as he was "rather cold," he started off at 12 p.m. with Nellie and walked the mile twice. The doctor, who had been frost-bitten a few days before, appeared to think he had taken leave of his senses! He describes that lonely midnight walk as producing curious and varied sensations:

The solemn stillness that reigned supreme, the impenetrable darkness, then the monotonous grinding and weird screaming of the ice, as the pack, goaded by irresistible pressure, squeezes and grinds against the hummocks and fast ice, and the clear, star-spangled sky overhead—all most impressive and, from the excessive contrast, awakening home memories and pleasant scenes from the past, with brightest hopes and aspirations for the future.

He was now seldom in bed before 3 a.m., for, owing to his many occupations, he rarely had any opportunity for private reading before 1 a.m.; and he was always a great reader. At this time he usually spent the closing hours of his day in yarning with a sick and sleepless comrade. He was an ideal visitor in sickness or sorrow.

On February 28th a general holiday was given to enable all hands to go out to some neighbouring hill and view the returning sun. But alas for human calculations!—clouds persistently obscured the southern horizon, and all that could be seen—an exceedingly beautiful sight—were the exquisite prismatic tints that illumined the sky to the north. It was not until March 2nd that the bright orb of day really gladdened the waiting, watching eyes, and Markham records that, though only a third of its disc was visible, "still, it was bright and *appeared* warm!" His method of securing a sight was to ascend the mizen rigging, and as soon as he announced its appearance the rigging was swarming with men, and the floe crowded with those who had not the energy to go aloft in a temperature of about 70° below zero, the watchers in the rigging "looking more like animated bales of fur than human beings!" The beautiful tints of rose and violet in the northern sky seemed to belong more to Italy and the Mediterranean than to those sterile regions. For more than half an hour he gazed until warned, by a peculiar sensation in his feet, that the temperature was 100° below freezing point. Even Nellie grew ecstatic over the return of light, and tore about through the snow like a mad dog.

The *Alert* was now in a position to boast of having already carried off the palm, so far as temperature went, for the month of February, and the lowest for March was now being registered. It was amusing to see the eager excitement of everyone when they received the latest intelligence regarding the thermometer, and when it was announced that the temperature was lower than that recorded by Kane, the lowest hitherto experienced, there was a general shout of exultation. As it steadily went down (some of the thermometers registered as low as 81° below zero) Markham remarked that it would soon not be able to fall much lower, or it would have to come out at the bottom of the bulb!

Now that daylight had fully returned, the school, which had proved very successful, was closed, and the entertainments were brought to an end on March 3rd.

Throughout the winter the Captain and Markham had been busy with arrangements for the spring sledging, deciding the programme and going closely into all details of equipment. The adjustment of the weight each man had to carry was a matter of the utmost importance and required minute and careful calculation. Some improvements, resulting from the experiences of the autumn, were adopted and proved to be an advantage when put into practice. One important problem had been the cooking apparatus, the type supplied taking more than thirty-four minutes to boil water from the snow, and consuming 10 ozs. of fuel—

spirits of wine or stearine. This was serious from every
point of view. The office of cook, held in turn for twenty-
four hours, was no sinecure. The cook had to be up two
hours before his companions and was never able to settle
into his sleeping-bag until three or four hours after the rest.
One of the officers constructed a kettle and stewpan which
was a decided improvement on those in use, taking only
nineteen minutes to boil the water and using only 6½ oz.
of fuel, but the mechanism involved some difficulty in
cleaning, and took up valuable space; still, economy in time
and fuel meant much.

The unusually low temperature made it impossible to
think of making a start until it moderated, and a rise was
impatiently awaited. At last, on April 3rd, they were able
to set out. Their available force was much smaller than
that of previous expeditions, so that, although practically
the entire ship's company took part in the sledging operations, it was only possible to send out two extended parties,
the remainder of the men and sledges being used as
auxiliaries. One party, under the command of Aldrich, the
First Lieutenant, was to carry on the discoveries of the
autumn by taking the coast line to the west. The other,
and larger one, consisting of two sledge crews, was placed
under the command of Markham, and theirs was the
extremely difficult work of pushing across the vast polar pack
in the effort to reach as high a northern latitude as possible.
Captain Nares had given his serious attention to the name
that should be given to this ice, as neither "polar" nor
"frozen" sea fully described it; the ice, composed of
massive floes of from sixty to eighty feet in thickness, was
not ice of a few seasons' formation but, as he thought, the
ancient "thick-ribbed" ice of centuries. He therefore
decided upon the term "Palaeocrystic" Sea.

To traverse this immense tract of ice presented no
ordinary difficulties. In addition to the almost insurmountable obstacles presented by the massive hummocks that
barred their progress, there was the danger of disruption
of the pack suddenly taking place as the season advanced,

for which reason it was imperative to take two boats with them, as their only means, in such an event, of reaching the ship. This naturally added seriously to their work and the weights they had to drag. In view of all this they dared not hope to reach a very high latitude; 84°, or at the most 85°, was the utmost to which they could aspire.

It will be readily understood that it was impossible for this northern party to lay depôts; they were obliged to carry with them all the provisions they would require for the period of their absence, which necessitated their taking with them another sledge. But as this additional weight could not be imposed on the men, the measure of whose strength had already been carefully calculated, they would be obliged first to advance with two sledges and then to return over the same ground for the third.

The limits of the present book will not permit of our following the fortunes of the other gallant explorers of the *Alert* or *Discovery*, the story of whose heroism and sufferings has won a high place in the annals of Arctic exploration, and of which Markham wrote and spoke with the highest admiration. We must concern ourselves here solely, and all too briefly, with the story of the northern party.

The last day on board was a Sunday, and, being the first in the month, the Service of Holy Communion was held, at which there was an unusually good attendance, seven out of the fourteen present being members of the crew; the men generally were too apt, Markham considered, to regard it as an officers' service, and he was always glad to notice the presence of any of them. Let us try to picture the scene upon the floe on that bright but bitterly cold morning of April 3rd with a temperature 33° below zero. Seven sledges, fully equipped and laden, were drawn up in single file, manned by the fifty-three officers and men who formed the expedition. The whiteness all around was relieved by the gay standards that floated from each sledge in the gentle breeze—swallow-tailed flags bearing the armorial colours and crests of their separate commanders, each charged with the red cross of St George. In addition, the northern party's two boats bore Captain Nares's Union Jack and a white ensign.

Before the start was made, all hands being assembled on the floe, prayers were read by the Chaplain, and "Praise God from Whom all Blessings Flow" was sung. The command to "fall in" was then given, and the little expedition started, headed by Markham's sledge the "Marco Polo," the staff from which his standard flew surmounted by a naval crown and the north star in silver. The "Marco Polo" carried a boat as did also the "Victoria," commanded by Lieutenant Parr, which was the second sledge of the northern division. With hearts beating high in anticipation, the cheers of their comrades ringing in their ears, to which they heartily responded, the little party set out, accompanied for a short distance by the Captain and officers who were to remain on board.

Hardships were their lot from the first, a steadily decreasing temperature causing continual frost-bites, which rendered the work of fastening the frozen strings of their moccasins a most difficult and painful task; the keen air also causing intolerable thirst, which could not be quenched during the march, as the water, supplied to each man in a tin bottle covered with duffel, persistently froze in spite of being carried inside the waistbands of their trousers, and they were never allowed to indulge in the dangerous practice of putting snow or ice into their mouths. Imagine their feelings when the warm tea or cocoa to which they had been looking forward when they reached their encampment was found to have been made with water melted from sea ice, which had either to be discarded altogether, or served only to increase the thirst it was meant to allay! Often the cold was so intense that it was quite impossible to sleep, and tent robes and sleeping bags were frozen so hard that they resembled sheet-iron, and caused an abrasion of the skin if they came in contact with the face. Their bacon froze so hard that it was like a piece of granite, and it was only possible to eat it after thawing it first in the warm tea. This did not make the bacon very palatable and converted

the tea into a sort of soup. These, however, were but minor
evils compared with what they had yet to face.

By April 8th they were having continuous day, though it
was still extraordinarily cold; when they could record a
temperature of 24° below zero they called it "high"! The
comfort of the sun's rays, which were warm enough to dry
wet bags, etc., was counteracted by its effect on the skin
of their faces which were rendered very sore by the combined
action of sun and frost. Also there was the fear of snow-
blindness, from which, in time, several of the party suffered,
Markham and Parr included; one of Markham's eyes was
particularly bad. The use of goggles was imperative. Captain
Nares had suggested that each man should have a black
patch on his back as a relief to the eyes of the men immediately behind him, and several weeks before the starting
of the sledging expeditions Markham had put up a notice
on the lower deck ordering that "some design should be
painted on the back of each person's duck jumper, the
design to be left to the artistic imagination of each individual.
Straight lines and initials should be avoided." The result
was quaint and amusing.

One day was very much like another. Markham himself
always called the cooks at varying hours, according to the
day's programme, sometimes at 6 o'clock, sometimes as
early as 4.15, for about two hours were needed to thaw and
cook the breakfast, which consisted of cocoa, biscuit, and
pemmican. The latter article found no favour with them
at first, but hunger proved a good sauce, and stewed
pemmican was soon voted a savoury dish.

Every morning Markham read prayers with the men, and
on Sunday, and on Good Friday, which fell on April 14th,
they were of longer duration. Then the order was given to
strike camp, the sledges were packed with due regard to the
adjustment of weight, the drag-ropes were manned, and
the start was made. After a march of about five or six hours
a halt would be called for lunch. This was always considered
their most enjoyable meal, but its one drawback was the
long cold wait of an hour or an hour and a half while the

water was being prepared to make tea. To sit was impossible in the intense cold for fear of frost-bites, so that they were obliged to move about the whole time. Lunch over, the march was resumed, continuing usually for ten, eleven, or even twelve hours. Then, a suitable site having been chosen, while the cook prepared the evening meal, all the rest worked at the erection of the tent. Footgear was changed, the officer having first examined all feet to discover possible frost-bites. If any were found, friction was resorted to and a little glycerine ointment on lint applied. Then, having settled into their half-frozen bags, they were ready for supper, consisting of tea and pemmican. And now came the social hour of the day. Supper over, pipes were lighted, and the daily allowance of grog served out. This Markham believed was an absolute necessity to the men in these abnormal conditions, provided it was always given at night, and not during the labours of the day. And so the hard day's work closed with cheerful conversation, singing, or reading aloud.

Before long Markham found it advisable to arrange the time for marching from noon to midnight, so as to avoid the sun in their faces, except just about midnight. They therefore rose much later, as their day closed later. This, however, made no difference, night and day being alike.

On the fourth day of their journey the small sledge "Bloodhound," which had gone with them to carry three days' provisions, returned to the ship, taking back one of the men whose strength did not appear equal to proceeding with the rest. The other six sledges now went on to Cape Joseph Henry where, finding the depôt established in the autumn intact, they transferred the provisions to the sledges. On April 11th the supporting sledges, "Bulldog" and "Alexandra," also returned to the ship, and the two extended parties went on their different ways; the western division, consisting of the "Challenger" (Lieutenant Aldrich) and "Poppie" (Lieutenant Giffard), went by land along the coast westward; the northern, consisting of the "Marco

Polo" and "Victoria," went straight forward over the rugged polar pack.

From the outset Markham's division experienced nothing but difficulties and obstacles. They had to cut a path with pickaxes and shovels, sometimes through ice piled up to a height of between twenty and thirty feet. For this a gang of road makers would go on in advance, the remainder of the party dragging the sledges one by one over the immense floes of enormous thickness. This method of progress, which they called "double banking," had to be maintained the whole time. On one occasion Markham records having been obliged to cross a certain floe on which the snow was knee-deep no less than thirteen times, and once, after three and a half hours' marching, they had barely done 300 yards, and again, in ten hours' marching, they had only made about a mile! They considered half a mile in two hours "good work." Sometimes they had a drop of six or seven feet from the top of one floe to the surface of another, and then the sledges had to be hauled up another of equal height. This operation needed great care lest damage should be done to the boats. In some places they sank deeply into the snow at each step, which added greatly to the exertion of travel. The snow sometimes concealed treacherous fissures into which they frequently fell, but, providentially, they always escaped without fractured limbs. Sometimes a piercing wind from the north seemed to cut them in two, of course causing frost-bites. Occasionally the fog was so dense that it was impossible to proceed, and Markham would relieve the tedium of enforced encampment by reading aloud from Dickens or Scott—*The Old Curiosity Shop* gave much pleasure.

Easter Sunday, with a fierce gale blowing and the temperature 67° below freezing point, was spent tied up in their bags in the utterly vain attempt to keep out the cold, and was, they all agreed, the most miserable one they had ever known.

But the worst trial of all was the awful scourge of sickness. As early as April 14th the first member of the Expedition

AN INVALID IN THE SLEDGE

was attacked, one of the crew of the "Marco Polo." The premonitory symptoms were pains in the ankles and knees, which Markham discovered on examination to be slightly swollen, and he treated him according to the directions given to the sledging officers by the doctor. This man was not again able to render any assistance, and, a few days after, one of the crew of the "Victoria" fell ill in the same manner. It was a serious matter not only to lose two workers but to have to carry two invalids, a load for which no allowance had been made in the distribution of weights. Gradually, as more sickened in the same manner, the terrible fear forced itself upon the leader that the foe with which they were seeking to grapple was the dreaded disease of scurvy, although they had been assured that there was no likelihood of their being attacked by it. The two officers only dared to breathe the word when they were by themselves, as they considered it essential that the men should not suspect its presence among them.

On May 7th their working force was reduced by one-third, five of the men having now to be carried, though they had made gallant efforts to struggle on. The strength of all the rest was daily decreasing, whilst the weight on the sledges was growing heavier. Markham had already decided, after mature deliberation, to abandon the larger boat, for under the circumstance it was only an encumbrance, and he felt, in case of a disruption of the ice, the boats would be of little use, except as a ferry from one floe to another, and for this purpose the smaller one would suffice. The travelling was worse than ever, if that were possible, the snowdrifts deeper, the hummocks higher. The fear of injury to the invalids was an added anxiety, when, as sometimes happened, the sledges were overturned in dragging them over the almost insurmountable barriers. However, happily, no harm came to them.

Markham's tent at night was like a hospital, where, after rubbing the swollen legs of the invalids, and modifying the application so as best to alleviate their sufferings, he had to bathe with sugar of lead the eyes of others who were suffering from snow-blindness, and attend as far as could be to the general well-being of all. On the return of the Expedition fault was found with Captain Nares because lime-juice was not supplied as a daily ration to the sledging parties. But this had never been done previously in similar cases, and Sir Leopold M'Clintock, the greatest living authority, declared publicly that Sir George Nares had acted in this matter as he himself would have done. Also the lime-juice was put up in a form that made it impossible to take it away from the ship for the spring travelling, as it was in bottles or very large, heavy jars; also had they been put near a fire they would immediately have gone to pieces. Markham had, however, furnished himself with a limited amount which he daily administered to the sick men instead of their grog. He could only thaw it by the warmth of his own body when in his sleeping bag, and then only a very small portion could be thawed at a time. This, it was afterwards demonstrated, was useless as, in order for it to be of any service, the whole volume needed to be thawed and remixed, and this was only possible when the weather became warmer in June and July.

His patience was sorely tried at the enforced delays, when the weather would have favoured progress, but he dared not risk over-fatiguing the men who were still available. Finally, on May 10th, the painful fact had to be faced— further advance was impossible. In addition to the five men already prostrated, four more were exhibiting symptoms of the same dread complaint, everyone was more or less ailing, and their provisions were nearly half consumed. Very reluctantly, after serious deliberation and consultation with Parr, Markham arrived at the unwilling decision that to push on further north would be folly, nay, sheer madness. The bitter disappointment revealed in his private journal was, perhaps, never known to anyone, for, once his judgment was convinced and he faced a situation as inevitable, he always rose to it and did his best to look on the bright side.

Having decided upon taking this step, he resolved to try

the effect of two days' perfect rest for the invalids. During
that time all who could work were not idle. The two officers
busied themselves, as they had already done whenever the
weather permitted throughout the march, in taking observations for determining the magnetic force and the inclination
of the needle, for which purpose they were in the habit of
erecting a pedestal of solid snow for their instrument. Sights
were also taken in order to fix their position by latitude
and longitude, and for the variation of the compass. Further,
a hole was cut through the young ice between the hummocks so that deep sea temperatures might be taken, a
work which occupied three hours. In taking soundings they
were surprised to find bottom in 71 fathoms (426 ft.). By
means of various contrivances they were able to obtain a
specimen of the bottom, and this was carefully bottled so
as to be taken to the ship for examination under the micro-
scope. In the hope of securing specimens of any animal life
that might exist in so high a latitude Markham sent down
a bag filled with the scrapings of the stewpans and pannikins
and bacon bones, and had it lowered to the bottom. To
their great satisfaction when it was hauled up next day
it was swarming with small crustaceans and foraminifera,
specimens of which were collected and preserved, as being
the most northern animal life hitherto discovered. Temperatures were also taken at every ten fathoms, and the specific
gravity of the surface was obtained as well. That there was
a tide was evident, so far as they could discern by the rough
means at their disposal—a small lead and line. Both
soundings and temperatures were matters of great importance, and altogether the time of "rest" was satis-
factorily and profitably spent. An attempt at fishing with
a baited hook through the hole that had been cut was made,
but this was unsuccessful, and hopes of "a nice cod for our
invalids" were disappointed.

The sun at intervals during the day was so bright as to
thaw their clothing, but, as soon as it was obscured by the
frequent snow showers, the clothing froze again and soon
became covered with ice which was difficult to brush off.

HIGHEST NORTHERN CAMP

May 12th was destined to be a red-letter day in the lives
of all the members of the Expedition, and, indeed, in the
annals of British Arctic exploration. Immediately after
breakfast all, with the exception of two men left to look
after the five invalids, started to the northward, and after
more than two hours' very hard walking a halt was called,
and the flags and sledge standards displayed, fluttering
out in the fresh south-westerly wind. At noon with the
artificial horizon they got a good altitude and found
their latitude to be exactly 83° 20′ 26″ N., or just 399½ miles
from the North Pole—the highest point yet reached by any
Arctic Expedition. This was duly announced, three cheers
given with one cheer more for Captain Nares, then they all
sang "The Union Jack of Old England," the "Grand
Palaeocrystic Sledging Chorus," written expressly for the
Alert by their chaplain, ending up with the National Anthem.
On their return the flags were displayed at the encampment
and kept flying for the remainder of the day. The event was
celebrated by a special supper consisting of a hare, shot
by Dr Moss before he returned to the ship with the
other sledges, which was cooked with the evening meal of
pemmican. Markham writes: "Both my invalids, I was
glad to see, were able to go a whole pannikin full of the
hare itself, whilst we all benefited by the flavour of it with
our pemmican, and uncommonly good it was." Absent
friends were toasted, and a cigar served out to each man,
given for the purpose by Lieutenant May, himself disappointed of taking part in the sledging expedition on
account of illness. The evening closed with songs, even the
invalids joining in. All were the better for the long rest,
except the sick men, who shewed no signs of improvement.

A start homewards was made at 3 o'clock the next afternoon, a couple of records enclosed in tin cases having been
placed, one as near the centre of the floe as possible, the
other secured on the top of a hummock, stating the latitude
and longitude of the position, with a few words concerning
the condition of the party. As they proceeded, further
signs of failing began to shew themselves among the men,

although they struggled manfully on, dragging their weaker comrades, to whom they devoted themselves with wonderful tenderness, suppressing their own feelings. As to Markham himself his journal records: "I am afraid to look at my own legs for fear of seeing the same" [red spots on the calves and a discoloured livid hue round the knee joints] "as they feel stiff and uncomfortable. Please God to spare me this affliction until, at least, I have conducted my brave companions back to the ship." In point of fact both he and Parr were found on their return to have the symptoms, though, fortunately, they did not develop. This was attributed, in part, to their having taken more exercise during the winter than the men.

The sledge crews began to have a suspicion of the nature of the malady that had attacked them, but its true name was never uttered. With the proverbial humour of the British seaman they dubbed it the "Joseph Henry mange," and their lameness went by the name of "the Marco Polo limp"!

At length, as the strength of the party weakened, it became necessary to abandon the second boat, a very serious decision in view of the danger of the pack breaking up before they reached land, ominous signs of which were now manifesting themselves. The whole band, with the exception of the two officers and two men, were now affected in greater or less degree, and even they were aching all over. Added to this, Markham's anxiety for the sick men was daily increasing, and he much feared they would not live to reach the ship. But for their sakes he dared not dwell upon this thought. He endeavoured to keep up their spirits by reading aloud to them Scott's *Pirate*. They found the road they had cut on their outward journey of the greatest service to them, but there were times when, owing to the heavy drifts, it was completely obliterated and they lost their way. Again and again Markham went forward to try and find a path, floundering up to his waist and occasionally up to his neck in deep snow. One object of cheer at this time was the appearance of a snow-bunting

whose chirp sounded very sweet in their ears, the first
living thing they had seen since leaving the ship; even the
invalids asked to have their faces uncovered that they
might see the welcome sight. Traces of lemming and hares
had now and again been met with; what had brought these
little animals so far from all means of sustenance was a
marvel.

On June 5th, to their great relief, they at last reached
land. Arriving at Cape Joseph Henry they discovered the
depôt of provisions intact, a great matter, as theirs were
fast diminishing, but it was coupled with a bitter disappointment, for here they learned from a record that a
sledge party with Captain Nares had only left for the ship
two days before! One of their direst needs was help to drag
themselves onwards. Captain Nares had thoughtfully left
three hares in a crevice among the hummocks, which
furnished them with fresh meat for two days. On the 7th,
as help was imperatively required, Parr pushed on alone
to the ship, Markham accompanying him a little way
to wish him God-speed. The details of this heroic walk
cannot be entered into here, though the record of it
deserves a place in the country's list of golden deeds.
Markham's journal records little of his own feelings at this
terrible time—the one anxiety he mentions is to hear of the
safe arrival of his gallant comrade. But we can well imagine
the heavy weight of care resting on the lonely officer,
deprived of the companionship of the only friend with
whom he could talk over the situation, and with the onerous
charge of so many invalids, some of whom were in a very
precarious condition.

The heaviest blow fell on June 8th, when death, hovering
over them for so long, at length visited their little encampment. George Porter, the second to be taken ill, died about
noon in the arms of Markham, who had watched beside
him all night. Pathetic indeed was that little funeral procession of feeble, crippled men, most of them in tears, as
they laid the body of their late comrade, with the Union
Jack for its pall, in its last icy resting place, the white

ensign flying at half mast. The grave was cut through six feet of frozen snow and two feet into the solid ice of the floe. Markham read the Burial Service over that strange and lonely grave. He had been doctor, nurse and chaplain to his little band. He then improvised a rude cross made of a boat's oar and a spare sledge batten, on which he wrote the following inscription:

Beneath this cross lie buried the remains of
George Porter, R.M.A., who died
on June 8th, 1876.
"*Thy Will be done.*"

On the following morning all were interested and encouraged by the unusual appearance of a rainbow, and this beautiful presage of hope was actually the precursor of the end of their troubles. Their eyes, ever searching the dreary wastes to the southward, were cheered by the sight— they could hardly believe it—of something moving among the hummocks. Relief at last! It was a dog-sledge with Lieutenant May and Dr Moss come to their succour. The relief party, the *avant-coureur* of a larger band headed by the Captain himself and nearly all the officers, raised a hearty cheer. The little band tried to respond, but their hearts were too full, a sound more like a wail than a cheer broke from their poor, sore mouths. Plenty of lime-juice and fresh meat, and, above all, the presence of a medical officer, acted upon their health as well as their spirits.

On June 14th, after an absence of seventy-two days, they at last reached the ship. Friendly hands were ready to drag in the "Marco Polo," but Markham and his indomitable crew, three only of whom were able to walk, and that with great difficulty, would allow no one else to touch a drag-rope except Parr. They had pulled the sledge so long and so far that they were determined to drag it alongside the ship. But what a contrast to the cheerful, enthusiastic party who had started out ten weeks before was the band of stricken men, eleven of whom had to be carried! Their experience had been wholly unexpected and unparalleled in

the annals of Arctic sledging. Arrived at the ship, Captain
Nares called for three cheers for the wayfarers, which they
returned, and then he gave thanks to God for preserving
them through so many dangers and privations, and enabling them to return to their ship with no further loss of
life.

Having first attended to the carrying of his men below to
be consigned to their snug hammocks, Markham was able
to think of his own refreshment, and the enjoyment of a
warm bath and a comfortable bed in his own cabin may be
imagined, after the misery of a frozen bag, and the un-
wholesome foetid atmosphere of a tent full of sick men. The
next day he declared himself, with the exception of a little
stiffness, perfectly refreshed and as fit for sledging again as
when he started! That this was not the opinion of Captain
and doctor was made clear by his not being permitted to
accompany the search party sent out some days later to
look for Aldrich and his western division, about whom some
anxiety was beginning to be felt. This party, under the
leadership of Lieutenant May, consisting of a dog-sledge
and three men, was despatched on the evening of June 18th.

For a week nothing was heard of them, but on Sunday,
June 25th, after Service, the Captain, Markham and others
walked to a hill whence they could view the surrounding
country. They were on the point of turning back in despair
when Markham, looking through the long telescope, descried
a black object among the hummocks several miles off. As
he gazed it resolved itself into a tent, and he could see men
walking about near it. His observations having been
verified by the others, a party was made up to go out to
them. Only four men out of the whole ship's company were
available, the rest had to be officers—the Captain, Markham,
Lieutenants Giffard and Egerton, and Dr Moss. It was as
they thought—all, except the officers, were suffering from
scurvy, although curiously enough they only collapsed after
Lieutenant May's party reached them. It had been a successful expedition, the disease not having attacked them
nearly as early as in the case of the northern division, and
they had explored 220 miles of new coast line.

The ship was now like a hospital, and others besides the sledge parties fell victims, proving that there was nothing in the actual work of sledging that was the cause; indeed, it was soon decided that the seeds of the disease had doubtless been sown during the winter months when it had been impossible to obtain sufficient fresh meat and vegetables for their diet. There was unfortunately a singular dearth of animal life in the locality.

Only a few men were available for the ordinary work of the ship, and there was much to be done in preparation for breaking away from winter quarters; those who were not laid up were needed to look after their sick comrades, who were now, however, making progress towards recovery. Poor old Nellie and the cat appeared to be afflicted with the same malady, and Markham was very troubled and anxious on account of his faithful dog. He attributed her sickness in part to her inveterate habit, of which nothing could ever cure her, of catching lemmings and swallowing them, fur and all! Both animals, however, recovered.

The only other man who died, besides Porter, was Petersen, the Danish interpreter, who was severely frostbitten during the first unsuccessful attempt to reach the *Discovery* before the spring sledging started, and whose death occurred after his return to the ship, in spite of the efforts that Lieutenants Rawson and Egerton had made in his behalf. A headstone of teak was erected over Petersen's grave in memory of both men, bearing the following inscription:

In Memory of
NILS CHRISTIAN PETERSEN, Danish Interpreter, aged 38,
who died in the faithful discharge of his duty
on board H.M.S. *Alert*, 14th May, 1876,
and lies buried beneath this stone.
Also of
GEORGE PORTER, Gunner R.M.A., aged 27,
of H.M. sledge "Victoria,"
who laid down his life in the service of his country 8th June, 1876
and was buried on the floe in latitude 82° 41'.

"*Thou shalt wash me and I shall be whiter than snow.*"

Owing to the condition of the ship's company Captain Nares announced that he considered it would be imprudent to remain out another winter, and though from one point of view it was a great disappointment, yet all acquiesced in the wisdom of the decision.

Shooting parties on shore were now organised, and the fresh meat of various kinds thus obtained aided materially in establishing the health of the crew, to say nothing of the pleasant relaxation of the sport.

A channel of water having appeared, the ice between it and the ship was blown up; this involved hours of laborious endeavour, but at length, on the morning of the last day of July, the way was clear before them, and amid great excitement hurried orders were given to raise steam as quickly as possible and prepare for sea. A large cairn, ten feet high, had been built on the summit of "Cairn Hill," containing a record briefly describing the work accomplished by the Expedition, and bearing a list of the names of the officers and men of both ships, each officer adding his signature to his name. All was not yet plain sailing, the ship had to be steered with difficulty through the ice, and at one time they were even in danger of losing their vessel after all.

Lieutenant Egerton, accompanied by one of the men, having been despatched to the *Discovery* to announce her consort's approach, brought back word that the *Discovery* had been visited by the same terrible malady as the *Alert*, and the story of the sledge parties had been much the same as theirs. Markham's great friend, Lieutenant Beaumont, whose division had explored the north-west coast of Greenland, had suffered very severely, and he had the grief of losing two of his crew, who were laid to rest in Polaris Bay. As the days went by a good deal of anxiety was felt on his account, as, his men not being well enough to travel, he had been forced to remain at Polaris Bay, and no tidings had been received of him. Captain Nares finally decided to make an exchange of men between the *Alert* and *Discovery*, so that the former, with a crew as able-bodied as the two ships could muster, could proceed to search for him. On August 15th a report was made of a tent seen on the floe about three miles to the southward of the ship, and a relief party including Markham was sent out. The joy and relief of the meeting may be well imagined.

The two ships' companies were now readjusted, and they felt they were really homeward bound. But still the struggle against impeding ice continued, and it was not until September 9th that they were at last in the open sea, though not yet wholly free from their persistent foe.

Space forbids any attempt to describe details of the homeward voyage—a trying and tempestuous one. There had been disappointment in the mail they had hoped to find at Cape Isabella; it was a very small one, the bulk of the letters having apparently been left elsewhere, and the few Markham received contained sad news. The beloved aunt, Mrs David Markham, who had been as a mother to him ever since he had come over from Guernsey as a boy, had died; also another aunt to whom he was deeply attached, Mrs Crompton Stansfield, whose country home in Surrey was a family *rendezvous*, and with whom he had always been a favourite. Public news was also grave; the air was full of rumours as to the possibility of war with Russia, which made him the more impatient to reach home.

On October 16th a vessel was sighted which proved to be the *Pandora*, Allen Young's yacht, which had brought out their letters—the very ship, as it happened, they wished to avoid meeting until they reached Disco, as their desire was themselves to bear their news to England; but here they met in mid Atlantic, out of the usual track of homeward bound vessels, 1500 miles from England! Unable, on account of the force of the wind, to hold close communication with her, they signalled the information that they had reached an impenetrable polar sea, but not the Pole, and that their sledges had attained the highest latitude ever reached. After exchanging congratulations and thanks they each went on their way, Markham hoping that the Captain who had taken such trouble on their behalf would gain the feather in his cap of being able to report the Arctic Expedition as being homeward bound.

As the long-absent explorers drew near home they were everywhere greeted with enthusiasm and hospitality, whilst their enjoyment of the sight of green fields and trees can only be fully appreciated by those who have for long been amidst the eternal snows. At Valencia Captain Nares left the ship, amid the cheers of all on board, and the *Alert* continued her voyage under Markham's command.

On October 29th Queenstown was reached, and on November 2nd the two ships entered Portsmouth Harbour in company, and were received with as enthusiastic demonstrations as had marked their departure. On reaching London, and seeing the doors of St Saviour's, Southwark, open, Markham went in to offer up his first thanksgiving in England for preservation through all the dangers and difficulties of the past seventeen months.

The public reception accorded to the members of the Expedition need not be described here. The heads of departments in every branch, and the senior lieutenants, were promoted, and Markham was made a Captain at the early age of thirty-five. He would, however, have received this recognition had he remained all the time in the ship, and not taken the prominent and important part he did in the sledging operations, so that, actually, he received no reward from the Admiralty for having attained the furthest northern latitude. The Royal Geographical Society, however, were more generous in their appreciation, and presented him with a magnificent gold watch, bearing a suitable inscription. Such a perfect time-keeper was it that, when, in 1916, the Daylight Saving scheme came into operation, Admiral Markham refrained from putting back the hands, saying he had never had to make the least alteration in it, and he did not like the idea of meddling with it.

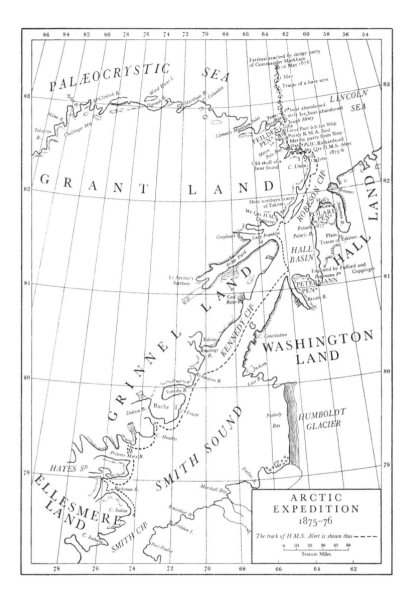

The material originally positioned here is too large for reproduction in this reissue. A PDF can be downloaded from the web address given on page iv of this book, by clicking on 'Resources Available'.

ON THE PRAIRIES

MARKHAM'S home had been for some years past with his cousin, Clements Markham, who had married and was living in Eccleston Square. He did not settle down for long, however. Shortly after his return from the Arctic regions, he went through a course of torpedo instruction at Portsmouth. Great had been the changes in naval conditions since he joined the Service twenty years before, when steam was a novelty and ironclads still in the future.

In May, 1877, he spent a few weeks in Guernsey, in company with Mr and Mrs Clements Markham, when he revisited his old home. When his torpedo course was over, he sought and obtained eight months' leave to travel in America, part of which time he proposed to spend in shooting on the prairies. For this purpose he made arrangements to join a United States Cavalry Regiment at Fort Sill, in the Indian Territory, with the nominal objective of scouting after a hostile band of Apache Indians.

He left England for New York by the Cunard steamer *Algeria* on September 22nd, 1877, arriving, after a somewhat tempestuous voyage, on the evening of October 3rd. On the forenoon of the previous day great excitement prevailed on board over the arrival of the pilot. This appearing to Markham utterly disproportionate to the apparent cause, he made enquiries, and discovered that numerous bets had been made as to which foot he would put first over the gangway. It seemed almost as if the man had received some intimation of their speculations, for he jumped down, arriving on both feet at once!

The first item in Markham's programme was a visit to his home people, and, after two days spent in New York, where he had business to transact, he started on his western

journey, with a short break at Chicago, where he made
the acquaintance of General Sheridan, who was kindly
arranging the details of his projected trip in the Indian
territory.

On October 10th he reached his mother's house near
Independence, a town that had sprung up since his last
visit, a product of the railway now about three-quarters of
a mile from "Ronceval." Nearly a fortnight was spent
with his family; then the time having come for him to
start on his trip to the Indian territory, he once again set
out on his travels, promising to return for a longer visit at
Christmas.

Leaving Independence at 7.15 p.m. on October 22nd, he
arrived at La Crosse at 11 o'clock, and drove at once to the
hotel to which he had been recommended. Here he was
informed that not a single room was vacant, and that it was
extremely unlikely he would be able to engage one any-
where else. But the clerk added that if he could wait until
2 a.m. he could have the room of a man who was leaving
by the train at that hour. With this he had to be satisfied,
and, sitting in the hall, wrote up his journal, whilst half a
dozen men sat smoking round the fire, with their feet either
on the stove or resting on the backs of chairs. Hotel
accommodation in the States fifty years ago was very
different to what it is to-day. At 2.30 he was conducted to
his room, feeling decidedly drowsy, but its aspect effectually
banished all idea of sleep. Two enormous beds, two broken
chairs, a basin, and a looking-glass with a large fracture,
completed its furnishings. The ceiling was in such a
dilapidated state that the laths were clearly visible through
the grimy plaster, whilst the paper, a decoration of bygone
days, was hanging in strips from the walls. The bed he was
destined to occupy was still warm from its late occupant,
who had risen hurriedly to catch his train, and it seemed
by no means unlikely that another unfortunate passenger
might presently appear and take possession of the other bed!

In the early afternoon of the next day he was again on
his way. The journey was tedious, and there was no sleeping

car. Drunken roughs boarded the train at night, and at one station, where there was a long wait, Markham preferred to sleep on a straw mattress in a small hotel. Next day's journey was more comfortable, and Markham's fame having preceded him (how he was at a loss to understand) he received much civility from the officials. At 8 p.m. St Louis was reached, and after being "interviewed" at his hotel by an enterprising newspaper reporter, Markham was able to rest in comfort. The next morning he was off again at 9 a.m.; as evening drew on, one gentleman beguiled the way by relating exciting stories of railway robberies by bands of armed men. The following day they were in the Indian Territory, but a thick fog prevented their obtaining any extended view of the country. At intervals they got glimpses of the vast rolling prairie intersected by muddy rivers and small creeks. Sometimes their way lay through lightly wooded country, where the only buildings to be seen were log houses. As they proceeded and the fog cleared, caravans of emigrants could be seen wending their way towards their new homes, the road being nearly parallel with the railway. The sumach, growing in wonderful profusion, its leaves almost vermilion in hue, resembled fields of the bright red poppy in England.

At 3.30 p.m. Markham, having reached the furthest limit of his journey by rail, alighted at Caddo, to find, to his annoyance, that the stage for Fort Sill had left the day before, and as it only went three times a week he would have a wait of two days! Caddo was a small settlement, consisting of about eighteen or twenty little houses, and owed its existence to the railroad. Its population was then about two hundred, consisting mostly of negroes. Its trade was entirely with the Indians in the neighbourhood. Shortly after reaching Caddo a message was delivered to him from General Mackenzie, at Fort Sill, inviting him to go straight to his residence upon arrival and be his guest. Markham received warm hospitality at Caddo, a bed in the house of a Mr Marchant, who kept a dry goods store, being placed at his disposal.

At 4.30 in the afternoon of the 28th Markham took his seat in the stage for Fort Sill. This vehicle was simply a rickety, tumbledown, military ambulance, with a duck covering, but open in front and at the two sides, and drawn by two horses. It was capable of seating four passengers, but when three heavy leathern mail-bags, a few packages, and Markham's own luggage were thrown in, he found his position, as sole occupant, a very cramped and uncomfortable one. It soon became dark, the fireflies hovered about the carriage lamps like bright sparks, a fugitive skunk ran across the track ahead, the crickets and grasshoppers chirped noisily, as the stage rumbled along—the way for the first two or three hours lying across a vast prairie, occasionally through dense thickets. Markham had taken the precaution of distributing his dollar notes about his person, and, with his rifle at his side and his revolver handy, felt tolerably secure, though robbery, generally accompanied by murder, was then by no means uncommon in the locality. At midnight they stopped at a log hut where coffee and tough beef were supplied by a repulsive-looking negress smoking a black pipe. Here they changed horses, but although the team was double two were lame, and all in a wretched condition. The night was oppressively warm; the moon rose bright, though surrounded by wild-looking clouds. Markham remarked to the driver that a storm was brewing, but he answered very surlily; and in half an hour they were again on their way.

By 4 o'clock in the morning the prediction was verified, and a heavy thunderstorm broke upon them in all its fury, the most severe Markham had ever witnessed, even in the tropics. So vivid was the lightning that it illumined every blade of grass on the prairie, and every branch of the trees was distinctly visible. It played about the harness until almost every buckle could be counted, and then left them in complete darkness. With the vivid flashes came almost simultaneously the loud roar of the thunder. Then the floodgates were opened, and a deluge descended which seemed like an unbroken sheet of water. The unfortunate horses, half-starved, half-drowned, and wholly paralysed with fear, refused to go on, and the travellers were compelled to remain on the open plains. The entire prairie now resembled a sheet of water, and with the storm a cold northerly breeze sprang up, causing a considerable fall of temperature.

The driver lashed and swore at his exhausted team, and at length the jaded horses started again. At 7.30 a.m. they reached Mill Creek, and pulled up at the house of Governor Harris, a full-blooded Indian, and ex-governor, under the United States, of the Chickasaw nation. The prospect of warmth and food was very alluring, for Markham was wet through and shivering with cold. But, alas! no fire had been lighted and he had to sit down to an exceedingly meagre breakfast, with his teeth chattering with cold. Here driver and horses were changed, the latter being substituted by four mules; and, just as they were about to start in the rain and sleet, another man flung himself into the ambulance with saddle-bags and revolver, a Texan who had just ridden a hundred miles, and the crazy vehicle proved a tight fit for two passengers with the luggage. The Texan smoked the worst of cigars continuously, and his manners were such that it was an intense relief when he left the stage at a later point.

It was evening before they reached Erin Springs, where they had supper and took their third and last driver and two horses. The road improved as they went on, but not the weather; still cold and wet, Markham arrived at General Mackenzie's house at Fort Sill at 4.30 the next afternoon.

General Mackenzie threw himself most warmly into the arrangements for the Indian trip, and shewed the greatest kindness and attention to his visitor during his three days' stay. At half past six in the morning of Saturday, November 3rd, a start was made, the "detail," as a small force attached on special service is called, consisting of two large waggons drawn respectively by eight and six mules, and guarded by a sergeant, two corporals, and twelve troopers; three cavalry officers, Lieutenants Thomson,

Rogers and Parker, fifteen soldiers, and two teamsters; while a citizen going to Fort Elliot, Lieutenant Parker's negro servant, two Indians and a squaw made up the party. They took with them five greyhounds. The orderly detailed to look after Markham proved to be an Englishman, hailing from the neighbourhood of Eccleston Square. He turned out to be an excellent servant. The equipments of the little expedition were quite luxurious for ordinary scouting, comprising tables and camp stools, and two wall-sided tents for the officers, the men's being bell-shaped.

And now followed four weeks of keen enjoyment of camping and sport along the Red River. The game was very varied, including buffalo, elk, deer, antelope, wild turkeys, duck, teal, and quail. Wolves, too, howled around their encampment at night. Large herds of buffalo were often seen, and these afforded that spice of adventure Markham loved, for the huge bulls would occasionally turn and charge their pursuer, and a firm seat in the saddle, dexterity in managing the horse, and a true steady aim were required to ensure safety of life and limb. Markham soon became skilled in this sport, and was always sure of killing.

There were two other dangers to be guarded against besides the charge of a maddened bull, or indeed of the whole herd. One lay in the presence of the numerous holes leading to the burrows of the prairie dogs. These little animals—which are not really dogs at all, and which reminded Markham of the Arctic lemmings—abound in these parts, and their habitations are known as "towns," honeycombing the prairie for miles, and proving a terrible trap for horses. The other danger was from rattlesnakes, which were very numerous. Markham had several narrow escapes, but, fortunately, the "rattle" always warned him just in time. These snakes often took possession of the burrows of the prairie dogs, and came out to warm themselves in the sunshine. Wild turkeys were found in abundance, and one place in particular was named by the officers "Markham's Roost." On one occasion five fell to his gun at one shot, as they peered out inquisitively from a bush. These birds are usually very shy, and shooting is by no means tame from the sportsman's point of view; but the practice of going out in the evening to shoot roosting birds did not appeal to Markham at all. "Thanksgiving Day" was, of course, celebrated with the proverbial turkey, and of their own shooting, with a tin of cranberry jam reserved for the occasion.

For the first part of the time the weather fulfilled all the traditions of an Indian summer. Early rising was the order of the day, and then the plains were scoured for game, twelve hours in the saddle being not unusual. The sportsmen would return to find a savoury supper cooking at the camp fire, round which the day's adventures would be discussed. The two Indians, wrapped in gay blankets, would sit silent and unmoved, unless positively addressed, when their stern muscles would relax and they would shew themselves interested and intelligent. They were the sons of the chief Mow-a-way, and, after several attempts to discover their names, Markham dubbed them "Timothy Tugmutton" and "Tippiti-witchet," soon abbreviated to "Timothy" and "Tip," to which appellations they always gravely responded, and, in their turn, bestowed names on the pale-faces—Lieutenant Thomson, Markham's tent-mate, being "Ohe-ni-kut," the left-handed (that being one of his characteristics), and Markham, by contradistinction, was "Tibbi-chi-kut," the right-handed. The squaw who accompanied them did all their work, for they scorned any employment other than that of hunting as beneath the dignity of a red man.

In about a fortnight the weather grew colder, with frosty nights and clear days, and then heavy rain set in, which, unfortunately, put a stop to a projected trip to Llano Estacado Plains. Travelling with the waggons became very difficult. The creek rose twelve feet in thirty-six hours, and so endangered their encampment that they had to be prepared to strike camp at a moment's notice. After forty-eight hours of steady rain the weather cleared and a hard frost set in; the nights under canvas were terribly cold, and when a driving wind from the north-west was added, it was dreary and uncomfortable in the extreme. They had no thermometer, but Markham estimated the temperature at 15° or 16° below freezing point, at the least.

On December 1st they returned to Fort Sill, and, after three days pleasantly spent among his military friends, Markham again started out, his immediate objective being Fort Reno, some sixty miles to the north. His luggage was sent on in an ambulance, and General Mackenzie allowed Lieutenant Miller to drive him all the way in his buggy. Miller was a most entertaining companion, having a rich fund of hunting and Indian stories. Part of the way lay through the Wachita Valley, a fine bit of scenery after the monotony of the prairie. Unfortunately rain came on later in the day, and rendered the roads so heavy that they had to give up all hope of reaching Fort Reno that night.

They therefore drove to the hut of the chief of the Caddoc tribe, who rejoiced in the name of "George Washington," and received a hospitable welcome from the old man and kindly attentions from his daughter, and after supper (the remnants of their lunch) supplemented by coffee made by the Indians, they wrapped themselves in their buffalo robes and laid down by the fire, where they passed a comfortable night. The following morning being bright and fine, they again pushed on, and following the old Indian's directions succeeded in crossing the Canadian River in safety, reaching Fort Reno shortly after 10 a.m. Here Markham experienced, during his two days' stay, the same kindly hospitality as at Fort Sill.

On Friday, December 7th, he started on the next stage of his journey, to Camp Supply; an ambulance with four mules was placed at his disposal, conducted by a civilian teamster, whilst a private attended as cook and general factotum. Major Clapp, of the 16th Regt., shared with Markham the interior of the ambulance. A tent was taken in which the two officers were to sleep.

The weather was fine and cold. About sixteen miles from Fort Reno they crossed the north fork of the Canadian

River, and continued to travel along its course for the rest of the way. So far as sport was concerned the journey was a dull one, as it was their misfortune to follow in the trail of 3500 Indians, who had not only frightened away the game, but had set fire to the prairie, thus effectually depriving the animals and birds of both cover and food. Markham managed to shoot enough to supply their party with a certain amount of fresh meat and also got an occasional shot at a stray wolf. Journeying over the charred and blackened prairie was sufficiently monotonous, and the smell of burning clung to them and their clothes for some time afterwards. It was about the time of year when the grass is usually fired so as to ensure good forage for the horses and cattle in the following spring. Markham describes one such fire he witnessed as a very fine sight, the long tongues of flame leaping to a height of twenty feet, and the grass crackling with a loud sharp sound. Even as far off as six or seven yards dead to windward the heat from the fire was unbearable, and at night the distance was reddened with the fierce glow.

Four days' travelling brought them to Camp Supply, where they experienced the usual warm hospitality, and after a short stay of a day or two, Markham took leave of the Major and went on in the stage bound for Dodge City. Their way lay due north in the face of a bitter wind, and the conveyance was an open waggon. The only other passenger was a sergeant of the 4th Cavalry Regt, going on to Larned to be married. This man, being under the impression that his fellow-traveller was a Major in the English Cavalry, always addressed him by the title, and as Markham had now become accustomed to having various ranks and appellations applied to him—Colonel, Major, or "Lootenant"— he did not think it worth while to correct him, though later he had occasion to doubt the wisdom of this omission. The road was a monotonous one over the rolling prairie, and at 1 o'clock a brief halt was made, and Markham shared the contents of his liberally stocked lunch-basket with the sergeant and the driver.

Just after sundown, they crossed the Cimarron River and passed a "cow camp," that is, a camp composed of cowboys who were driving cattle from Texas to Kansas. This camp consisted of a party of twenty-six, with 7000 head of cattle. As the stage jogged quietly along there came suddenly a peremptory summons to halt, and a couple of the roughest-looking fellows it was possible to meet, each armed with a Winchester repeating rifle and a "six-shooter," and each carrying a saddle, intimated their intention of taking passage with them as far as Dodge! The waggon was fairly crowded as it was, with two passengers and a good deal of baggage, but the driver evidently thought it better policy to acquiesce and thus avoid a brawl. One of the men was a negro, the other a white man, a Swede, as it afterwards appeared. Their clothes, such as they were, hung about them in tatters. On their legs they wore stiff leather leggings, and bandages of old flannel and cloth about their feet took the place of shoes. One wore a crownless sombrero whilst the other was hatless. Jack, the white man, had long flowing hair reaching to the shoulders. It soon became evident that the appearance of these roughs did not belie their characters. Three days previously Jack had had the "misfortune" to shoot his boss, and was bent on putting a reasonable space between himself and the murdered man's friends. Of the long arm of the law he appeared to have no fear. Life was held cheap enough by these outcasts from the civilised world. Bob, the negro, also proved to be a lawless and desperate character, who had murdered a man about eight years before, and had eluded justice by escaping to these parts, which were a common refuge for the criminal. In Dodge City he was well known and he felt he would be quite safe there.

Night was now coming on, and, at the instance of their new acquaintances, all alighted at a miserable ranche for supper and lodging for the night. The place was known as "The Soldiers' Grave," seven or eight soldiers having been killed there a few years previously. On entering the ranche they found about fourteen or fifteen men inside, of the same stamp as their fellow-passengers. These, though they made room for the new comers near the heap of wood burning at one end of the building, scowled ominously at Markham on hearing him addressed as "Major." The conversation soon shewed him that he was in a regular den of murderers and thieves and he found himself classed with them in an unexpected manner when the woman of the ranche, coming up to the table at which he and the negro murderer were seated, enquired if "both you gentlemen will take coffee?"

Before settling down for the night Markham strolled out to get a breath of pure air, and was looking down at the soldiers' grave when the sergeant and driver came up to him, advising him not to stroll away so far from the ranche. It was midnight before the miserable supper was over. The only light in the place was from the fire. Flooring was also a thing unknown, but, spreading his buffalo robes on the dirty ground, Markham wrapped himself in them, and composed himself to sleep, having first taken the precaution of buttoning his coat well over his watch and purse, and of placing his revolver rather ostentatiously ready for action. He had hardly laid himself down when Bob, the negro murderer, spread his blanket and lay down at his side! He managed to sleep fairly well, but was glad to rise with the rest at five, and after a wretched apology for breakfast they were again on their way. Jack confessed that his main intention in returning to Dodge was to kill a man who had once cheated him of half a dollar! Bob's objective was to steal a horse and ride "home"; he did not divulge the locality.

At sunset they crossed the Arkansas River, and drove into Dodge City, which had then the reputation of being the rowdiest of all rowdy western towns. Markham found it far worse than rowdy. Life was held so cheaply that a gentleman from the east actually met his death through wearing a high hat, a loafer at the railway station betting a friend he would put a bullet through it; but, the aim being rather too low, the unfortunate man received it through his head. It was merely regarded as a misfortune, and no steps were taken to arrest the murderer. In spite of a placard to the effect that "anyone found with loaded weapons will be fined," pistol shots were by no means uncommon at night, and shooting in the saloons was of frequent occurrence.

It was a real pleasure to Markham to take the train at midnight, get into a comfortable sleeping-car, and leave Dodge City far behind. Travelling viâ St Louis and La Crosse he reached home on December 20th, where he stayed six weeks with his family. During this time he received many requests from different towns to lecture on his Arctic experiences, to three of which he was able to accede. He also took his mother for a few days' trip to St Paul, visiting the beautiful Falls of Minnehaha.

He left Wisconsin at the beginning of February, and went to stay with an old Australian friend at Shelbyville, Illinois, with whom he took a trip to Cave City, Kentucky, and visited the famous Mammoth Caves. They then went on to Cincinnati for a day, where they parted, Markham journeying on to Washington, where he found his old comrade of the whaler, Dr Bessels, and, in his company and that of other friends, saw the sights of the political centre of the United States. After a week or so at Washington he and Dr Bessels went to Baltimore for a day, and here they parted, the doctor returning home, and Markham proceeding to New York, where another week was spent. He then bade farewell to the States, and embarked for England, arriving off Queenstown on March 8th.

Chapter XI

April 1878–October 1879

A CRUISE TO THE KARA SEA

IN the latter part of April, 1878, in anticipation of war with Russia, which appeared imminent, the large garrison and seaport towns of the country were busily engaged in warlike preparations on a big scale. The Naval Dockyard at Devonport was especially occupied in the completion of several large ships and in the fitting out of others. On the 24th no less than five turret ships were put in commission— the *Prince Albert*, the *Cyclops*, the *Gorgon*, the *Hecate*, and the *Hydra*. Markham, though a very junior Captain, was selected for the command of the last.

This ship, a coast-defence ironclad, was one of what was called the "Particular Service," or "Jingo" Squadron, under Sir Cooper Key. The conduct of the ship's company left much to be desired; leave-breaking and other delinquencies were frequent, and the new Captain found himself reluctantly compelled to take stern measures. He gave careful consideration to the subject of leave and planned out a system which eventually worked very well. As time went on, he was much pleased with the general improvement of the crew at their drills and other duties. As the ship might be called upon to go into action, he organised boarding drill, though he thought it unlikely that the *Hydra* would ever require either to board an enemy or resist a similar attack. Nor did he overlook the need of wholesome recreation; "Thursday Pops" were instituted and at these his magic-lantern was again in evidence.

On the second anniversary of his having attained the highest northern latitude, May 12th, he invited two of the *Alert's* old crew, who were serving in the Squadron, to dine with his steward. After dinner one of them proposed the health of their old commander; and after tea on board they went off to their own ships, having spent a very happy day. Markham also came across an able-bodied seaman who served with him in the *Camilla*, and invited him to his cabin for a yarn, much to the astonishment of the sentry and some of the officers.

In view of modern developments it is interesting to find an entry in Markham's journal about this time with regard to H.M.S. *Triumph*, which anchored in Plymouth Sound on her way to the Pacific as flag-ship. He was dining on board the *Valiant*, and writes: "The *Triumph* exercised her electric light—it is certainly a wonderful invention, and for action at night-time is perfectly invaluable. Every ship should be fitted with one. Although the night was intensely dark, when the light was turned on the *Hydra*, we from the *Valiant* could distinctly see every person on deck and even read quite easily the ship's name, whereas the *Triumph* herself was perfectly hid from view."

On June 14th the *Hydra* joined the Squadron in Portland Roads, a formidable fleet with no less than fifteen post-captains' commands. On the 18th they went out to sea for the purpose of performing several evolutions. It was gratifying that the *Hydra* was the only ship in the Squadron that had no signal addressed to her to "keep station," and Markham was afterwards complimented by the Admiral on his steering. Further, to her Captain's great satisfaction, when the ships were ordered to "prepare for action and report when ready" (that is, to prepare for sea and to ram), the *Hydra* was the first to report. When peace had been assured by the Treaty of Berlin, the ships, after being reviewed by the Queen at Spithead, were paid out of commission at Sheerness in August, and Markham was again his own master.

After a few weeks' tour in Brittany, he paid a visit to Holland, in company with Clements Markham and his wife, to welcome the Dutch explorers de Bruyne and Koolemans Beynen, who had just returned from traversing the Barentsz Sea. His friend Beynen was able to give him a detailed account of the ice in the neighbourhood of Franz Josef

Land. On Markham's return from the Arctic regions he
had given close attention to the best route to be followed
in future Polar explorations. His own experience had proved
the soundness of certain canons already laid down by
Sherard Osborn and others, one of which was that in order
to make any substantial advance into the unknown regions
of the north a coast line must be found trending in a northerly
direction with a western aspect. Further, although much
could be done in the summer, a winter in the ice with
extended sledge parties was a necessity, in order to carry
out to the full the scientific objects of the expedition. As
Markham closely studied the subject, he came to the conclusion that the best route would be by the west coast of
Franz Josef Land. It was important, therefore, to discover the navigability of the ice-laden Barentsz Sea under
ordinary circumstances. Several voyages of reconnaissance
had already been made, by Payer in 1872, and by various
Norwegian captains, the last expedition being that of the
Dutch explorers already referred to.

It was consequently with alacrity that Markham, seeing
no chance of immediate professional employment, accepted
the proposal made to him at this time by Sir Henry Gore
Booth to join him in a voyage to the Arctic regions in the
little 40-ton Norwegian cutter *Isbjörn*. They left Hull on
May 1st, 1879, reaching Bergen on May 4th. At two o'clock
that morning the Captain of the steamer called Markham
by request. It was a lovely morning, and although the sun
did not rise until nearly 4 o'clock, it was perfectly light,
and the water smooth as a looking-glass. Korsfjord was
from half a mile to two miles in breadth. Here and there
were primitive-looking villages and small wooden houses
of much the same construction and architecture as those
in the Danish settlement in Greenland. As he stood watching
the sun rising over the eastern hills, tingeing their summits
with gold and shedding its rays into the deep fjords on
the opposite side, Markham was roused from his reverie
by the stentorian tones of the mate giving the order to
"half the watch" (the other half was the man at the wheel!)

to "turn the hands up." At this the half of the watch gave
three loud knocks at the foremost hatch and called out
"All hands!" After a short interval one man and a sleepy-
looking boy made their appearance. "These ships," remarks
Markham, "are not over-manned."

At Bergen a Norse grammar was purchased and here also
a chronometer was tested. Over this instrument Markham
had watched with the utmost care throughout the journey.
On the way to Hull it had occasioned great alarm to a
fellow-passenger who had been warned as he took his seat
in the railway compartment to be careful of it. "Good
gracious!" said he, with a horrified expression, "it won't
go off, will it?" Markham hastened to allay his fears, but
it was some time before he seemed to regain his ease, eyeing
the chronometer and other curious-looking parcels with a
great deal of anxiety. Had the incident occurred in Russia,
the owner would, in all probability, have been arrested as
a Nihilist! Bergen was left on May 5th, but unfortunately
the weather now changed to wind and heavy squalls of snow,
the thickness of the atmosphere effectually obscuring the
scenery. On May 8th Markham crossed the Arctic Circle
for the third time, in weather befitting the occasion, snow
falling heavily and icicles hanging from the weather side
of the deckhouse. He devoted a good deal of time to
careful perusal of Payer, and was more than ever charmed
with his graphic descriptions of Arctic life.

They had now changed into another steamer, the Captain
of which displayed the qualities of a dormouse. On three
separate occasions at different times of the day when
Markham and his companion went on deck to take a good
walk, an officer came up politely requesting them to desist,
as the Captain was asleep. On Markham's expressing surprise at seeing so little of him the mate explained that he
was "a very old man and very fond of the bottle!"

Tromsö was reached on May 10th, the whole voyage
having been a rapid one, occupying only eight days and a
half. As they neared the town a large and gay flag was
seen flying from the mast-head of a black cutter with a

yellow ribbon round her. On this flag, fluttering in all the glory of new bunting, was a Norwegian jack in the upper canton and in the fly the letters ISBJÖRNEN (The Polar Bear). This was the little vessel that was to be their home for the next five months. She looked quite attractive in the beauty of fresh paint and varnish. In one of the boats put off from shore was a respectable-looking old man who saluted the two Englishmen as he came alongside, advancing and paying his respects as soon as he stepped on board. Being unable to speak English he very wisely refrained from attempting a conversation, and it was not until some time after that they discovered that he was Jorgensen, the skipper of the *Isbjörn*. Farewells were now said, even the " dormouse " being visible, and a *douceur* given to the steward, which, Markham says, "so completely surprised him that he looked at it twice and then at us, before he could really comprehend our insane act, then, realising the fact, shook us heartily by the hand and disappeared."

On landing they were introduced to Captain Carlsen, who had circumnavigated both Spitsbergen and Novaya Zemlya, and had served in the *Tegethoff*, in the Austro-Hungarian expedition. Later he called to see them. He was plainly much displeased at not having been asked to accompany them and was unable to conceal his jealousy of Jorgensen who, he said, had not only not been in the ice, but was no sailor. It rather looked as if envy had prompted this estimate of the skipper's qualifications, but later events proved that it was not altogether false.

The two travellers stayed for a week at Tromsö at the Grand Hotel. The days were spent in buying cabin-fittings, stores, etc., visiting the Museum, and learning to walk on Norwegian snow-shoes, identical, of course, with the now well-known *skis* of winter sports. A *ukase* was procured which, when translated from Russian into English, proved to be to the effect that all subjects of the Czar must be civil to the two voyagers and permit them to kill as many walruses as they desired without interference.

On May 28th a start was made. Preferring to sail under

British colours, the ensign of the Royal Harwich Yacht Club
was hoisted, the Club having made Markham an honorary
member before he started on his second Arctic Expedition.
The accommodation on board was, to say the least, somewhat cramped. The cabin was raised about two feet above
the upper deck, and was reached by a little half-spiral ladder
leading into a small passage-way, which was fitted with
cupboards and lockers; one of the former was assigned
to Markham for the precious chronometer and his other
instruments. The cabin measured 5 ft. 6 in. × 5 ft. 9 in. In
the centre was a table, a cushioned locker occupied the fore
end, and on each side was a bunk, with cupboards under-
neath, while shelves and stow-holes were ranged along above
the bunks. An objectionable shelf, which came in contact
with Markham's nose every time he turned round, had to
be removed so as to give him a little more air and room!
The bunk was entered through a small octagonal hole; this,
however, he had cut, so as to obtain more light and air.
Light was admitted into the cabin through a window looking
out on deck assisted by two prisms overhead, and a certain
amount entered by the companion ladder. Various contrivances had to be resorted to in order to make the most
of the limited space, and the result was fairly successful.

The crew, though eminently polite, taking off their caps
and saying "Good-day" to the two Englishmen when they
came on deck every morning, were a rough, uncouth set
of men, and of uncleanly habits. They were of a musical
turn; the two helmsmen invariably relieved the tedium and
monotony of steering by humming or chanting some very
melancholy ditty. The skipper, Lars Jorgensen, was an
intelligent old man, totally unacquainted with the mysteries
of navigation and nautical astronomy, but evidently a fair
and careful seaman. Except when in the vicinity of land
or ice he was extraordinarily cheerful, manifesting his
hilarity by dancing about the deck and singing to the
accompaniment of the beating of a tin dish or the bottom
of a bucket!

The *Isbjörn* was not a clipper, and even in a breeze and

GROUP ON BOARD THE *ISBJÖRN*

close-hauled, her progress resembled that of a crab! Her
extreme slowness sorely taxed the patience of the two who
were eager to go forward beyond the haunts of man
into the ice region. Markham declares that in no part of
the world he had visited were the winds so variable, both
as to direction and force. Now becalmed, now rolling
uncomfortably, they proceeded, but so slowly that the
scenery they passed, beautiful as it sometimes was, became
all too familiar to them.

Whilst becalmed off Sörö, Gore Booth and Markham went
on shore, partly for the purpose of procuring fresh milk and
if possible a sheep, as a variation to the perpetual beef.
Seeing a habitation hardly deserving the name of a house,
they approached it, and as it appeared quite deserted, the
old skipper and one of the crew who had accompanied them
opened the door without further ceremony and walked in.
Then the strange stillness was explained—everyone was
asleep. The owner soon awoke to the fact that his dwelling
had been invaded, but far from resenting the unceremonious
intrusion, bade them welcome. They were the first
Englishmen he had ever seen, and at first he refused to
believe their nationality, until they informed him that they
were bound for Novaya Zemlya for pleasure—then he was
quite prepared to accept them as natives of Great Britain!
Here they succeeded in purchasing about half a gallon of
milk for the sum of one shilling, but the sheep were too
small and ill-conditioned to be worth the price asked for them.

The *Isbjörn* was next compelled to put into Hammerfest,
some sharp squalls having proved her to be insufficiently
supplied with ballast. The trade of this port was proclaimed
as soon as the harbour was entered by a strong smell of salt
fish and cod liver oil, but they were assured it was nothing
to what it was in the summer. The ballast taken in here
was soon found to be still insufficient, so another halt was
made in a secluded fjord called Havö Sound. Gore Booth
and Markham availed themselves of the opportunity to
take a walk on shore and buy milk. After the addition of
five tons of ballast, they resumed their journey, with the

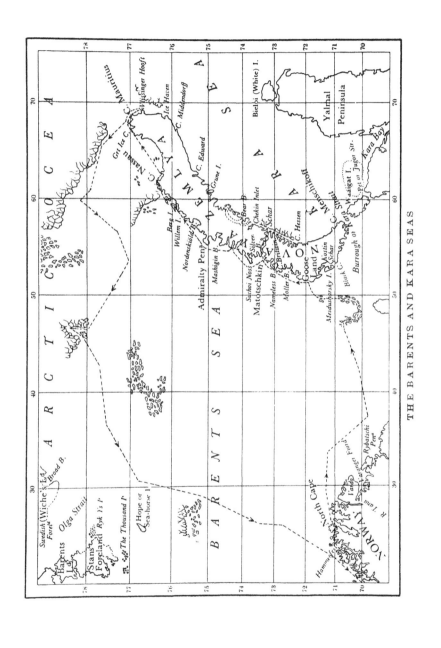

THE BARENTS AND KARA SEAS

hope, at last, that the little vessel's sailing qualities would be materially improved, and at midnight on the same day, May 27th, they entered the Mageroe, the last channel they had to pass before getting out into the open sea. Markham describes the *Isbjörn* as the "liveliest of 'little bears'" and as they proceeded with the wind against them through a nasty, confused sea, having doubled the North Cape, and shaped their course for Novaya Zemlya, the voyage at this point was not very delightful or comfortable. The breeze began to smell very ice-like and the temperature was becoming lower, accompanied by heavy snow squalls.

On June 4th, when in the vicinity of South Goose Cape, and about ninety miles from land, the cry of "Ice!" put all on the *qui vive* and soon they were passing through streams of loose, brashy ice, sufficiently packed in places to necessitate considerable *détours*. The crow's nest was "a bungling affair"—nothing more than an ordinary sized barrel entered from the top instead of from below. Just after reaching the ice Markham got soundings and a specimen of the bottom, soft mud, which he carefully bottled.

Two days later, after penetrating into the loose ice through which there were broad "leads" radiating in all directions for about twenty-five miles, the old skipper, over-careful, not to say timid, decided that it was better to get clear of it altogether; and so, while his passengers were in bed and unable to remonstrate, he headed off to the south-west and all that had been gained was lost. As soon as they were made acquainted with the state of affairs the cutter was tacked, and they began working up along the edge of the ice against a fresh north-westerly wind and a confused sea. Had he been in the *Alert* or the *Arctic*, Markham would not have had the slightest hesitation in boldly entering, and forcing his way through. Old Jorgensen and his crew, influenced, as they discovered, by the two harpooners, shewed a decided objection to coming to close quarters with the ice, and as sport was the primary object at the moment, there was nothing to be done but to submit to their inclination and be content to cruise along the edge

of the pack and occasionally into the bights. This un-
willingness to encounter the ice was one of the greatest
difficulties they had to contend with throughout the cruise.
  The beautiful ivory gull was seen for the first time, also
looms and other birds. Walrus-hunting now began; Gore
Booth took an early opportunity to go off for the greater
part of the day, whilst Markham remained on board taking
serial temperatures, obtaining sights to fix position, and
skinning specimens: one a beautiful little *Cyanecula*, about
the size of a robin, its neck and breast a brilliant blue, an
ivory gull, an Arctic tern, a guillemot, and a pomatorhine
skua. Soundings revealed the bottom to be hard gravel,
unlike the soft mud of two days back. The temperature was
in a gradual proportion from 29° at the bottom to 31° at
the surface.
  The following day Markham took off the crew in the other
walrus boat to try their luck, and so make up to them for
having had to spend one day on board hauling up his deep-
sea lead line whilst the others enjoyed the sport. They
started at 5 o'clock in the morning, as he had to be on board
again at 10 o'clock to wind up the chronometer. The
expedition resulted only in one seal and one dovekie, both
shot by Markham. The bird appeared as they were cautiously
approaching the seal, and as it was the first Markham had
seen in the Barentsz Sea he was much tempted to secure
it rather than the larger, and, to him, less interesting prey.
But certain that such a proceeding would cause him to
lose caste in the eyes of his companions, he turned his
attention to the seal and was rewarded; for on bringing down
his first quarry, he instantly dropped his rifle, seized his
gun, and bagged his second. Markham's reason for making
a collection was that he was not quite sure that the fauna
of Novaya Zemlya had ever been thoroughly studied;
indeed there had been no one, with the exception of the
Russians, to do it, and although some of the specimens
appeared to be common enough and well known, he thought
there might be some peculiarity or difference with which he
was unacquainted.

Although the voyage was on the whole monotonous, owing to the extreme slowness of the vessel, and the over-caution of her Captain, yet, with all his various interests and employments, Markham's days were filled to their utmost capacity. Divine Service was held every Sunday in the cabin.

The *Isbjörn* proved herself as handy as a little dinghy in navigating the loose ice, and, on June 9th, they suddenly emerged into a "land-water," which is the name Markham gives to a channel of water found in the summer between any large body of ice and the land, where a heavy sea was encountered. Snow was falling heavily, but on the fol-lowing day they caught their first glimpse, on the star-board bow, of Goose Land, the southern portion of Novaya Zemlya. On the 12th they anchored in a large bay, vaguely designated on the chart as "Nameless Bay." "Loom Bay" would have been more appropriate, for it harboured thousands upon thousands of these birds, the constant whirr of their wings producing a sound as of surf beating upon some rockbound coast. In rather less than two hours, the two sportsmen bagged no less than six hundred, and it may be add-ed that the fresh meat was absolutely necessary for the health of the crew. The birds rose in a great cloud at the first shot, completely hiding the face of the cliff, with a sound like that of a gigantic waterfall, while the victims fell like hail. One day the cry of "Ren!" from one of the men apprised them of the presence of reindeer, and the desirability of procuring some venison sent them hastily on shore. Gore Booth, the first to approach within range, shot four fine bucks, the entire herd. With regard to the food of these animals Markham was inclined, from his personal investiga-tions, to agree with Dr Lindsay that the so-called "reindeer moss" is possibly their only means of sustenance in winter when their favourite food, the willow, is unobtainable. Before leaving Nameless Bay they had the luck to find a nest and eggs of a king eider (*Somateria spectabilis*). Very rarely had these eggs been identified.

An improvised dredge gave very satisfactory results,

though their limited appliances—a piece of iron, a wooden hoop, and a bread bag, made it impossible to reach a greater depth than about forty fathoms.

Throughout Novaya Zemlya they met with traces of former inhabitants. In one spot, Cross Island, Willem Barentsz, in 1594, had found two wooden crosses which pointed to the fact that white men had visited this island before he discovered it. They landed on Cross Island to inspect the sad relics of the *Freya*, the ship of the unfortunate Norwegian walrus-hunter, Tobiesen, who, unable to extricate his vessel from the ice, determined to remain by her, his only companions being his little son and two seamen who gallantly stayed with him. Very touching was the sight of the frail house in which they had spent that terrible winter, and the graves of the father and son who had both succumbed to scurvy.

On June 20th they entered the Matyushin Shar, which bisects Novaya Zemlya into two islands. Here they replenished their stock of water at a fresh-water stream at the head of the bay, but, unfortunately, the Norwegian sailors carelessly put it into empty salt barrels, which caused intolerable thirst. At the beginning of the cruise the water had been put into rum barrels, which made it the colour of sherry and gave it a decidedly spirituous flavour; later, a further variation was made by the use of unwashed vinegar barrels.

The channel of the Matyushin Shar is very narrow with sharp turnings. They erected on shore a large cairn surmounted by a cross on which they engraved in large letters *Isbjörnen*, and in this was placed a record recounting their movements for the benefit of Captain de Bruyne, as previously agreed. They now hoped to pass through the strait into the Kara Sea, but were stopped by a barrier of ice, which proved that they had arrived too early in the season. They were therefore obliged to remain in the Matyushin Shar, cruising backwards and forwards between the ice barriers and the spot they had named Cairn Bay, from the number of cairns in the vicinity. The time was, however, profitably employed in excursions by boat and on land, for the purposes of sport and natural history, including marine zoology. Markham verified the opinion, commonly held among Norwegian sailors, that the "burgomasters" (glaucous gulls) act as sentinels to the seals, warning them of the approach of danger. He was watching his friend, gun in hand, cautiously approaching a seal, and saw a couple of these birds soaring above the intended prey, coming down from time to time as though whispering something into its ear. As the sleepy seal refused to be roused, one of the gulls, alighting, deliberately pecked it, and the seal, at last appreciating the situation, disappeared.

It was at this time that Markham observed a curious incident with regard to the freezing of sea water. Newly-made ice, known as "pancake ice," was actually forming in a certain and limited locality on the surface of the water, when the air temperature was as much as 39°, the surface water being 31°. As this happened at the mouth of a large valley through which flowed a quantity of fresh water, its precipitation into sea water at a lower temperature might have accounted for it. Thunder was heard at this time, an unusual occurrence in the Arctic regions.

Unable as yet, owing to the barrier of ice, to advance farther through the Matyushin Shar, they proceeded to the northward along the western coast of Novaya Zemlya. Bad weather and contrary winds hindered their advance, but, on July 25th, they crossed the 75th parallel and anchored in Lystina Bay. Here various species of birds were found, and, barren though the island was, there was a varied flora. By careful search Markham found as many as fifteen botanical specimens—saxifrages, poppies, etc., besides grasses, mosses and lichens.

Fogs were very prevalent, sunshine being the exception. The sun had now passed its greatest northern declination, and though they were still too early in the season to get through the ice, the winter was fast approaching. Had their little vessel been a steamer she would have had small difficulty in forcing her way through; as it was, the danger of besetment was too great to be risked. They therefore relinquished all hope of circumnavigating the north island of Novaya Zemlya for the present, and attempted once more to reach the Kara Sea through the Matyushin Shar. Here a delightful change had taken place during the four weeks that had intervened, and their hopes rose high, only once more to be dashed by soon again meeting that impenetrable barrier of ice. They determined, however, to remain in the neighbourhood for a short time in order to discover its nature and extent. They were also able to determine approximately the point of junction of the tides of the Barentsz and Kara Seas.

The ice now gradually clearing, nearly every day saw a slight advance, though disappointments were still frequent, and the surrounding country was explored in the time of waiting. Concerning some of his solitary rambles Markham says he never remembers to have felt such a sense of loneliness and quietude, which brought him "face to face with the wonderful works of nature and the power of the Almighty."

On the last day of July they succeeded in pushing through into the Kara Sea, only to find themselves once more held up by the solid impenetrable pack. This was far heavier than what is usually seen in Baffin's Bay; they therefore turned south, with the object of hunting walrus, which were said to abound in the vicinity of Yalmal Peninsula. As they were working along by the land-water they had frequent opportunities of going on shore, and botanical and other studies were pursued with zest. The weather during this time was delightful and they had some good fishing. The condition of the ice, however, and the small prospect of obtaining game in a southerly direction decided them to return to the Matyushin Shar. They re-entered it on August 18th and, to their great surprise, on reaching Gubina Bay, on the south side of the strait, they encountered Captain de Bruyne in the Dutch exploring schooner, *Willem Barentsz*. Apart from the pleasure of seeing him they were delighted to find he was the bearer of letters and news from home.

One sad piece of news was that of the death of the Prince Imperial whilst serving with British troops in Zululand. The greatest kindness was received from the Captain and officers of the *Willem Barentsz*, who did all in their power to supply the many needs that had arisen during the cruise of the *Isbjörn*, crockery, leather, etc., being among the gifts. The *Isbjörn* was able in return to make them a very acceptable present of fresh meat. The two vessels remained in company whilst passing through the Matyushin Shar, and frequent visits were exchanged, the Englishmen even rising to a dinner-party in the confined space of their little cabin! On the 23rd, they parted with the Dutch, and each went their separate ways northwards. Signs of winter were now unmistakable, and from this time they were obliged to employ artificial light below and in the cabin.

Magnificent glaciers were seen and visited as they sailed along the western coast of Novaya Zemlya, in a northerly direction. After rounding Cape Nassau the wind, which had been freshening considerably, increased to a gale, and so violent did it become that the safety of their little vessel was seriously imperilled in a futile attempt to tack. The heavy sea on the weather bow caused her to "miss stays" and the old skipper, who happened to be steering at the time, put the helm hard up in order to wear, but the little cutter refused to pay off, and rushed headlong towards the ice and destruction. The skipper's orders to "lower the peak" were inaudible in the shrieking of the wind, but one man, perhaps more intelligent than the rest, seeing the danger, let the peak halyards go. The vessel's head immediately paid off and the danger was averted, but so close were they to the ice that it could easily have been touched with the hand as the vessel flew past.

That afternoon they anchored off the Barentsz Islands, and when the wind subsided somewhat, Markham landed in order to determine, with the prismatic compass, the respective positions of Capes Nassau and Troost, concerning which they had been in some doubt. They put to sea again on September 5th, still going north, and on the following day passed Ice Cape, and reached the Orange Islands, by rounding which they had the honour of flying the British flag for the first time to the north of Novaya Zemlya. The wind being favourable and no ice being encountered, they had great hopes of reaching a much higher northern latitude, and even succeeded in enlisting the interest of the timorous old skipper. But, alas, a few loose streams of ice proved too much for the crew, who absolutely refused to proceed any farther north. This was a great disappointment, as it was their only chance of sighting Franz Josef Land; they had at least sailed nearer to it than any other ship, which shewed what could have been done by a well-provided and well-conducted expedition. They had now only four weeks' provisions on board and were in the midst of the ice which might at any moment shut them in. They therefore reluctantly saw their vessel turned to the north-west and making for the Barentsz Sea. Their highest position attained was latitude 78° 24′ north, that is to say, six miles farther north than the Dutch had reached the previous year, though fourteen miles short of the highest latitude of Weyprecht and Payer in 1871. At least the *Isbjörn* could claim that no other vessel not wintering in the Arctic had ever been in such a high northern latitude at such a late period of the year.

The crew were now happy in the extreme and sang all day long, each man his own separate song, as the little *Isbjörn* sped along on her homeward way. On September 22nd they reached Tromsö, where a few days later news was received of Captain de Bruyne's safe return and that he had telegraphed to the English Consul for news of the *Isbjörn*. Markham at once wired his congratulations and received an answer informing him of the success of the expedition, which had reached Franz Josef Land, finding no ice whatever in the vicinity when they reached the 55th meridian! Whilst rejoicing in a fellow explorer's success, Markham speaks of it as very aggravating to think that they also might have reached Franz Josef Land, and undoubtedly would have done so, had they had a different crew. "But," he adds, "it is no use repining, and, as we have not done it, I am very glad the Dutch have."

As it was, they had a very interesting and successful trip. For one thing it had proved that in ordinary years a steamer could easily reach and explore the coast of Franz Josef Land, which Markham considered the best route for future polar research. This view was fully confirmed by Leigh Smith in 1880. Markham had also with untiring zeal collected numerous specimens of plants, birds, crustacea, mollusca, echinodermata, fishes, insects, rocks and fossils; reports and catalogues of which have been published.

On October 6th he reached England, where he found he had been selected as Flag-Captain to Rear-Admiral Stirling, recently appointed as Commander-in-Chief of the Pacific Station, and was ordered to proceed forthwith in a mail steamer via Panama to take command of his ship, the *Triumph*, then at Callao, on the coast of Peru.

On November 3rd, 1879, Markham left Southampton in order to go out and join the *Triumph* on the Pacific Station, less than a month after reaching England from his cruise in the *Isbjörn*. At Southampton he had been introduced to Whymper, the celebrated mountain climber, whose object was the ascent of Chimborazo. He was accompanied by a couple of Italian guides, who, with himself, were so accoutred with water bottles, mountain barometers and various other *impedimenta*, that "they seemed prepared, then and there, to ascend any mountain that came across their path!" One of Markham's fellow-passengers, whom he came to know later in the voyage, finding that he collected butterflies, not only presented him with those he caught at St Thomas, but gave him all the necessary apparatus, besides various instructions on the subject. Markham's time during the voyage was mainly spent in reading Trollope's *West Indies* and writing for *Good Words*.

One afternoon, just before entering the tropics, a very unusual rainbow was observed—a perfect bow, but instead of being in the heavens, it lay spread out on the sea.

Anchoring on the 15th in the harbour of St Thomas, he found his old ship, the *Blanche*, lying at anchor and on the following day, which was a Sunday, went to Service on board. He found many alterations in the rig and armament of the *Blanche* and also in the arrangement of the cabins; but the beautifully inlaid hatchways, which owed their existence to him, were still preserved, though no one knew with whom they had originated.

At Jamaica he paid a visit to Dr Colan, one of the doctors of the *Alert* during the Arctic Expedition, who had become Deputy Inspector-General in charge of the Royal Naval

Hospital at Port Royal. After a long talk on Arctic topics Markham was taken over the hospital, and every detail, in particular of the treatment of yellow fever patients, was explained to him.

Rather disturbing news was received before leaving harbour, to the effect that a severe "norther" had visited Colon, where Markham was to disembark, that several steamers were on shore, and that the wharf of the Royal Mail Company was destroyed. He afterwards learned that such an inundation had never occurred before in the memory of man. This would mean difficulty in landing, but the alternative was to go to Portobello which would entail a week's delay in joining his ship. When the following day they reached Colon, they found that the gale and floods had so injured the permanent way that all communication with Panama, whither he was bound en route for Callao, was suspended. As the *Don*, the vessel in which he had come out from England, had to go on, and there was a chance of his being able to catch a steamer at Panama by landing at Colon, Markham decided to do this, in spite of the evil reputation the place had for sickness and bad hotel accommodation. The delay of one week in taking up his command was not to be thought of. Accordingly he spent five days in a hotel at Colon, of which he writes: "Of all the dirty, rickety, tumble-down houses of entertainment for either man or beast commend me to the Howard House....What a relief it will be to leave this dreary, fever-stricken hole, and get to Panama!"

The railway ran right through the main street in front of the door of the hotel. The only safe place to walk was under the verandahs of the houses, where one was hustled by negroes, coolies, Chinese, and people of all nationalities. Miserable, ugly-looking pigs roamed about the streets, as common as dogs in England. Even here, however, Markham was able to enjoy some study of bird life; especially attractive were the exquisite little humming birds, scarcely larger than bumble bees, their beautiful plumage glittering in the sunshine as they flitted from flower to flower. He was also interested in the swarms of red ants which seemed to prefer the railway line to any other part of the road. Streams of these insects would occasionally be met, each carrying an enormous piece of green leaf entirely covering its body. Dead horses and mules were lying in the swamp on each side of the track, with vultures gorging themselves on the decomposing carcases. No wonder Colon was an unhealthy place! Markham's visit synchronised, unhappily for the peace of his nights, with the annual observance of the independence of the State of Panama, which, before being incorporated in the Republic of Colombia, had proclaimed its own individual independence. The uproar produced by the letting-off of crackers, the cheering, and blowing of brass trumpets, over and above the ordinary noises of the town, made sleep impossible, and drunken men and women danced in a booth immediately under his bedroom.

At last, however, owing to the kindness of the manager of the railroad, for whom a train was being sent off to take him on a tour of inspection, Markham was able to make a start in company with one of his fellow-passengers, his farewell comment on leaving Colon being, "I do not think my heart will break if I never see the delightful place again!"

But his difficulties were not yet over. At a place four miles from Colon they were obliged to stop as the track had been undermined by water. Fortunately Markham had taken the precaution of putting on his long porpoise-hide boots, so that the trudge through thick alluvial deposit was managed, at least, with dry feet. They soon reached the first serious "wash-out"—the wrecked appearance of the bridge across the river Mendy was almost indescribable, and so were the scenes of desolation and destitution through which they passed. They were fortunate enough to be able to secure a "hand-car," propelled by three negroes. Markham had thought that his only way of reaching Panama would be to take a canoe up the turbulent Chagres from Gatun to Matachin, a distance of about eighteen miles, spending one, if not two nights on the journey. This would have been both an uncomfortable and rather hazardous voyage, but thanks to the kindness of Mr Woods, the railroad manager, who gave him all the assistance in his power, it was unnecessary.

Occasionally, as they rattled along in the hand-car, they came to places where portions of the road had been washed away and they were obliged to lift the vehicle off the lines and carry it to where the rails were intact, while at one spot three large water tanks had been washed off their iron foundations and deposited many yards down the road immediately on the track. These obstructions had to be circumnavigated, no easy matter, as the hand-car weighed at least five or six cwt. and it had to be lifted and carried round the obstacle. The San Pablo, or Barbacoas Bridge over the Chagres, was seriously damaged; two of the stone piers had subsided, each about six feet into the bed of the river, so that the bridge had assumed a zig-zag shape. With care, the hand-car with one passenger was taken across, but Markham and Mr Woods crossed it by jumping from one girder to another.

The rain now came down in torrents. After an hour they reached another serious "wash out," but, on the other side, they had the satisfaction of seeing a train and engine. They could only reach it by walking about two hundred yards through mud up to the knees. This train was placed at the disposal of the travellers to carry them to Panama, which they reached at 4 o'clock that afternoon. Here accommodation was certainly better, but the good people of Panama were also celebrating their independence! The whole town was given up to the masqueraders who took all sorts of liberties with everyone they met; mummers invaded even the room where the travellers were dining. In the Plaza, of which the Grand Hotel where Markham stayed formed one side and the Cathedral the other, the unpleasant spectacle of bull-baiting could be seen. Markham, after having crossed the Plaza several times, heard that some men had been fatally gored, as those in charge of the animal had an unpleasant habit of letting it loose upon any stranger crossing the Plaza in order that the people might have the amusement of seeing the foreigners run!

After another five days spent in Panama Markham embarked on the P. & O. steamer *Payta*, en route for Callao. A voyage of a week brought him to his destination. His first view of the coast of South America compared unfavourably in his estimation with that of Novaya Zemlya; it looked barren and sterile in the extreme. In the harbour of Callao was a large assemblage of warships of different nationalities—United States, French, German, and Italian, besides British, and conspicuous among them by reason of her size was the *Triumph*. Taken altogether they were a very formidable array of fighting ships. As the ensigns were hoisted at 8 o'clock every morning, each ship played her own national anthem. In addition to the other ships in the harbour there were two Peruvian men-of-war, the *Union*, which had won for herself an unenviable notoriety for the way in which she had succeeded in running away from the enemy, and a monitor, the *Atahualpa*, a bargain Peru had acquired from the Americans—she could barely steam four knots, and was not able to put to sea!

It must be borne in mind that Chile and Peru were now in a state of war, though operations at this time were being carried on in a very desultory manner. The British ships were therefore necessarily detained in the port of Callao as a protection for the British residents in Lima, the Chilean Fleet being daily expected.

Markham's time was now very fully occupied with his new duties and his leisure was scanty. He was also trying to write the story of the cruise of the *Isbjörn*, besides various magazine articles. As usual, he threw himself with energy and zeal into the task of promoting the thorough efficiency of the ship and her crew. The men gave him great trouble at first and he was obliged to be very strict in the matter of punishments for leave-breaking and other insubordination. The temptations of such a port as Callao furnished an added reason for firm discipline. An entry in his journal at this time reveals the kindly heart beneath the stern exterior: "I wonder if the men have any idea that I feel the punishment I inflict upon them as much as they do themselves. I was very much distressed to-day at having to punish those who have been otherwise well-behaved, but I am determined to put a stop if I possibly can to leave-breaking."

Among his midshipmen in the *Triumph* was a young Japanese named Goro Ijuin, sent by his Government for a course of instruction in the British Navy. When in after years he rose to high rank in the Navy of his own country, he always expressed himself grateful to Markham for all he had done for him while serving in the *Triumph*.

A curious marine phenomenon connected with their present location was what is known as the "Callao painter." Its effect was two-fold; it was always accompanied by a very nauseous odour, and the white paint on the boats and any parts of the ship that had come in contact with salt water were discoloured a chocolate hue. At times the sea water also became discoloured and this was attended with the same obnoxious odour, so that it all seemed to have a connection. The bodies of myriads of small fish resembling sardines could be seen floating on the surface. No satisfactory solution of the phenomenon could be discovered. Darwin does not even mention it. Markham's own opinion was that it must be due to a volcanic disturbance in the ocean-bed, and that the effluvium arose from decomposed animal matter.

The unsettled condition of the country kept the ships some time at Callao. Prado, the President of Peru, suddenly dropped the reins of government and slipped away in the *Payta*, under cover of taking important despatches to Europe which must be delivered to the Captain with his own hand. On December 20th the *Triumph* left Callao, shaping her course to the southward; but on the night of the 22nd they were recalled by a telegram in cipher from the British Minister at Lima stating that a revolution had broken out, and that the insurgents, headed by Nicholas de Pierola, were in possession of Callao, and that Lima was about to be stormed. It was therefore necessary for the ships to be on the spot for the protection of British subjects. On their arrival, however, they found that the gravity of the situation had been exaggerated, the revolution was already ended by an act of stratagem on the part of Pierola, who had marched to Callao, told the people that Lima was his (an utterly untrue statement) and called upon them to surrender. This they did, and Lima following their example, Pierola proclaimed himself supreme chief, and nominated a Government. He proved himself, at any rate, a despotic ruler.

On New Year's Day, having gone to Lima to pay some calls, Markham was interested to note the effects of the brief revolution. Many houses, as well as the Cathedral, had suffered from the fusillade. From the summit of one of the towers of the Cathedral he and his companion espied Pierola, the self-constituted ruler of Peru, and his staff crossing the Plaza, followed by a crowd of ragged little boys. They shouted "Viva Pierola!" but being at such a height no one could hear them; they therefore proceeded to ring the bells in the belfry as hard as they could! One of the bells was a monster, and must have been heard some miles off; it weighed over 30,000 lbs. and the clapper alone weighed over a ton. Its date, so far as Markham could decipher it, appeared to be 1645.

About this time, at the invitation of Mr Backhouse of Lima, Superintendent of the Railway Company, Markham made a very interesting expedition up the Aroya railroad. Starting at 5 o'clock in the morning, he reached Lima at 8 and found Mr Backhouse waiting to receive him. The little *Favorita*, the special train in which they were to travel, consisted of a small engine and carriage, not unlike a wagonette, all in one, and not more than fifteen feet long. It held comfortably about eight people, but on this occasion the party consisted of four, in addition to the engine-driver and fireman.

The construction of the Aroya railroad struck Markham as one of the most marvellous feats of engineering skill ever achieved. The line was taken as far as possible along the valley of the Rimac, which it crossed many times; one of the bridges over which they passed had a centre pier 252 ft. high, the bridge being 575 ft. long. The Rimac is a turbulent, foaming rapid which, in less than eighty miles, rushes down a declivity of 12,000 ft. In some places the tunnels appeared one above the other like little black holes in the clefts of the rocks. In one particular spot three different lines of railway appeared from above to be winding up the ascent. So sharp was the zig-zag that the train was unable to turn, and, after going up one incline, had to back up the next, and so on. Where practicable the turns were made, or else the engine was turned on a turn-table. In the last forty completed miles of the road there were no fewer than forty tunnels, one the shape of a horse-shoe, which gave it its name. In some places the train ran at the base of sheer cliffs, rising perpendicularly to a height of 3000 or 4000 ft. One spot was pointed out, the apex of a triangle by which one of the zig-zags was formed, over which a car and several wagons had jumped. They were attempting to apply the brakes at the upper part of the zig-zag when the cars took charge and rushed down the hill with fearful velocity. Fortunately the few men who were engaged in adjusting the brakes had time to leap off before the cars had attained any great speed, and received little injury, but such was the velocity of the train that, when it reached the summit of the cliff at the base of which the Rimac was rushing 1000 ft. below, it leaped completely over the river and lay, a mass of *débris* and wreckage, on its opposite side.

At 11 o'clock they reached Matucana, nearly 8000 ft. above the sea level, and here they had breakfast in the Cristoforo Colombo hotel, kept by an Italian. Matucana is a very old village, and was even at one time of such importance as to have its own private revolution, a fashion not uncommon in South American towns! The tower of the old mud church, built more than three hundred years ago, was still standing, though the church itself had been partially restored.

Markham had noticed up to this height a great number of small butterflies and moths, a large bumble bee, and two kinds of birds, a pigeon and a species of small swallow. Patches of verdure were few and far between, the general scenery being bold and rugged, with barren hills and cliffs of lofty grandeur. The terraces, or "hanging gardens" of the Incas, which lined the hills on both sides of the railway, specially caught Markham's attention. They are called *andenes*, and give their name to the range of mountains which divides South America into two separate regions.

At half-past twelve they left Matucana and reached Chicla, the terminus of the railway, shortly after 2 o'clock, having travelled over eighty-six miles since leaving Callao and ascended to a height of 12,220 ft. It seemed strange to Markham that, although during his life he had climbed several mountains (Etna for instance), he had now reached a higher altitude by rail on the Andes than in any mountaineering excursion. During the last hour of the ascent they were at times enveloped in clouds, and rain fell during the time they were at Chicla. The temperature here was 40° Fahr., whilst at Chosica, the first stopping-place, it was as high as 78°. Some of the party suffered from *soroche*, caused by the rarefaction of the air, but the only effect Markham experienced was a certain drowsiness. After lunch at the hotel they started on their homeward journey at 3 o'clock, and, shutting off steam, the *Favorita* rattled down at a good rate, reaching Lima at 6.45 p.m. They found everything quiet in the streets, and there was no sign of the revolution of a few days before.

There were actually at one time five English men-of-war in Callao harbour, probably a larger fleet than had ever been assembled there before, and, curiously enough, there were no fewer than six "Alerts," men and officers, on the Station.

On January 24th the *Triumph* left Callao, and reached the Lobos Islands on the 27th, anchoring off the southern group. On first landing Markham had thought the islands were of volcanic formation, but on noting the composition he concluded that they were formed of quartz and felspar. One of Peru's chief sources of wealth is from guano; Markham saw one cutting 25 ft. deep. The island on which Markham landed was entirely barren. The colour of the soil was a dirty grey, relieved only by the richer hue of the guano deposits. However, he collected what specimens he could, though there was a great dearth of animal life. The men had begun to realise their Captain's passion for collecting, and everything that struck them as curious was always brought to him.

Amongst the expeditions made at this time perhaps one of the most interesting was to the Galapagos Islands. When, or by whom, the Galapagos Archipelago was discovered seems uncertain. It was used as a sort of head-quarters by the buccaneers of the seventeenth century. The first authentic reference to the group is on a map of 1570. The present names of the islands were evidently given by Englishmen during the Stuart period; Charles, James, Chatham, Hood, Albemarle, and Marlborough being the names of the principal ones. The less important islands are also called after Englishmen. The whole archipelago derives its name from the Spanish word for the freshwater tortoise, *galápago*.

Landing on Charles Island, Markham discovered in a hut on the beach a nest containing four small eggs, which had been left for him by one of the crew of the despatch boat which had conveyed the Admiral on shore in an advance party. The nest belonged to the beautiful little yellow wren peculiar to this group. The island was entirely without inhabitants, but was famous for the number of wild cattle, dogs, pigs, donkeys, and other animals to be found there. They were probably introduced by Senor Valdizan, who rented the island from the Government of Ecuador, and whose grave, bearing the date July 23rd, 1878, they found at a short distance from the little settlement.

The islands are undoubtedly of volcanic origin, with cone-shaped peaks, which, although now dormant, might at any time break into activity. Though bare and sterile

on the lee side, the windward side of the islands was clothed
with dense vegetation, and in addition to the trees indigenous to the locality were the orange, lemon, lime, fig
and vine, probably introduced by the late inhabitants.
These conditions can only be accounted for by the fact that
the thirsty soil of the weather side absorbs all the moisture
brought by the trade wind before it can reach the other.
Turtles and sea birds were seen in abundance, and there
were large quantities of fish in the bay, chiefly a kind of
cod. The lizards, which are very scarce, belong to a genus
entirely confined to these regions. A peculiar kind of locust
was also found, and various other insects, including beetles,
cockroaches, dragonflies, and a large sort of bumble bee,
also numerous moths, but only three distinct species of
butterflies. An interesting find was a freshwater lobster of
a greenish hue, about six inches in length, and as it was
discovered 450 ft. above sea level and a mile and a half
from the beach, it seemed to point to the fact that fresh
water is to be found in the island all through the year.
Amongst the interesting collection of specimens made by
Markham at this time were a petrel (*Puffinus obscurus*)
and nine species of Lepidoptera[1].

Penetrating several miles into the interior of the island,
they found some caves, which proved to be cavities in the
lava, some forming passages having natural walls on each
side from 8 to 10 ft. in height. Nothing better adapted by
nature for defensive purposes could be conceived. Traces
of fires proved that these caves had been used by the
inhabitants as dwellings.

The one drawback to this interesting expedition was
the nights, the only beds being the hard floors of the huts;
and the incessant braying of the donkeys and rush of wild
boars through the camp was only less annoying than the
persistent attacks of mosquitos and other insects, which
effectually deprived them of sleep. By day the flies were
a terrible pest.

Markham wrote a brief history of the Galapagos Islands,

[1] Appendix A.

which was read at one of the ship's entertainments, and afterwards published in pamphlet form.

The *Triumph* now proceeded to the coast of Mexico, anchoring off Acapulco. From here Markham made an interesting excursion into the interior of Mexico, and was able to add largely to his collection of butterflies. Their next anchorage was off San Francisco, on April 2nd, 1880, which was reached after one of the heaviest gales that had been experienced in the vicinity for many years. The Admiral complimented Markham on the manner in which the *Triumph* was brought into harbour.

San Francisco, where they remained ten days, was a delightful change after South America, and the people were most hospitable. On April 17th they reached Vancouver, and anchored in the harbour of Esquimalt. Victoria, the capital, was then but a poor place, and not to be compared with some of the cities in the "far West." The houses were all of wood, with no pretensions to size or style of architecture. The streets were broad, with paved side-walks, but there was a distressing air of poverty about the town. One of Markham's first concerns at Esquimalt was the erection of a Seaman's Club House and a Recreation Ground. He was also made a J.P. for the Esquimalt district, as it was thought advisable for an officer to be on the bench when questions connected with the men or the Navy came before the magistrates.

The *Triumph* left Vancouver on October 2nd and proceeded south. They experienced very hot weather in the tropics, the heat off Acapulco being so great that the stokehold thermometer registered 130°. The coolest part of the ship had a temperature of 88°, whilst the sea water was 86°.

In November after the United States Government had failed to mediate between Chile and Peru, owing to the exorbitant demands of the Chilean representatives, the war was resumed, and the *Triumph* had again to take up her station at Callao. In December, officers of different nationalities were appointed to the conflicting armies to

M   12

watch operations. The *Triumph* provided one for each side. On December 6th there was a small naval action between Chile and Peru off Callao, causing a stampede amongst all the neutral vessels! It ended by the Peruvians taking shelter under the batteries, upon which the Chileans drew off out of range. Christmas found the war still raging. Markham comments in his journal on the ironic contrast between "peace and goodwill" and the "struggle between the Peruvians and Chileans in which quarter was neither asked nor given."

As the Chilean army threatened Lima, Markham was sent by the Admiral on two occasions to carry a message to General Baquedano requesting that neutral property in the town should be respected. He describes the Chileans as men of fine physique, intelligent, and full of energy and enthusiasm, well clothed and fed, and in the best of spirits; whilst the Peruvian army struck him as dispirited, wretched, and apathetic.

Markham was the only person who visited the advance line of both armies, and he was actually there twenty-four hours before the battle of Chorillos. The Peruvians suffered a total defeat in this battle, and the Chileans advanced upon Lima, where the Peruvian General Gonzales de la Cotera, war minister at the time of Prado's flight, attempted to raise a revolution and proclaim himself President. He was only rescued with difficulty from the enraged mob, and placed for safety in the British Legation. From there he was sent on board the *Triumph*. The Chileans had requested Markham to surrender him, but he replied that the General was under the protection of the British flag, and that if the Chileans wanted him, they must come and fetch him. He was eventually shipped off to Guayaquil, and Markham was glad to be rid of him!

Closely following on the battle of Chorillos came the startling news that the English Admiral and Minister had both been shot by the Chileans at Lima; but the report was contradicted the next day.

The Peruvians still hoped that Lima would have been

saved, for they had a strong position at Miraflores. A deputation from the Corps Diplomatique succeeded in securing a temporary truce between the contending parties. The British Minister, Mr St John, had worked hard for a peaceful settlement, but the Chilean General, whilst inspecting his troops, advanced, perhaps unintentionally, outside his own lines, and the Peruvians immediately opened fire on the Chilean Headquarters Staff. Thus began the battle of Miraflores, which resulted in the complete defeat of the Peruvian army. The President of Peru was at the time entertaining the foreign ministers and some of the naval officers at luncheon at his suburban residence at Miraflores. The party broke up abruptly and without ceremony. Helter-skelter they rushed towards the comparatively safe shelter of Lima. The English Minister was slightly wounded in the hand by a stone hurled by an exploding shell. The French Admiral, attacked by a Peruvian who did not know him, behaved with great coolness and courage, and narrowly escaped with his life. The German Minister, a portly figure, had to be dragged along by the English Minister and Admiral. As he could not climb the walls himself, and was too heavy to be lifted over, the Admiral "parbuckled" him over them, that is to say, dragged him up one side of the wall and rolled him down the other. The unfortunate man could only utter the single monosyllable "Ach!" to express his distress. "That's German for water!" cried someone; a top-hat was promptly filled with water at a neighbouring stream and the contents thrown over the Minister's head and face! The drastic remedy proved effectual, and so revived him as to enable him to push on to a place of safety. Another diplomat trusted his coat to a Chinaman while he climbed over a wall, but, on alighting on the other side, saw the Chinaman two fields ahead making for Lima with the coat and the contents of its pockets!

On January 17th the Chileans, about 3000 strong, marched into Lima, which was undefended, and General Baquedano and staff rode in the following morning. This put an end to hostilities, though peace was not formally concluded until later. Markham made a report to the Admiralty on the torpedo used by the Peruvians during the war.

On February 14th the *Triumph* arrived at Coquimbo. From here Markham made various expeditions into the country, visiting copper-smelting works and mines. A month later they anchored off Valparaiso, and Markham made an expedition to Santiago, travelling first by rail through wild and mountainous country, then emerging upon a perfectly level plateau, an amphitheatre surrounded by the Cordilleras.

They continued to cruise along the coast of South America; the monotony of six weeks at Coquimbo was relieved for Markham by the interest of compiling a history of the war between Chile and Peru. This, however, he never published as, on his return to England, he found that Clements Markham was engaged on the same project.

At Caldera a guanaco hunt was organised by the Vice-Consul. These animals Markham describes as "rather graceful, more especially when seen on the crest of a hill, their long, almost birdlike, necks standing out in bold relief against the sky." Being very suspicious creatures, who always keep a sentry posted on the summits of the hills, they were very difficult to hunt, and Markham found that it was almost useless to stalk them. The only chance of a successful shot was by coming upon them suddenly, or by having plenty of beaters to drive them towards a certain point. This he did himself, so that one fell to the Admiral's gun, the only shot that took effect throughout the day. Its head was given to Markham, who preserved it as a valuable addition to his museum.

The ship called at Taltal and Antofagasta, the latter famous for its nitrate and silver works, and also for being the scene of the actual outbreak of hostilities in the late war. Markham describes the desert of Atacama, through which he passed after visiting the above mentioned works, as "the very acme of sterility...not a blade of grass...not a

single bird, beast, or reptile; it was one vast plain of solitude
...talk of the dreariness of Arctic lands—they are gardens
of Eden compared with the desert of Atacama!"

Cruising northwards along the coast they reached Iquique,
the second town of importance on the Peruvian coast, and
from Mollendo, the port of Arequipa, Markham and seven
others made an excursion to Lake Titicaca, the sacred lake
of the Incas. The landing at Mollendo was a very dangerous
one, huge rollers and heavy surf breaking over the rocks
with a deafening roar. However, following the pilot boat,
they pulled through a mass of broken water and succeeded
in getting alongside a dilapidated kind of pier on which was
a large crane suspending a chair in mid-air. Seizing this
dexterously, they were hauled up and landed safely in
Mollendo. A scene of desolation met their eyes, for every
kind of Government building had been destroyed by the
Chileans. It was even now strictly blockaded, and the
running of trains prohibited. A little engine and carriage
had been placed at their disposal by the Superintendent of
the railroad, and, in order to escape being fired at, Markham's
party had arranged with Captain Uribe, of the Chilean
warship *O'Higgins*, to hoist a certain flag on the carriage.
Travelling along the coast for about four or five miles they
passed through a fertile plain to Tambo. From Tambo they
gradually ascended by an extraordinarily winding road to
Cachenda, a station 3250 ft. above sea level. Here they
lunched at a primitive hostelry, and obtained their first
view of Mount Misti, the volcanic mountain at the foot of
which is situated the city of Arequipa. In shape it is a
perfect cone, not unlike Fujiyama, the sacred mountain
of Japan. Cachenda is situated in the great desert of
Arequipa, a desolate expanse of sand, strewn in places
with large stones and boulders, probably thrown out by
Misti in some period of eruption. La Joya, situated in the
centre of the desert, is half way to Arequipa. The water
pipes supplying Mollendo run parallel with the railroad
for about eighty-five miles. The sandhills, composed of
fine white sand, which cover the desert about Cachenda,

presented a strange sight; each was formed in the shape of a perfect horseshoe, the convex side being toward the south, the quarter of the prevailing wind. These sand accumulations, varying in height from 5 to 20 ft., are called *medanos*, and are formed by the sand collecting on some object, a stone or the carcase of a dead mule, and gradually increasing in bulk as more and more sand is drifted by the wind. A curious contrast to the general sterility of the desert was afforded by the sight of an isolated fig-tree, and a few geranium plants. This, it was found, was the result of a leak in the water-pipes utilised by some of the people connected with the railroad.

Passing Uchumayo, a large village on the opposite side of the River Chile, and looking down on the valley below and the fertile plain of Arequipa, the party could see extensive fields of maize, wheat, beans, and alfalfa, with pepper and willow trees in the foreground.

At Arequipa they received a great welcome from at least three hundred people, including all the Englishmen in the city. The day was a *festa* and many idlers strolled down to the station to get a sight of the foreigners. Colonel Solar sent an A.D.C. to welcome them and offer all the civilities in his power. Accompanied by the English Vice-Consul and a small retinue of their countrymen, they drove through the town in a tram-car, called on Colonel Solar, and engaged rooms at a hotel. Here, after a tour of the city, they passed the night, and proceeded the next morning to Puno, in spite of warnings of the danger of the dreaded *soroche* if they attempted to rush straight from the coast line to a height of nearly 15,000 ft. above the level of the sea. But, their time being limited, they were obliged to take the risk.

They left Arequipa punctually at 5 a.m. on a dark and gloomy morning. The railroad wound first in a southerly direction, then to the westward, round Mount Charcani, and so on to the Cordillera to the northward and then eastward! The highest altitude of the line is 14,660 ft. above sea level. At dawn they had a magnificent view of the snowy peaks of Charcani. At 8 o'clock they reached Pampa do Arriero, or the "Pampa of the Muleteer," where hot coffee was served to them by a "most charming old lady," in a tumbledown house, dignified by the name of a hotel. This old lady was the owner of a little vicuña, which Markham wished to buy as a pet for the ship's company, but nothing would induce her to part with it. As they proceeded on their way they saw herds of vicuñas, alpacas and llamas, the department of Puno being the greatest wool-producing province of Peru.

When they stopped at the hotel at Vincocaya they were conscious of a certain oppression of breathing, but were not yet further affected by the rarefaction of the air. After a height of 14,660 ft. had been reached, the country assumed a different character. Hitherto the view had been bounded by lofty peaks, but after descending a short distance they reached an extensive plateau, cultivated with grass, wheat and maize. This huge tableland had evidently been thickly populated in the days of the Incas, for traces of the *andenes*, or terraced gardens, were plainly visible on the upland slopes. After leaving Colco they passed several small lakes, on which they saw numerous wild-fowl of various kinds, among them one that was apparently a snow goose (*Anser hyperboreus*); it was a surprise to Markham to find this bird at such low latitudes.

Juliaca was next reached, and half an hour after leaving it they obtained their first view of Lake Titicaca. Markham owned to a feeling of great disappointment as he did so, for, instead of an enormous expanse of water, such as he had expected, for the lake is eighty miles long and forty wide, they saw only an arm, not much more than ten miles across. In order to see the lake properly it is necessary to embark on a steamer and, leaving the Bay of Puno, to proceed to the lake proper, but for this, unfortunately, there was not time. They saw a few of the *balsas*, formerly used by the Indians in navigating the lake; these were made of rushes rolled up and plaited and then sewn together and were sufficiently buoyant to carry fairly large cargoes. The lake is reported to abound in fish. There is a tradition that the wonderful gold chain or rope which Huayua Ceopac caused to be made on the birth of his eldest son Huascar was thrown into Lake Titicaca to prevent it from falling into the hands of the Spaniards. The bottom of the lake is very uneven, the water being excessively deep in some places, whilst in others it is so shallow as to be barely navigable even for the light-draft *balsas*.

Puno they found to be a quaint, old-fashioned, dirty town, with about 4000 inhabitants. They ordered dinner at the "Grand Hotel Ynca," and almost immediately Markham was prostrated by a violent attack of *soroche*. The symptoms were excruciating pains in the head, sickness, and a general sensation of lassitude and depression. Nearly all the party were affected to some extent, but Markham suffered most, probably because he had had so little sleep for several nights previously. They left Puno at 8 p.m., and by the time they reached Vincocaya the ground was covered with two or three inches of snow. At the hotel one of the officers was informed that the bed assigned to him had been occupied by a man who had died of *soroche*! Markham was only too glad to lay his head on the hardest of pillows in the coldest and dreariest of rooms, but sleep was impossible, and next morning he was scarcely able to walk to the little train, a distance of only about fifty yards. It had been an unwise step to sleep at such a high altitude as Vincocaya, but it had been done in order to give a rest to their engine-driver. As they descended to Arequipa they gradually recovered but it was some days after he got on board before Markham threw off the effects of the attack. After a night at Arequipa, including a dinner-party, which was hardly enjoyed by the afflicted travellers, they went on towards the coast. In the desert of Atacama they saw a wonderful mirage. Pools of water, clear and fresh, appeared to be close to them, and so identical was the resemblance to water that they could even see the summits of the distant hills plainly reflected on its placid surface; yet, on approaching nearer, all vanished, leaving nothing but the dry soft sand of the desert.

Rejoining the ship they proceeded on their way to Callao, where they remained about three months, and, amongst their other manœuvres, they carried out a grand night attack with torpedoes. Markham was at this time preparing a paper on the defences of Callao. From Callao they went south again to Coquimbo, and here they learned from English newspapers brought in by the mail that the *Swiftsure* had gone into dock to prepare for sea, and was coming out to relieve the *Triumph*. Admiral Stirling was now at the head of the Rear-Admiral's list and was expecting his promotion and news concerning his successor on the Pacific Station. A telegram from the Admiralty shortly after this informed him that he would be promoted to Vice-Admiral on January 1st, 1882, and that Rear-Admiral Lyons would arrive about that time to take over the command.

Whilst at Coquimbo a very sad accident occurred on board the *Triumph*, on November 23rd. A tin of xerotine siccative, a new preparation for drying paint, caused an explosion in the fore part of the ship, resulting in the death of three men and the injury of seven others. The explosion was thought to be due to the escape of inflammable gas through a defective tin. Markham felt the loss of his men very keenly and daily visited the injured, who had been transferred to the *Liffey*, the *Triumph's* sick-bay being a complete wreck.

The *Triumph* now began to make her way northwards in the direction of Panama. In January Rear-Admiral Lyons arrived to relieve Vice-Admiral Stirling, and Markham took leave of his old chief with much regret, accompanying him across the Isthmus of Panama to Colon, whence he took passage home in the *Nile*. They saw the beginnings of the proposed canal; Markham comments upon it as "a very gigantic undertaking," and adds "unless the Chagres is diverted from its natural bed, I cannot understand how it can ever be a successful accomplishment."

Turning south again they anchored off Juan Fernandez, and Markham and his friend Stephens made an expedition on shore. Here he found a humming bird peculiar to the island, besides other specimens. He was interested in "Selkirk's look-out," situated in a gap in the range of hills, but on the whole he was disappointed in the island.

After months of uncertainty as to the date of his return to England, which was dependent on the arrival of the *Swiftsure*, he was at last to take leave of the Squadron, and start with the *Triumph* on what was to be the homeward voyage. His way now lay south through the Straits of Magellan to Sandy Point, or Punta Arenas, where he was to await the *Swiftsure*, which did not arrive until August 2nd. The *Triumph's* band greeted her with "O Willie, we have missed you!" and "Where have you been all the day?" to which the *Swiftsure* responded with "Tommy make room for your uncle!" Finally, on October 2nd, Spithead was reached, and on the 13th the ship was paid off.

Most of Markham's large natural history collection is now in the Natural History Museum at South Kensington. It included two new species, an albatross (*Diomedea irrorata*), still the only example possessed by the Museum and, in consequence of being a "type specimen," not exhibited in the public galleries, and a petrel which bears his name (*Cymochorea markhami*)[1]. The albatross was a source of no small anxiety to Markham, as his chief shared the sailor's well-known superstition with regard to the killing of these birds, and its presence on board had to be kept a dark secret.

[1] Appendix A.

WITHIN three weeks of paying off the *Triumph* Markham was sent for by Sir Cooper Key, and, to his astonishment, was offered the command of H.M.S. *Vernon*, the Naval Torpedo establishment at Portsmouth. At first he hesitated about accepting the post, but his objections were set aside by Sir Cooper, and two days afterwards he was appointed. It was curious that Captain (afterwards Lord) Fisher, who was keenly interested in torpedoes, was sent to the *Excellent*, which was the Gunnery School at Portsmouth, whilst Markham, who was a gunnery man, was put in charge of the Torpedo Establishment. He described himself "a square man in a round hole."

He was for three months with Captain Gordon as additional Captain, and worked very hard in order to acquaint himself with his new duties. He held this important command for over three and a half years, and his conduct during that time so met with the approval of their Lordships at the Admiralty that he was invited to remain at the post for a further extension of time. This he declined, as he felt it would be better for the Service that there should now be a change; the strain, moreover, was beginning to tell upon him. During his tenure of office the torpedo, as a weapon of offence, was immensely developed, as was also submarine warfare in all its branches. Electricity was also largely introduced into our ships for lighting and other purposes, this being due to Markham's suggestions and recommendations from the *Vernon*.

This home appointment gave Markham an opportunity for the exercise of his love of hospitality, and he was scarcely ever without visitors in his cheerful rooms on the Hard, overlooking Portsmouth Harbour, and later in a furnished house at Southsea or in the Isle of Wight. He was always good company and in a circle of intimate friends he let his capacity for boyish amusements have full play. He thoroughly enjoyed being mistaken for a railway official at a station and never undeceived his questioners. He liked to tell the story of how, when shewing a small boy over Portsmouth Dockyard, he once vaulted over all the small posts he came to, much to the boy's delight. While he was in command of the *Vernon*, his steward, contrary to regulations, married without leave. Markham sent for the man to his office and asked severely, "Are you married?" The steward falteringly pleaded guilty. After having gravely reprimanded the breach of discipline, Markham concluded by saying, "Go into my after-cabin, and you will find a box. Give it to Mrs —— with my compliments!" The box contained a china tea-set which had been chosen with elaborate care.

On giving up the command of the *Vernon*, in May, 1886, Markham applied for six months' leave for the purpose of travelling in the northern parts of North America. He was in communication with Mr Sutherland, Chairman of the proposed Hudson Bay Railway Company, who suggested that he should make the round trip from St John's to York Factory, through Hudson Strait, and then on to Winnipeg by land, with the object of reporting to the Company on the navigability of the Straits as an ocean route for commerce, adding that, if he agreed, he could go in the *Alert*, as the Company had the privilege of sending two representatives in her. After due consideration Markham consented to this plan. To be employed again in the old *Alert*, although not in command of her, and to be battling once more in her with the ice, was a fascinating prospect.

The Hudson Bay Company was not sympathetic towards the scheme for the railway, so a considerable amount of tact would be needed when he came in contact with its agents in Canada.

Whilst these negotiations were going forward, he was informed by Lord Walter Kerr that he would be offered the command of H.M.S. *Imperieuse*, shortly to be commissioned for an experimental cruise in the Channel, in order to decide whether she was to remain a masted ship, or whether her masts were to be removed, and as their Lordships required a sound judgment and report they had resolved to offer it to him. This was a flattering invitation, for the appointment was an important one, but the call of the north was too strong.

On June 8th Markham left Liverpool in the S.S. *Carthaginian*, bound for Halifax. When in the neighbourhood of Newfoundland he descried, when going on deck in the early morning, a faint white shimmering in the rising sunlight which was very familiar to him—it was an iceberg which had drifted from Davis Straits, or possibly even from farther north. They reached Halifax on June 19th, where he stayed for a few days, joining the *Alert* on June 25th. When he came down to the ship he found that one of the old "Alerts," now a leading stoker in the *Garnet*, had come to see him off, and he was much touched by this mark of attention. The Blue Ensign which was flying at the peak was the third ensign Markham had seen on the *Alert*. The first "our own grand White Ensign, then the Stars and Stripes of the United States, and now the Blue Ensign of the Dominion of Canada." There was a marked contrast between the present *Alert* and the ship as he had once known her, for her accommodation now was of a very rough and ready nature.

Their way lay by the Gulf of St Lawrence through the Strait of Belle Isle, along the coast of Labrador, which reminded him very much of the land about Cape Farewell. He was mainly occupied during the voyage in reading books on Hudson's Bay, and making copious notes, and much of his time was spent either on the bridge or aloft. He was again doomed to suffer from the vacillation of those responsible for the navigation of the ship, loose streams of ice being regarded as "the pack," and progress being retarded in consequence.

On July 5th they reached the entrance of Hudson Strait,

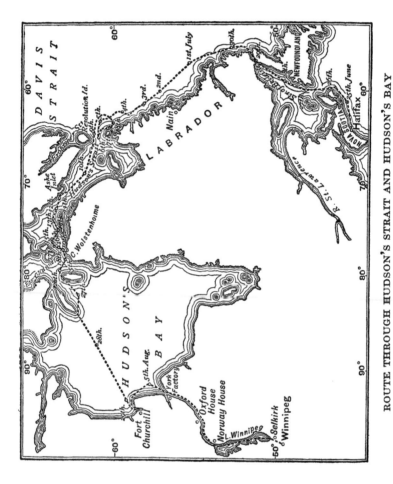

ROUTE THROUGH HUDSON'S STRAIT AND HUDSON'S BAY

where they were detained several days, partly by thick weather and partly by soft, brashy ice, which was never packed sufficiently to prevent even so slow a steamer as the *Alert* from making fairly good progress. Whilst delayed at the entrance of the Strait they noticed the same turbulent eddyings mentioned by Davis, Parry, Back, and others, called by Davis the "Furious Overfall." From the 9th to the 11th scarcely any ice was seen, and they were able to accomplish a distance of over 200 miles in about thirty-six hours, a fact which proved how free the eastern part of the Strait is from ice; for the *Alert*, even at full speed, could only steam about six knots an hour. On the 11th they anchored in the snug little bay called Ashe Inlet, where the officer in charge of the meteorological station informed them that ice did not form in the Strait before December, and that the channel was navigable during the whole of November.

After leaving Ashe Inlet their progress was retarded by ice, only 400 miles being accomplished in nine days; this was mainly due, in Markham's opinion, to the absence of sufficient steam-power to enable the ship to thread her way through the loose ice, but he also felt there was a tantalising lack of enterprise on the part of the navigators.

The ice encountered in the western part of the Strait was somewhat heavier than that at the eastern entrance. It consisted of small pieces packed loosely, as if the floes had been broken up and had afterwards drifted together. This peculiarity was one he had never observed in other northern seas, and he considered it had an important bearing on the report he had to make. These innumerable small pieces would very largely deprive the pack of sufficient force to cause serious injury even if a vessel were beset. In the case of a "nip" the small pieces, being composed of soft brashy ice, would act as a cushion between the ship and the larger floes. During the time they were in the Strait the weather was generally fine, the average temperature being 35° Fahr., and on some days even rising to 50°; the prevailing wind was from the westward, but from whatever direction it blew it seemed to have little effect on the movements of the ice.

After being for upwards of eight days in the ice, the *Alert* arrived at Digges Island, and then proceeded through the open water of Hudson's Bay, and from that time, with the exception of a few loose streams of broken-up ice, no more was seen. On July 29th they dropped anchor in Churchill Harbour. Here Markham made the acquaintance of Mr and Mrs Lofthouse, of the Church Missionary Society, and found that they had no house to live in, and were seriously thinking of taking up their abode in the little church, where some of their luggage was already deposited! The timber for the construction of a house had arrived the previous year, but the materials were in three different places, and no labour could be obtained to bring it together and set it up. The Hudson Bay Company was opposed to anyone, even missionaries, settling on its territory. The men of the *Alert* were happily able to render some assistance in rafting the timber, and towing it up to the port with the steam pinnace.

The mosquitos at Churchill were a terrible pest, night and day; the Ward Room was swarming with them, for the skylight had to be opened owing to the heat from the stoves which were still kept going, and it became difficult to eat without the risk of swallowing some of the insects.

Markham saw various kinds of birds in this neighbourhood, but refrained from shooting them as he had no means of carrying the skins. He was able, however, to make some botanical collections, and had various other specimens given to him.

On Friday, August 6th, York Factory was reached and Markham took leave of the *Alert*. As there was a difficulty in obtaining canoes and Indians he was forced to remain until Monday with the Chief Factor of the Hudson Bay Company and his wife. On Sunday, having attended the Presbyterian Service at the church belonging to the Company in the morning, he went in the evening to the C.M.S. church for Crees, where, the resident missionary being on furlough, the service was conducted by a Cree Indian in his own language in a very earnest manner.

YORK FACTORY

CREE CHURCH

Having made such purchases as were necessary at the store, including a Hudson Bay coat, made of blanket with a blue hood and capote, he set out on Monday, August 9th. He had managed to secure the services of two men, and was glad to find that the tent lent him by the Chief Factor was not considered too heavy for the canoe. The costumes of the little party were sufficiently varied and picturesque— Jem, a half-breed and interpreter, boss, cook, and general manager, wore a blue jumper; Tom, a full-blooded, long-haired, good-tempered Cree, who could not speak a word of English, but was a capital canoeist, was more or less in rags; Alf, a half-caste boy of fifteen, who was being given a free passage at the factor's solicitation, had made himself a jumper out of a bright scarlet blanket; Markham was arrayed in his Hudson Bay coat, a three-cent Zulu hat, and moccasins. The two Indians were very devout and every morning and evening Jem read aloud to Tom a chapter from the Cree Bible.

Their way lay up the Hayes River. They were towed by ropes on shore for about 150 miles, but their progress was slow owing to the river being unusually low, and their canoe, not having been in use for some time, leaked considerably. Markham would have been perfectly happy but for the venomous insects that assailed them throughout the day, flies, sandflies, mosquitos and "bull-dogs." The tent was a great comfort, which was only spoiled by the mosquitos which took possession of it before its rightful occupant. Markham said that if anything would induce him to smoke it would be the hope of thus ridding himself of these pests, but the smokers did not appear to be any freer than he, and though he asked Alf to come and smoke in his tent it made no difference.

The Indians were much impressed by Markham's importance, for it appeared that the factor had told them that he was rolling in wealth, and that he must push on quickly as the Queen had sent for him!

Alf was a great encumbrance; although he took his share on the tracking-line he was practically useless in the canoe, and the weight of his baggage seriously retarded their progress. Markham had to walk almost all the way, over very unpleasant ground, either rough pebbles, soft sand, or marshy quagmire. One day a canoe with three Indians overtook him and, steering across to the opposite side, came back to him later with a quantity of yellow berries, not unlike wild raspberries, which he found most refreshing. The following day, as they passed their camp, the Indians followed up their considerate act with a gift of venison. Markham in return presented them with tea and tobacco. The steward of the *Alert* had unfortunately put all his provisions in paper parcels; these soon burst in the canoe, and the tea was mixed up with pepper, salt, and sugar! But Markham could not afford to throw it away and was obliged to infuse the curious compound.

From the Hayes River they branched off into its shallower tributary, the Steel. In the evening Jem and Tom informed Markham that owing to the condition of the river it would be impossible to proceed, but Markham refused to be put off by difficulties. He accordingly despatched them in the canoe, lightened of its load, to the nearest Indian camp to procure, if possible, another canoe and another Indian. As they were unsuccessful in their quest, the only thing to be done was to send Alf, with all his baggage, and a portion of Markham's own, to the friendly Indians they had passed the previous day, requesting them to take him back to York Factory for a couple of dollars. This left Markham in solitude, which he found pleasant enough for awhile.

On a fine moonlit night the bushes made a fairly comfortable bed, but when the rain came down in torrents, accompanied by a cold northerly wind, Markham sorely missed the tent and plaid which he had been obliged to send back. When, by 6 o'clock on the following evening, his Indians had not returned, he began to wonder whether they had played him false and to contemplate walking on alone to Oxford House, a distance of 240 miles! But at 8 p.m. the canoe returned with a third Indian, who proved to be the man who had supplied him with the yellow berries a few days back. He was a merry fellow, who worked like a horse and rejoiced in the name of Nichi (pronounced Neeshy). They now made capital progress. The nights were rapidly getting longer, and the days proportionately shorter. As they went south they came across signs of a more temperate and genial climate. The pine forests were thicker, the willows larger; birch trees and poplars were seen, and also a pretty little flowering pea. Animal life was also much more plentiful; the fulmar petrel and silvery gull were observed, and a flock of wild geese of a dark plumage. Markham mentions a tortoiseshell butterfly which for size and brilliancy would have done credit to the tropics.

He was much struck with the way in which the Indians handled the canoe up the rapids, when the slightest blow on the frail hull would have been fatal. One man would track, up to his waist in water, another in the bows with a pole pushing for dear life, and the steersman aft with his paddle. Markham was sometimes in the canoe and some- times on shore. The passage through the rapids was most exciting, and once or twice it seemed as if the torrent must overwhelm the boat; but the skill and strength of the Indians were quite equal to any emergency.

The changes in the weather were very sudden, and a difference of 60° in the temperature during the twenty-four hours was by no means uncommon. At times, after a sharp frost in the night, they would start in a dense cold fog, which would be followed later by tropical heat.

They rose each day at about half-past four, and had a cup of tea. Then Markham would walk on in advance, carrying his gun, and was thus able, from time to time, to provide the party with fresh meat. After about four hours he would stop and wait for the canoe to come up. They would then have breakfast, Markham's usually consisting of a slice of ham fried by himself, some ship's biscuit, and tea. After an hour's halt he would start off again, and walk until about 2 o'clock, and directly the canoe came up they would have dinner; then off again until nearly sundown, when they would halt for the night, and while the men were preparing camp and their own supper, Markham employed the time in writing up his journal. He found it a delightful life, but for the intolerable nuisance of the mosquitos. On Sunday he rejoiced the hearts of his men by giving them for their dinner two pots of New Zealand mutton from his own stores, and some cheese which the steward had put up for him.

The Indians shewed him a new way of making bread, or "cake," as they called it. The kneaded dough was placed on the flat end of a stick and flattened out by the hand, with occasional moistening from the mouth of the cook. The other end of the stick was then thrust into the earth before the fire, and the cake thus roasted. Markham was also interested in watching Tom catch a fish, which his keen eyes detected asleep in the water. Seizing an axe and cutting a branch from a neighbouring tree, he pointed it and in less than two minutes had transfixed the fish. It was about two feet long, and something like a ling, but without scales. It made a pleasant change for breakfast, its flesh, which was white, tasting good and sweet. They often found gooseberries, raspberries, and red and black currants, which though small were very refreshing.

At Point Douglas the River Steel forks into two branches, the Fox River to the west and the Hill River to the south. The Hill River, which they followed, was very narrow, with many shallows and rapids; consequently their progress was slower. Reaching the first falls, Markham was informed that there would now be no more tracking; here also they made their first portage. As they had come away without any portage-straps, the tracking-line had to be cut up to supply the deficiency; the different articles slung in these impromptu straps were hung round the heads of the Indians, who were thus able to carry a load of 200 lbs. at one time, trotting along much faster than Markham could walk, and running back for their next load at the double. Laden as the canoe now was, it was necessary to make two journeys, of 200 to 400 yards, to each portage.

Between the falls and the rapids the water was nearly

still, and canoeing was easy. Sometimes there were as many as ten portages in the day, some half a mile in length. The majority of them went by certain names, such as "Mossy portage," "Half-breed portage," "Dead-man's portage." Some were provokingly close to each other, two being only 100 yards apart, so that they had barely settled down in the canoe when it was time to get out again and carry their loads once more. In one place the canoe was lightened by the "cacheing" of some of the Indians' provisions for the return journey. These were placed in a hole at the foot of a tree and then covered over with moss and ashes from the fire to protect them from wolves and other animals. For a time they were untroubled by mosquitos, but were attacked by them again on reaching Swampy Lake.

Many wild ducks were found in this vicinity. Whenever the Indians saw birds or animals they invariably imitated their cries, and attracted them within range of their guns.

The next stage brought them to Knee Lake, so called from its fancied resemblance to a knee—a long expanse of water, about forty miles in length and about five miles broad at its widest part. Here the sun's rays beat down upon them from a cloudless sky as they paddled across, and the heat was so great as even to drive away sandflies and mosquitos. The lake was studded with an immense number of rocky islets, one of which had the reputation of influencing the compass very perceptibly. The Trout River, at the end of the lake, was reached after six hours' hard paddling. Here they had to make a portage round Trout Falls, a fine cascade of water about ten feet high. Several more portages, and then a succession of rapids opening into still water, marked their further progress, and at half past seven on August 21st they arrived at Oxford House.

Oxford House was a small post compared with York Factory or Churchill, consisting of the little residence in which the chief trader, with his wife and five children, and the accountant lived, and two other houses—one the shop and office, the other the meat and lumber house. Like all the other forts this one was surrounded by a stockaded fence, once affording protection from Indian raids, now serving to shut out thieves. Various vegetables and fruit flourished in the garden. Markham's bedroom, rather grandly styled "the spare room," was simply a loft, with one window, which did not open. His couch was a couple of blankets on a wooden truckle bedstead, but the room seemed cosy enough after many nights spent on the moss of a North American forest. The chief trader was away and the accountant appeared somewhat sceptical of Markham's identity, and positively refused to accept his cheque.

Here, as at York Factory, he was hindered rather than helped in his efforts to proceed on his journey. However, he succeeded in securing the services of two Indians (Muskegans) for the journey to Norway House, paying them $25 and rations for both journeys; he also hired a canoe from an old woman for $3. The two Indians could neither speak nor understand English, and, as Markham was unacquainted with the Muskegan language, communication between himself and them could only be by means of signs. They appeared stolid and apathetic, but, at times, broke out into extraordinary loquacity, belying the opinion commonly formed of the North American race. Markham thought the change was probably brought about by contact with the white man. The Indians demanded five meals a day, but were not particular as to their quality. Markham once shot a huge musk rat, the skin of which they said was good; apparently they thought the body good too, for they made a meal of it!

The new canoe was much smaller and frailer than the first. Markham and his companions were closely packed, and for a man who detested tobacco-smoke it was not pleasant to have a man smoking the worst possible tobacco two feet in front, and another doing the same thing two feet behind. But for the Indians smoke was an integral part of existence. The portages with the lighter canoe were less tedious, and they made thirty miles the first day.

Rather more than a day's journey brought them to Pine Lake, where a thunderstorm burst upon them, and they were forced to land and improvise a kind of tent with the oil-cloth from the bottom of the canoe. When they resumed their journey they passed through a long, rocky gorge, and rapids and falls made portage necessary. Forest fires were seen from time to time, the smoke being sufficiently dense entirely to obscure the sun at its rising and setting for at least 10° above the horizon. This had at any rate the good effect of banishing mosquitos for the time. "Robinson's portage," the longest on the whole route, being a mile in length, came as a welcome change after a long time of being cramped up in the canoe. The falls here were the finest they had yet passed. One lake was a mass of bulrushes, but happily, the wind being fair, they were all bending in the direction in which they were going; had it been otherwise it would have been "like charging a square of infantry with fixed bayonets"! Another fork of the river brought them to another change of name, and they pursued their way along the Ech-a-ma-mish (winding river), which proved to be the most difficult they had yet had to negotiate, as it eventually degenerated into a narrow, marshy swamp, and a thick black muddy ditch, where the canoe had to be pushed and shoved along on the top of the mud. Of all the uninteresting work that could be conceived, Markham thought that of conveying a canoe for miles on thick black mud, or through long, dank weeds was the dullest!

On August 27th Norway House was reached, thirty-eight portages having been made during the trip, an unusual number owing to the excessive shallowness of the rivers. The previous evening, seeing a white man on the bank with a canoe, they approached him, and Markham, for want of something to say, called out "How do you do?" He replied, surlily, that he was quite well. Somewhat rebuffed, Markham announced that he was going to Norway House, and inquired if he had any message for Mr McDonnell. "Mr McDonnell is no master of mine," was the reply, "I'm a free man." It seemed strange that he should evince neither surprise nor interest on seeing a fellow-countryman. Markham's comment is: "Perhaps I am rather ruffianly-looking!" It was 6 o'clock in the morning when they arrived at Norway House, but the inmates of the Fort were all asleep, regardless of the lusty crowing of a cock, which Markham hailed with pleasure as being the first he had heard since leaving England. An hour or so later Mr McDonnell came out and welcomed the traveller, giving him a packet of letters and papers from England.

A steamer had recently left Old Norway House, twenty-five miles away at the entrance of the river, but he was told it would almost certainly call again for him. This, however, was too vague, and he made arrangements with some Indians who were going on to Winnipeg to give him a passage in their boat. Even then difficulties were raised about starting, but, eager to push on, Markham overcame all objections, offering himself to take the steer oar in place of one man who had failed—and very hard work he found it. At the last minute, to his surprise and consternation, he discovered that they were going to embark two entire families! But there was no help for it, so, putting the best face he could on it, he assisted them and their belongings into the boat. The party consisted of an old Indian, his bachelor son, two married sons with their wives, each with three children, all under six, and two of them infants in arms. The children were almost as great a trial as the mosquitos had been and the women were of no assistance, even in cooking, their whole time being given up to their children. The whole party were unspeakably dirty, but the older members of it extremely devout. Every morning and evening there were prayers, hymns, and Bible-reading.

The families occupied the stern sheets, and Markham sat where he could, principally on his luggage. The boat was about 40 ft. long, sharp at both ends, with about 10 ft. beam in the centre, and drawing about ten or eleven inches of water—essentially a fair weather boat. The mast was very primitive, with a square sail; and, when the wind was favourable, the little craft flew before it at the rate of about ten miles an hour. But when it was against them they could not use the sail at all, whilst to row in the wide waters of Lake Winnipeg against a head wind was impossible, so that they were forced to camp until it changed. The Indians were adepts in the art of wasting time, and opportunities afforded by fair winds were lost again and again by their interminable meals. As time went on, their provisions began to run lamentably short, and Markham put himself on half rations. On one of the islands he came across an Icelander who, for half a dollar, provided them with half a sack of potatoes and some fish called "gold eyes," about the size of a whiting.

They reached Selkirk on September 11th, and none too soon, for they had subsisted on little but tea for the previous three days. Here Markham parted from his Indians with real regret, and put up at a primitive hotel, where he had a tiny room, lighted by an evil-smelling kerosene lamp. He left Selkirk the following day and crossed the river on a very primitive kind of ferry, a floating stage hauled over by one man, and then drove through the forest to the depôt, a distance of about four or five miles. He found several people interested in the proposed railway waiting to receive him at Winnipeg. Here he was given the best room in the hotel; visitors, reporters, and invitations to dinner poured in upon him, and it was with difficulty that he escaped a public banquet.

Both the Premier and the Attorney General shewed themselves very keen about the proposed railway, and were delighted with Markham's report on the navigability of Hudson Strait. This was pronounced to be of "inestimable value," and Markham eventually received the official thanks of the Canadian Houses of Parliament.

The trip had been as successful as he could have wished. He had travelled from England to Winnipeg by water, and had the satisfaction of knowing he had achieved the distance in a very much shorter time than it had ever before been done. He spent two or three pleasant days at Winnipeg, where he was hospitably entertained. The main street of

MAIN STREET IN WINNIPEG

the town, though it had some excellent blocks of buildings, was marred by a lack of congruity; for, side by side with a fine building, would be seen, perhaps, a wretched little wooden tenement. Someone remarked to Markham: "We want a good fire to make Winnipeg a really fine city!"

On September 15th Markham left for Wisconsin. A visit to his family was cut short by a cablegram from the Admiralty, on October 11th, offering him the command of the Training Squadron, which carried with it the rank of Commodore. It was too good an appointment to be lightly refused. He telegraphed his acceptance and hastened home. Reaching London on November 1st, he took command of the Squadron on the 5th, and left Portsmouth in the *Active*, his flag-ship, on the 10th—not a bad record.

STARTING FROM NORWAY HOUSE

Chapter XIV

November 1886–August 1891

MARKHAM'S new appointment was an important one. Following such an able man as Commodore Fitzroy, who had successfully organised the Squadron and established a routine, he was anxious that there should be no retrogression. Lord George Hamilton, in an interview before he left London, requested him to keep him informed as to how things were going, and to submit to him his views on the value of the Training Squadron and on Naval education in general.

The Squadron consisted of the *Active* (his flag-ship), the *Volage*, the *Rover* (subsequently relieved by the *Ruby*) and the *Calypso*. They cruised as much as possible under sail, and their first voyage was to the West Indies; this occupied a period of between five and six months, during which time they visited Barbados, Tobago, Trinidad, Grenada, St Vincent, St Lucia, Dominica, Guadeloupe, Montserrat, Antigua, Nevis, and St Kitts.

At Barbados they made an excursion to Bathsheba, and walked out to see some petroleum wells. These were then being worked in a very primitive fashion, eleven of them producing an average of 350 barrels a year, all bought by Russia.

Markham described the Gulf of Paria, which separates Trinidad from the mainland of South America, as the grandest sheet of water he had ever seen. At Trinidad he met Froude, the historian, at a dinner-party at Government House. The Chief Justice, Sir John Gorrie, invited Markham and two of his captains to accompany him on an expedition to the Blue Basin.

At Grenada Markham was joined, to his great pleasure, by his cousin, Clements Markham, who spent the rest of the voyage with him. Owing to heavy squalls encountered between St Vincent and St Lucia it was impossible to anchor in Gros Islet Bay, and they were obliged to go into Port Castries. Markham was disappointed at not being able to take the Squadron into Gros Islet Bay, as it was here that Rodney used to keep his fleet ready to pounce out upon the French if they attempted to leave their anchorage at Martinique. However, he was able to visit Martinique and to shew the Diamond Rock to his young officers. This rock had played a very important and unique part in naval history. In 1804 it was armed and actually put in commission by Sir Samuel Hood, as H.M.S. *Diamond Rock.* The command was entrusted to Lieutenant Maurice of the *Centaur,* and the rock rated as a sloop of war with a corresponding ship's company! The guns, two 24 prs. and two 18 prs., with some smaller ones, were landed and placed in position in a novel and most ingenious manner. The *Centaur* was brought close into the rock and a hawser was taken from the masthead to the summit of the island, which is 570 ft. above the sea level. This hawser was used as a jackstay along which the guns were hauled. The party from the Training Squadron could see what they took to be the platforms of some of the lower guns, and the ruins of the officers' quarters. The French were so annoyed at the establishment of the little outpost that they sent a portion of their fleet to subjugate it, but the little garrison held out for twelve months, and it was not until their provisions were giving out that they were at last compelled to surrender.

As Markham was anxious to pay a visit to Les Trois Îlots, the birthplace of the Empress Josephine, he anchored off Fort de France. Accompanied by his cousin he went on shore, and immediately on landing they found a large savannah enclosed with trees, in the centre of which stood a marble statue of the Empress, presented to the island by Napoleon III, in 1868. On the pedestal was a bas-relief in bronze of her coronation by Napoleon. At the time of their visit the statue was in a sadly neglected condition, and they were told by the British Consular Agent, who was also American Consul, that he was trying to get the statue, in order to send it to New York. This he fully expected to do, as Republican feelings were paramount in Martinique.

The following day the two cousins crossed the bay to Les Trois Îlots, where, to their astonishment, the Mayor and Corporation, the Curé, the officer commanding the gendarmes, and others were all assembled to receive them, and immediately the bells of the church began to peal in their honour, and continued ringing until their departure. They were conducted first to the mairie, where some speeches were made, and then to the military headquarters where the Commodore was requested to inspect the cavalry soldiers, seven in number. After a visit to Josephine's birthplace, the whole population came to see them off and there were more speeches. When the ships took up their berths off St Pierre the French flag was saluted with 21 guns, and the salute was returned by some small guns in a fort entirely hidden by foliage.

Off Antigua the *Rover* caught a large shark, measuring 12 ft. in length. When opened it was found to contain, amongst other things, a champagne bottle, an empty sardine tin, a rat, two chickens, the hindquarters of a calf, two balls of spun-yarn, and a *Times* of January 22nd! By March 5th, 1887, the Squadron was back at Barbados, and Markham and his cousin were invited to take up their quarters at Government House.

The Admiralty having telegraphed to Markham so to dispose of his time as to arrive at Portland on May 8th, he took the Squadron to Bermuda, where they remained six days, and then to the Azores, anchoring in Horta Bay, in the Island of Fayal. As they approached the land, steaming between Fayal and Pico, Markham thought that Pico was one of the most perfect cone-shaped mountains he had ever seen. They experienced very bad weather on the homeward voyage, but, whenever practicable, the usual exercises were carried out by the Squadron. Markham tried some interesting experiments with the electric light, by hoisting signals and illuminating the flags by directing the light on them, and the *Active*, in this way, succeeded in carrying on a conversation with the *Rover*, although the flags were not very easily distinguished. As they neared England a thick fog sadly interfered with their progress, but they were able to drop anchor off Portland at 10 p.m. on May 8th. Markham received a cordial reception at the Admiralty, and was informed that the recent cruise had been most satisfactory in all respects.

On June 21st he attended the Jubilee Thanksgiving Service in Westminster Abbey, and shortly afterwards the Squadron, with a fresh complement, went for a cruise in home waters. By July 18th they were again at Spithead, where the Fleet was assembling for the great Naval Review. Two more ships, the *Inconstant* and *Arethusa*, were added to Markham's Squadron for this occasion.

On the evening before the Review, Markham and the other flag officers of the Fleet were commanded to dine with the Queen at Osborne. They were a party of sixteen, consisting of Her Majesty, the Grand Duke of Hesse and his daughter, Princess Irene, the Duke and Duchess of Connaught, Prince and Princess Christian, Prince and Princess Henry of Battenberg, Lady Ampthill, General Ponsonby and the five naval officers. Markham was agreeably surprised at the absence of formality. When dinner was over they all rose together and went to the drawing-room, when the Queen came round and talked to each one separately. The conversation was chiefly confined to the Review, the ships, and the weather. They left at 11. For the Jubilee Review the weather was perfect. Before the departure of the Queen the following general signal was made: "Convey to officers and men under your command Her Majesty has great satisfaction and pride at the magnificent display made by Her Navy this afternoon." The Training Squadron now took part in the Naval Manœuvres, and Markham was complimented by Admiral Hood on the work of his Squadron.

His sailing orders for the next months were to proceed to Vigo, Arosa Bay, Gibraltar, and Madeira, to be forty-three

days at sea, and twenty-six in harbour, which only gave
time for forty-eight hours' leave to each watch. From
Vigo Markham and two of his Captains made an expedition
to Oporto where they saw much of interest, including the
Cathedral with its exquisite silver chapel. From Arosa Bay
they had the opportunity of visiting Santiago, and at
Gibraltar Markham was joined once more by his cousin,
Clements, who went on to Madeira with the Squadron, and
made the homeward voyage with them.

After a few weeks in England Markham once more took
the Squadron to sea, with orders similar to those of the
previous winter. His first anchorage was at Santa Cruz,
one of the ports of Tenerife, whence he proposed to make
his long-desired ascent of the Peak. To do this it was necessary to drive to Orotava, on the north side of the island,
about twenty-six miles from Santa Cruz. Five officers from
the *Active* and three from the *Calypso* accompanied him.
He met with little encouragement either at Santa Cruz or
at Orotava; he was told that the Peak was rarely ascended
so late in the season—it was mid-December. However, a
good guide was secured while they dined, whose only stipula-
tion was that they should be ready to start at 1 a.m.

Mounted on wiry little ponies and mules, the cavalcade
started—the nine Englishmen and six guides and mule-
teers, with four pack mules carrying provisions. The night
was fine but dark, and it was impossible to see the path
up which they toiled. As daylight broke they were rounding
a spur and there in front was the Peak, rising up in solitary
grandeur, and apparently close to them. They all raised a
shout of joy, but their guides and the barometer soon informed them that they had still more than 7000 ft. to climb.
At about 7 o'clock they reached a dreary-looking plateau,
covered with small and loose scoriæ, and here and there
enormous masses of obsidian. Here they saw a species of
broom, growing to a height of from 4 to 6 ft. At this point
they halted for breakfast; unfortunately the water had been
forgotten and they were obliged to drink beer instead—a
very bad substitute, in Markham's opinion. At a height

of about 10,000 ft. they came to a small level patch of ground, on which was a pile of volcanic rocks, or boulders. This was called the "Estancia de los Ingleses," a tribute to the adventurous spirit of the British race. Markham had noticed the same thing in 1865 on Mount Etna, where the last resting-place before the cone was called "Casa Inglese." At the Estancia de los Ingleses the guides told them the horses could go no further. As the guides themselves seemed

STREET IN OROTAVA

more inclined to take a rest than to push on, Markham and his companions decided to begin the final ascent without their services. The way was very laborious, over loose ashes and lava, which would have been insurmountable had it not been for the zig-zag track.

By this time the rarefied air was beginning to have a very painful effect upon the party. The heat, although it was winter, was intense, and all superfluous clothing was cast off, to be resumed on the way down. About noon they reached La Rambleta, and at its highest elevation found themselves at the very base of the cone, which rose up straight before them in a perfect pyramidal form. They had now reached an altitude of 11,680 ft., and, realising that they were within measurable distance of their goal, raised a cheer and a shout of "El Pico, El Pico!" to encourage those of the party who were struggling in the rear. Markham called a halt of about seven or eight minutes, after which they addressed themselves to the last 500 ft., the stiffest of all, for it was said to be at an angle of 44°. At length, after an arduous climb of at least half an hour, they found themselves at the very summit of the Peak, a height of 12,192 ft. Only Markham and four of his companions succeeded in achieving the final ascent. A little over eleven hours had elapsed since leaving the hotel.

They found the summit surrounded by a heap of rocks forming a circle, some 150 yards in diameter, composing the old crater. Evidences of volcanic activity were everywhere visible, and numerous jets of sulphureous smoke or steam were issuing in all directions. The interior of the crater, into which they descended, was covered with a kind of calcined chalk and efflorescence of sulphur. The view from the top was magnificent. Not a cloud was above them, nothing but the blue dome of heaven, and below and around was the equally blue ocean. Nearly all the islands of the Canary group were plainly visible, whilst at their feet lay Tenerife itself.

After about an hour spent on the Peak they commenced the descent, which, although trying to the legs was accomplished in far less time than the ascent. They made a slight *détour* to visit the ice cave, a cavern in the lava, from the natural arch of which long icicles and stalactites depended. At half-past two they rejoined the remainder of their party at the place where the horses had been left. The guides were mostly drunk, so Markham and one of his companions determined to push on, leaving orders for the rest to follow with the horses as soon as possible. After various misadventures in the darkness they reached the hotel about 10 p.m., thirsty, bruised, and thoroughly tired out.

After a night's rest Markham declared himself fit and fresh, though a little stiff, and returned to Santa Cruz with two of his Captains who had not made the ascent. The next day the Squadron put to sea once more, and proceeded somewhat slowly, owing to adverse winds, to the West Indies. On this cruise they visited the Dutch island of St Eustatius, the scene of Rodney's action in 1781. English was still the language spoken when Markham visited it, and the only one taught in the schools! The Squadron next anchored off St Martin, and then pursued its way to Bermuda, and, on March 12th, 1888, they were again homeward bound.

The sailing orders for the summer cruise of 1888 included a visit to Barcelona, in order to assist at the reception of the Queen Regent of Spain on the occasion of the opening of the Exhibition. They anchored amid a crowd of warships of all nationalities and the firing of guns continued from the time of their arrival at 8 a.m. until 1 p.m. The Training Squadron fired no less than 178. The Duke of Edinburgh was there in command of the Mediterranean Squadron, and, when he left, Markham was the Senior Naval Officer.

The Exhibition opened on Sunday, May 20th, "a Sunday less like a Sunday I cannot conceive," Markham wrote at the close of a long, fatiguing day. A capital place had been allotted to him in the front seat of the part reserved for foreign officers at the side of the Royal dais. After waiting for about an hour the sound of cheering proclaimed the arrival of the Royal party. First came a number of grandees in elaborate Court dresses, then a woman, dressed in a short scarlet frock trimmed with gold and carrying in her arms a baby—the King of Spain! Then followed two little girls, dressed in white, the sisters of His Majesty; then the Queen Regent, accompanied by the Duchess of Edinburgh, the Duke, Prince George (our present King), the Duke of Genoa, and Prince Rupert of Bavaria. His Majesty was safely deposited on the throne, the Queen Regent sitting on his left, his sisters on a footstool at his feet, and his nurse standing on his right—a novel and amusing spectacle.

Three long addresses were read, and the Exhibition

14-2

declared open; cheers were given for the Queen, and a National Anthem, composed for the occasion, was played by the band. Markham records that the infant king behaved excellently, until, getting bored during the reading of the last address, and attracted by something in the Duke of Edinburgh's uniform, a strong desire seized him to obtain possession of it, and one of his sisters had to pacify him.

The following day the Queen held a reception of all the foreign naval officers, of whom there were about 400 present. Markham was presented by the British Ambassador, Sir Clare Ford. A few days later the Queen visited Markham on the *Active* and surprised him by her nimbleness in boarding the ship on a rough day.

At a state dinner given by the Minister of Marine the Spanish Minister proposed the health of the Queen of England and referred in most complimentary terms to her and the British Navy. Markham followed and expressed the thanks of the Squadron for the hospitality they had received at the hands of the Spaniards while they had been at Barcelona.

When the festivities were over Markham took the Squadron to Minorca, and anchored off Port Mahon. On May 31st he received official intimation of his appointment as A.D.C. to Queen Victoria, and all the ships signalled their congratulations.

A few days were spent at Gibraltar and Vigo, and at the latter place the mail brought them the news of the death of the Emperor Frederick of Germany. Markham wrote in his journal: "I am afraid the event...may be fraught with much misery and suffering, for we cannot conceal from ourselves that Europe is in a very disturbed state, and the least thing may bring on a great and dreadful war."

Portland was reached on June 28th, and the Squadron was temporarily divided for the Manœuvres, the *Active* and *Rover* being attached to Squadron A, under Admiral Baird, the *Volage* and *Calypso* to Squadron B, under Admiral Tryon. Markham had command of the inshore blockading Squadron, with plenty of night work, as his duty was to prevent the escape of "the enemy" at night, being relieved in the day by the ironclads. At the close of the Manœuvres Admiral Baird paid Markham the compliment of a special signal thanking him for his valuable assistance and advice.

After a short leave Markham again left England with the Training Squadron for the North Sea and the Baltic. Copenhagen was the first place visited, and here he found that his fame had preceded him. Both the Minister of Marine and the Minister of War seemed to know all about him and said that his name was well known in Denmark. Markham and his officers were taken round the Dockyard and the King invited him and his Captains to dine with him at his Palace at Bernstorf. Both the King and Queen were very cordial and Markham had several long talks with them both before and after dinner. The following day they were presented to the Crown Prince and Princess, to their eldest son Prince Christian, the present King, and to Prince Charles, now King of Norway. At a dinner given by the Minister of Marine a graceful allusion was made to Markham's Arctic work.

From Copenhagen the Squadron proceeded to Kiel. Passing Friedrichsort they noticed the great strength of the fortifications on each side of the harbour, though the guns were carefully concealed by matting or some such material with which the fortifications were covered. Markham would naturally have chosen to make the ships fast to the buoys, but did not like to come inside without permission, nor could he well make them fast without some communication with the authorities; he therefore anchored the Squadron within a cable and a half of the buoys. This was only just accomplished when a German officer came alongside and said that it had been arranged for them to go to the buoys. Markham was very nearly saying, "Why did you not come off and let us know before we anchored?" but checked himself, and at once signalled to the other ships.

At noon the following day he was presented to Prince and Princess Henry of Prussia, at the Schloss, and in the afternoon entertained them at tea on his ship.

The day on which Markham was presented to the Empress Frederick was, in his own words, a "regular day of feasting." He had been invited to dine at the Court Marshal's table at the Castle at half-past seven, and to be presented to the Empress afterwards. As he had already accepted an invitation to dine with Admiral von Blanc, the Senior Naval Officer, he went on shore at once to explain how he was situated. He found the Admiral in a similar dilemma, as he had also been invited to the Castle. However, it was arranged that they should all sit down to dinner with him at six, and then go on to the Schloss at half-past seven. After dinner at the Schloss the company were requested to place themselves in position ready for the arrival of the Empress, Markham being directed to be nearest to the door on the right. The doors were thrown open, and the Empress walked in, followed by Prince Henry and the Princesses Irene, Victoria, Sophia and Margaret, all in deep mourning. Her Majesty advanced at once to Markham and requested that the Captains should be introduced.

The following day the Empress, accompanied by her three daughters, Prince and Princess Henry and all their suite, having first paid a visit of about five minutes to the German ship *Kaiser*, came on board the *Active*. It had been a wet day, but, as they came alongside, the clouds broke and a bright sun shone out. "In England," said Markham, "we should call it 'Queen's weather.'" The Empress, in reply, asked him if he thought it was hereditary. She spent an hour on board, and was glad, she said, to see the Union Jack and English faces again.

Markham was invited to visit Herr Schwarzkopff's torpedo works, which were established on the beach near Bellevue. Although he could ill spare the time, it was an opportunity not to be missed.

When they left Kiel Prince Henry came off to see them go out, and sailed round the Squadron in his gig, stopping under the *Active's* stern for a few minutes to wish Markham goodbye. The German Admiral not only dipped his flag, but the National colours to the Commodore as he passed.

From Kiel they went on to Karlskrona, where Markham and twenty-two officers of the Squadron were entertained at dinner at the Officers' Club to meet the Admiral, Prince Oscar, and about forty officers of the Swedish Navy. While they were at Karlskrona, Baron Nordenskjöld came expressly from Stockholm to meet Markham and his cousin, and they had an interesting talk with him on the work upon which the Baron was engaged, the history of maps from the time of Ptolemy. The following day Baron Nordenskjöld lunched on board the *Active* and they had a long Arctic talk. Special permission was granted them to see the Dockyard at Karlskrona, where they were shewn everything. Prince Oscar dined one evening on board the *Active*.

The Squadron's winter cruise of 1888–1889 again took them to Madeira and the West Indies. On their return to England Markham occupied himself, during his ten days' leave, in obtaining material for the biography of Sir John Franklin, which he had undertaken to write. He went with his cousin, Clements Markham, to Spilsby, in Lincolnshire, and visited the little house in which Sir John was born, also the parish church, and Louth, where he was educated.

The summer cruise was to the Baltic once more. At Copenhagen Markham made the acquaintance of Dr Nansen, on his arrival from Christiania *en route* for England, where he was to read a paper before the Royal Geographical Society.

A warm welcome was given to the Squadron when they reached Stockholm; the people turning out *en masse* to cheer. Four days later Markham and his staff, with his cousin, had an audience of the King at the Palace. King Oscar was most cordial, and remembered having been shewn over the *Vernon* by Markham five years before.

From Stockholm the Squadron proceeded to Gothenburg, and Markham managed to get away with his cousin and some of his officers for forty-eight hours to visit the beautiful Trollhättan Falls.

The Squadron returned to England in July, and was at Spithead for the Naval Review on the occasion of the visit of the German Emperor, William II. The Review was held in very unpropitious weather, and the cheers with which the Emperor was greeted as he passed down the line were drowned by the violence of the wind! Directly the salute was fired, all the Captains proceeded to pay their respects on board the *Victoria and Albert*, where they were presented to the Emperor. After Markham's own presentation, by the Admiral of Squadron B., he had himself to present all the Captains of C, D, F, and G. He describes the Kaiser as "very genial and in the best of humours," and the Prince of Wales as "in his kindliest mood."

From the middle of August Markham again took an active part in the Manœuvres, and on September 25th started on his final cruise in the Squadron. They visited Spain and Portugal, and on October 21st Markham received a telegram from the Admiralty ordering him to proceed at once with the Squadron to Lisbon, to be present at the funeral of the King of Portugal. Reaching the mouth of the Tagus, they found the Portuguese and other ships with their yards topped, firing guns every fifteen minutes. On the day before the funeral the Duke of Edinburgh arrived to represent Queen Victoria, and Markham, with his Staff and Captains, went to the station to meet him. Owing to an accident the Duke was, after all, unable to be present at the funeral. Markham attended with his three Captains and Commander; a small gallery, or tribune, as it was called, was reserved for them, from which they had a commanding view. The church was draped with heavy black and gold embroidery, and three catafalques were erected, one at the entrance, one in the centre of the nave, and one at the east end, on each of which the coffin was placed in turn in the course of the ceremony.

Some interesting days of sightseeing were spent, and then the Squadron again put to sea on its homeward voyage. Spithead was reached on November 10th, 1889, and on November 12th his appointment came to an end. It had been a most delightful and independent command, upon which he looked back with pleasure. On two separate occasions he received the thanks of the Austrian and German Governments for the assistance he rendered to subjects and ships belonging to those nations, and on relinquishing the command he received a very flattering letter from the Admiralty expressing their approval of the way in which he had carried out his duties.

He had already been appointed Captain of the Portsmouth Steam Reserve, and entered upon his duties the very day he laid down the command of the Training Squadron. He held this appointment until he attained flag rank in August, 1891.

On the occasion of the visit of the German Emperor to England in 1890, he, as one of the Queen's A.D.C.'s, was selected to attend on Prince Henry of Prussia during his stay in England. The Prince was pertinacious in his questions as to the secret of the Whitehead torpedo. At last, when tired of parrying them, Markham determined to silence the inconvenient enquiries.

"I am not at liberty, sir," he said, with extreme courtesy, "to tell you anything myself, but I think I can suggest to whom you could apply for the information."

"Tell me, tell me!" cried the Prince, eagerly.

"Write to the Admiralty, and say you would like to be put in possession of the secret," was the dry rejoinder.

"I don't think he ever forgave me," he concluded, with a chuckle, when, long after, he told the story.

Markham had some interesting stories about the ex-Kaiser, one of which illustrates his dogged pertinacity. When he was at Cowes, in 1890, he was shewing Markham over the *Hohenzollern*; while he was explaining the working of the watertight compartments, one of the doors refused to yield to the efforts of his one available hand. Markham sprang forward, saying, "Allow me, sir." But the Kaiser waved him back imperiously, with the words, "No, no; I will do it myself," and after much exertion he succeeded.

On one of the visits of the Kaiser to Queen Victoria it was Markham's duty to accompany the Prince of Wales when he went to meet him. The *Hohenzollern* was descried steaming into port, and the Prince stood in readiness on the deck of his yacht to exchange greetings as he came up. But the Imperial yacht steamed by without taking the least notice. The Prince was furious, and exclaimed indignantly to Markham, "Why doesn't the beggar wait? Why doesn't the beggar wait?" A little later he had to receive his nephew with every shew of affection.

FLYING HIS FLAG IN THE MEDITERRANEAN

In January, 1892, Markham received a semi-official communication from the Admiralty, informing him that he had been selected by Lord George Hamilton to relieve Lord Walter Kerr as Rear-Admiral and second-in-command in the Mediterranean, and on March 4th his flag was hoisted on board the *President*, in the Thames, and struck the same evening on leave being given him until March 18th, when he took passage in the P. & O. steamer *Britannia* for Malta. He had been successful in obtaining the services of his old Training Squadron staff to serve with him again in the same capacity.

On arriving at Malta he hoisted his flag in the *Trafalgar* but almost immediately it became necessary for him temporarily to relieve Lord Walter Kerr, now in command of the Detached Squadron, off Egypt. Markham therefore proceeded in the *Phaeton* to Alexandria, where he hoisted his flag on board the *Australia*, but on the following day it was transferred to the *Nile*.

Our relations between Turkey and the Powers were, at this time, somewhat complicated. The Turkish firman for the installation of a new Khedive, which was daily expected, was continually delayed.

Markham now proceeded to Suda Bay with eight ships of his Squadron, the *Australia* being left behind to follow in forty-eight hours if, in the meantime, no telegrams of importance arrived; the *Phaeton* had been sent on to Syra for telegrams. The following day the Squadron was met by the *Scout* with a telegram in cipher, the purport of which was that the Imperial firman had left Constantinople in one of the Sultan's yachts. Markham therefore at once turned the Squadron round and shaped a course for

Alexandria, sending a message to the *Phaeton*, at Syra, to meet him with all despatch. On his return he transferred his flag once more to the *Australia*, which was in the inner anchorage, as it was absolutely necessary for him to be in close proximity to the telegraph wires. He then went up to Cairo to confer with the British Resident, Sir Evelyn Baring, on the situation. When the firman arrived it was discovered that the Turks had inserted a clause appropriating to themselves the Sinai Peninsula, which would practically put in their possession the Suez end of the Canal. Markham therefore remained at Cairo.

But it so happened that the powerful English Squadron now present at Alexandria, in reality merely to do honour to the Turkish Envoy, was viewed by the Sublime Porte as a demonstration of British power. This, and a fortuitous but entirely unexpected meeting of the *Phaeton* with the Imperial yacht, enhanced in Turkish eyes the British reputation for cunning, the equivalent of diplomacy in their estimation, and had a good effect. The Cairo Press insisted that the Squadron drew off from Egyptian waters for the purpose of luring the Sultan into despatching the firman, whereas, as a matter of fact, the firman actually left Constantinople before the Porte could possibly have been apprised of the departure of the ships. Markham was presented by Sir Evelyn Baring to the Khedive, and then presented his Captains and Staff, who had accompanied him to Cairo. He describes the Khedive as "a young and rather stout man" who seemed shy and appealed occasionally to Sir Evelyn "as a child would to his father!" Admiral Tryon telegraphed to Markham that he did not consider it advisable to keep the Squadron at Alexandria any longer than was absolutely necessary, while, on the other hand, Sir Evelyn Baring said its presence was most desirable, for the time being, as a moral support, not only to himself, but also to the Khedive and the Egyptian Government. The ships therefore remained for another ten days. Markham spent three days in Cairo and his time was divided between official visits and exploration of the town and neighbourhood. He returned to his ship at Alexandria on April 8th.

The objectionable clause in the firman was removed, though the Turks still tried to keep it intact. Finally, after much delay, it was read on April 14th, Sir Evelyn Baring insisting that the telegram expunging the obnoxious clause should be read also, and instructions were given that the English troops were not to salute until this had been done. The Egyptian Army, under the command of the new Sirdar, Colonel Kitchener, was drawn up on two sides of the square in front of the Palace, the two other sides being lined by British troops under General Walker. The stand reserved for the representatives of the British Navy was next to that on which the Khedive received the Turkish Envoy. The firman, wrapped in red silk, was presented to the young Khedive, who took it in both hands, pressed it to his forehead, and then gave it to his secretary, who cut open the packet, unfolded the firman and read it aloud. The reading occupied some eight or ten minutes, and at its conclusion the secretary produced the telegram and read it. Directly he began, the Turkish Envoy turned his back and walked into the Palace. When the telegram had been read, the troops presented arms and cheered three times for the Sultan and three times for the Khedive, the bands playing the Turkish and Egyptian National airs. The Russian Minister was especially sulky, and did not even salute when the troops saluted the Khedive, but Markham found the French Admiral most desirous of establishing cordial and friendly relations with the British.

On April 16th the Squadron left Alexandria and Markham's flag was again transferred from the *Australia* to the *Nile*. Later he was informed by the Commander-in-Chief that he thoroughly approved of everything that he had done in Egypt.

Immediately after they got into formation Markham exercised the Squadron at T. A. tactics, a new system invented by Sir George Tryon for manœuvring a squadron with as few signals as possible; it took its name from the flags

T. A. being hoisted as a preliminary, signifying, "Observe closely the motions of the flag-ship." The ships had to watch the helm signals and movements of the Admiral and follow them closely, the object being to move the Squadron about in the quickest possible time and in the shortest space. Markham considered the system a good one, though it required much practice, and he doubted whether it would work as well when the Squadron went into action, when helm and signals were liable to be shot away or obscured by smoke.

Early on April 19th they reached Crete and headed in towards Suda Bay, Mount Ida, with its snow-covered summit, just catching the rays of the rising sun and forming a conspicuous landmark. Markham's flag was saluted with eleven guns from the *Edinburgh,* and it was a great relief to him a little later to be able to hoist it finally on his own ship the *Trafalgar.* He was pleased with the condition of the ship and much struck with the general tone and good feeling which pervaded it, both among officers and men.

Not long after reaching Suda Bay, Markham, with two of his staff and the British Consul, paid his official visit to the Vali, the Governor General at Canea, who received them in person and the following day returned the visit, accompanied by the Turkish Commodore as interpreter. The Vali remained about a quarter of an hour and, in spite of its being Ramadan, did not refuse a glass of champagne and a cigarette, basing his acceptance of them on the plea that he had recently been under medical advice. The Commodore, however, would accept nothing. As they took their leave the latter, who had evidently been pondering over his final speech, turned to Markham and said, in his best English, "His Excellency begs me to thank you for your kind *hostility!*"

Markham's Squadron consisted, at times, of seven or eight battleships and five or six cruisers, and was stationed practically all the while in the Levant and in Egyptian waters. He had annually to meet the Commander-in-Chief with his ships, when the whole Fleet would cruise in company for about six weeks.

In the midst of the daily routine of the Squadron— gun and torpedo practice, steam tactics, and the various evolutions necessary to qualify the ships for the serious business of war—Markham organised many expeditions to places of interest. From Suda Bay the Squadron went on to Salonica, passing through the Zea Channel, along the western side of the island of Zea, the ancient Keos. The town, the only one in the island, situated on the slope of a high hill, consisted of a cluster of houses, built in tiers, giving a very curious appearance from seaward. The roofs of the houses were all flat, and so constructed that it was possible to walk all over the town on the housetops. The entrance to each house was through the roof.

Salonica, with its minarets, cypress trees, and white houses, was full of interest. Amongst other sights he saw a performance of dancing dervishes. The mosque was crowded, but a gallery round the top of the building, which was circular, was reserved for the visitors. In the centre was an arena, very much resembling a circus, set apart for the dervishes. About twenty-four of these, headed by a sheikh, marched solemnly in, whilst a man in the gallery chanted, in a drawling monotone, presumably extracts from the Koran. The dervishes were attired in long flowing dresses of different colours and went through certain prostrations and genuflections, which were carried out independently and without regard to time. They also assumed various positions indicative of prayer, besides occasionally holding the hands open in front, as if reading from a book. All this, which went on for half an hour, the onlookers found very monotonous, and they were all relieved when the beating of a tom-tom and the sounds of a wheezy flute announced that the dancing was about to begin. The performers then threw off their upper robes and appeared clad in white dresses with skirts reaching to their ankles. They then all marched solemnly round the arena, saluting the old sheikh, who remained standing, by stooping down and kissing his hand, he at the same time imprinting a kiss on the top of the long conical hat worn by each dervish! The performers stopped twice in the course of this procession and bowed, in a dignified manner to the one immediately behind. On the second round, as they came up to the sheikh, they suddenly turned off into the centre, spinning round with such rapidity that their skirts stood out straight from their waists. When they were all dancing the effect was very curious, and suggested a number of plates set in motion by a dexterous juggler. The majority scarcely moved from the positions on which they first began to spin, but some few moved round, though cleverly steering clear of each other.

From the mosque they visited the tobacco factory, and were struck with the rapidity with which the operators, principally Jewish, Bulgarian, and Greek girls, cut up the tobacco and made the cigarettes.

Before leaving, the Squadron held its athletic sports on shore, and the Admiral was second in the "veterans' race," in which some nine or ten started. He fancied that the Turks must have regarded them as a set of lunatics for taking such violent exercise in the heat of the sun!

From Salonica they put into Provato Bay for the purpose of seeing what remained of the Canal of Xerxes. It was a capital harbour, the only objection to it as an anchorage being the shallow water. Although occasionally, and at long intervals, visited by a single ship, this was, Markham believed, the first time a squadron had ever anchored there. The country both here and at Thasos was very attractive. Thasos was at one time famous for its gold, white marble, and wine; now, so far as Markham could discover, its only specialities were honey and spinach! After two years' cruising in the Levant Markham came to the conclusion that Thasos was by far the most beautiful of the islands.

On May 12th, the anniversary of Markham's attaining his highest northern latitude, he invited Mr Radmore, the carpenter of the *Australia*, one of his old sledge crew, to dine with him, in fulfilment of an invitation given sixteen years before.

On reaching the island of Lemnos, and anchoring in Mudros Bay, Markham was much struck with the admirable suitability of the island as a base for a British force in the event of complications in the East. As a coaling station and arsenal he considered it would be unrivalled. When anchored off Nauplia, they drove to Mycenae, a distance of ten miles, and saw the ruins of Tiryns on their way. At Mycenae they saw the "Treasure House of Atreus" and the other bee-hive tombs. When the Squadron was off Budrum, at the entrance of the Gulf of Kos, on the coast of Asia Minor, Markham was able, in company with his cousin, Clements Markham, and others, to visit the ruins of the old fortress of the Knights of St John, still in a wonderful state of preservation. Whilst at Vurla Bay a large party from the Squadron, one of the largest, indeed, that had ever made the excursion, was organised to visit Ephesus. From Ephesus they took the train to Magnesia, where they watched excavations in progress under the direction of a German archaeologist. Another excursion was made to Thermopylae.

At Athens the two Admirals and all the Captains were received in audience by the King, who further honoured the Fleet by dining, first on board the *Victoria*, Admiral Tryon's flag-ship, and later on board the *Trafalgar*. The King, who was accompanied by Prince George and Prince Nicholas, talked freely to Markham about his troubles with his late Prime Minister, going so far as to say that, had he been returned at the elections that followed his dismissal, he had quite made up his mind to abdicate. Markham and his staff also dined with the King at his country place at Tatoi.

About this time a party from the Squadron made the ascent of Mount Pentelicus, driving out in the early morning to the monastery at its base. They passed the famous quarries, which were still being worked, and reached the summit (4000 ft.) after a climb of two hours and a half.

While anchored in the Gulf of Kalamaki Markham was interested in visiting the canal which was then being constructed across the Isthmus of Corinth. The manager conducted them over the works in a trolley and engine, taking them from one end to the other. The canal had been begun eight years previously, had ruined two companies, and, up to that time, had cost £3,000,000! Over 30,000,000 tons of rock and soil had been excavated from it. Large blocks of stone under the water were pointed out as the paved way over which the ancient Greeks transported their vessels on rollers across the Isthmus. Corinth, Eleusis, and Rhodes were also visited. Of Rhodes Markham wrote:

It would be impossible to describe all we saw—the old Chancery, the Palace of the Grand Masters (only the lower story of which is now standing, and is, alas! converted into a penal establishment for the worst class of convicts, murderers, etc.), the site of the Church of St John, which was unaccountably blown up in 1856, the towers, the bastions, all were exceedingly interesting, while the vaulted chambers and passages leading to the different residences were very curious. It was impossible to help contrasting all we saw to-day, the ruin, the squalor, and the dirt, with what Rhodes must once have been in the height of its ancient splendour in the days of the Knights of St John.

On its visit to Samos the Squadron was first anchored off Tijani, but, on representations being made to Markham that the people of Vathy had made great preparations for its reception, he gave up his original intention of going to Patmos, and took the ships to Vathy instead. It was sixty years since an English fleet had been to Vathy, and this was the largest squadron that had ever been in the harbour. Markham describes it as something like a Chinese puzzle to find room for the eight ships to anchor. They were welcomed by the entire population with bands and ringing of church bells. Samos had a peculiar interest since, though owning allegiance to Turkey, it had complete autonomy; and although the Governor, called the Prince Governor, or Prince of Samos, was appointed by the Sultan, it was an understood thing that he should be a Christian. Markham paid his official visit on landing, and the following day dined with the Prince, accompanied by his Captains and Staff. The Prince paid two visits to the *Trafalgar* and explained to Markham the constitution of the island—a Parliament of thirty-eight members, elected annually, and only sitting for a few days each year. Their principal duty, apparently, was to elect four senators, also a yearly office, who, with the Prince at their head, formed the government of the island. From what Markham was able to gather during his stay, the Samians were very anxious to be under British protection, and were hoping and expecting that he was going to depose the Governor and proclaim a Protectorate! The Senate sent off three casks of Samian wine as a present, thereby putting Markham in a very awkward position, as he felt that, under the circumstances, it would be impossible to accept it.

In November, 1892, Markham and his Division accompanied the Commander-in-Chief to Malta, where they remained until early in the following year. He was asked by the Commander-in-Chief, at the request of the Governor, to investigate and report upon the submarine defence of the harbour. The report, which contained some novel proposals, was of course confidential. The Second Division left Malta on January 7th, 1893, and Markham was glad to be afloat again.

While anchored in the harbour of Volo, on the coast of Thessaly, Markham and a few others from the Squadron made an expedition to the celebrated, though seldom visited, monasteries of Meteora. The railway line lay through the fertile plains of Thessaly, bounded on each side by ranges of mountains, culminating in the summits of Olympus, Ossa, and Pelion. The rocks of Meteora spring up perpendicularly from the plain to a height of 1000 ft. After a journey of six hours they alighted at Kalabaka, a small town on the site of the ancient Aginium, which was captured and occupied by Julius Caesar in his march over Pindus to Pharsalia. Here they were received by the military commandant and a crowd of people. Of this reception Markham wrote:

I imagine they expected to see us arrive in full uniform, and were considerably disappointed when they saw some very ordinary-looking mortals descending from the train attired in anything but gorgeous apparel. . . . On our arrival at Kalambaka we found a number of ponies awaiting us—short, shaggy little beasts, equipped with wooden and leathern saddles, covered with large red rugs, and mine even had a pillow with an imitation lace pillow slip, on which I was to sit!

Escorted by Demetri, a Greek policeman, who let off a long gun at intervals for no apparent reason, they ascended a zig-zag path and approached the gigantic rocks. Some twenty or thirty in number, they towered up to the skies, some with sharp pointed summits, some with rounded tops; deep chasms divided them, and above them the eagles soared, their nests being plainly discernible in the clefts. A ride of an hour and a quarter brought them to the Convent of St Stephanos, where they had arranged to stay. This monastery, situated on the edge of a spur, was completely isolated on three sides, and on the fourth was approached by a drawbridge spanning a chasm about ten feet wide and about fifty feet deep. Their approach was heralded by the shouts of the pony boys and by Demetri firing his gun. At the same time the party dismounted, and, making their way over rocks, rendered doubly slippery by a coating of ice, they came up to the drawbridge. The door was opened and a hearty welcome was given them by the aged Agoumenos, or Father Superior of the monastery, and two or three other monks, all in long black cassocks and black hats, with flowing beards, and hair of such a length that it hung in plaits down their backs. At this time only ten monks were resident in the monastery, but there appeared to be a servant to every monk, besides some twenty labourers employed on the monastery farms.

Having been shewn over the chapel they were conducted to the guest-chamber—a small square room with a divan along one side of it. Their sleeping apartments (Markham was assigned one to himself) were clean and tolerably comfortable, but miserably cold, for there were no fireplaces,

ST BARLAAM MONASTERY, METEORA

and the temperature was several degrees below freezing-point.

At 6 o'clock they sat down to dinner at a table in the corridor, outside their rooms, the Agoumenos dining with them and the other monks waiting on them. The old man began with what Markham, for a time, thought was a long grace delivered in Greek, but as he kept nodding to his guests and laughing, he could only infer that it must be a harangue of welcome! The dinner, which was exceedingly good, consisted of a pillau of rice, hashed fowl, stewed mutton and leeks, a roast sucking-pig, very good bread, baked in the monastery, and wine. After dinner they repaired to the guest-chamber, where, seated round a *mangal,* or large brass brazier, filled with hot wood ashes and placed in the centre of the room, they spent a lively evening in company with the venerable Agoumenos, the old monastery resounding to the strains of "Hearts of Oak," "The Midshipmite," and other cheerful songs, which their host seemed thoroughly to enjoy. At 8 o'clock Markham, who had understood that monks retire early, as a large part of their night is devoted to prayer, suggested that the Agoumenos might wish to leave them. But the old man steadily refused, saying that he found himself in such good company that he did not intend going to bed before they did, and it was not until 11 o'clock that the party broke up!

On the following morning they found snow on the ground. Having prepared themselves a light breakfast from provisions which they had happily brought with them, for the monks did not appear to think it necessary to cook any food before the evening, they started off to visit some of the other monasteries. It was freezing hard and the morning was bitterly cold. Demetri proved a valuable guide, as the path was completely obliterated by the snow which had fallen during the night. About an hour's hard walking brought them within sight of two more monasteries, that of St Barlaam and the Great Monastery of Meteora, each perched on the summit of a huge mass of rock, and separated by a chasm of 400 to 500 ft. in depth. They made their

way to Meteora and at the foot of the rock sought to
draw attention to their presence by shouts, Demetri, as
usual, firing his gun. After a while a black-robed monk
with a long grey beard appeared on a small platform at the
top, and asked what they wanted. On their replying that
they wished to pay a visit to the monastery the answer that
came down to them was not very encouraging. The ladder
could be lowered, but, as all the monks were away, there
were not sufficient men to wind the capstan. There were two
methods of ascent, one by a rickety wooden ladder, swinging
perpendicularly against the face of the cliff, the other by
means of a net wound up by the monks above, a height
of over 150 ft. The ladder was lowered, and Demetri
started the ascent. Markham, unwilling to be outdone by
a Greek, and anxious to encourage his party, followed
quickly at his heels. It was by no means an easy task, as
the ladder swayed at every step, and the rungs were
dangerously slippery with ice. However, they both reached
the top in safety and, wriggling through the narrow aperture
in the masonry which formed the entrance, found themselves
with solid ground under their feet. Walking up a narrow,
tortuous path, they encountered two old monks, who received them in a very nonchalant manner, as if they were
quite accustomed to strangers. As soon as they realised that
one of their visitors was a British Admiral their demeanour
changed, and they became quite cordial. Another of the
party braved the dangers of the ladder, and the others
were hauled up by means of the net, Markham and Demetri
assisting in working the very primitive capstan. They found
the monastery very like that of St Stephanos. At one time
there had been 150 monks, but the number had now dwindled
down to five monks and six servants and there was a general
air of decay about the place. In the church lay the bones
of John Cantacuzene, Emperor of the East, who resigned
the Imperial throne at Constantinople to end his days
with the monks of Meteora. The visitors were served with
a jelly of dried grape-juice and water and coffee, and in
the descent Markham essayed the method of the net. The
passenger sat in the centre, and the upper meshes were

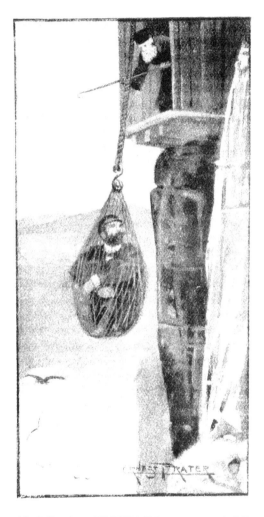

MARKHAM DESCENDS IN THE NET

drawn up over an iron hook at the end of the thick rope. The net was then swung out from the platform and during its passage spun round "like a joint of meat on a roasting-jack!" Markham described the sensation as "by no means unpleasant," and preferable to the use of the ladder.

At St Barlaam a monk made it so plain from the top that visitors were not wanted that they turned their steps to the monastery of Agia Triada (the Holy Trinity). Here their experience was very similar to that at the Great Monastery, save that the ladder there was easier, the one here being reached by a narrow gallery hewn out of the solid rock, not more than eighteen inches broad.

On their return the travellers sat down to another excellent dinner and enjoyed another cheerful evening. The old Agoumenos took his share in the evening's entertainment by contributing portions of the Prayer Book, chanted in a drawling monotone; he then asked for a dance and was highly delighted with the Highland schottische. Markham describes this as one of the most interesting expeditions he had ever made, though he formed no high opinion of the lives and characters of the monks.

Of the Vale of Tempe Markham wrote:

The magnificence of the scenery is almost indescribable— the cliffs, great granite cliffs, rising up perpendicularly on each side to a stupendous height; some being crowned by the ruins of old castles or fortresses, now the homes and resting-places of numerous eagles, who, disturbed by our presence, soared and wheeled above us. From the end of the pass, or defile, our eyes looked over a park-like country, an undulating plain covered with trees and vegetation, while beyond, in the far distance, could be seen, like a bank of blue mist, the range of hills in the neighbourhood of Salonica. Along the path on which we were walking Pompey had escaped after his defeat by Julius Caesar at the battle of Pharsalia, while on the opposite side of the river was Mount Olympus....Before we could get back to our carriages a violent thunderstorm burst upon us....Nothing more grand or sublime can be conceived than a thunderstorm, situated as we were—the vivid flashes of the forked lightning and the heavy crashes of thunder reverberating along the perpendicular cliffs....

Early in February, 1893, Markham was taken ill with a sharp attack of Mediterranean fever, followed by acute rheumatism. The Commander-in-Chief placed the *Scout* at his disposal, and Markham went with his Flag-Lieutenant to stay with some friends at Fiume. He rejoined the *Trafalgar* at the Piraeus on March 24th, but stayed for a few days at the British Legation at Athens. In spite of persistent rheumatism, he could not resist the temptation of a visit to the excavation camp of Professor Waldstein (the late Sir Charles Walston), at Heraion, near Argos; 210 men were employed, and already several portions of the temple together with statues and pottery of various periods had been unearthed.

Markham was now ordered to proceed to Malta, where he was to turn over to the *Camperdown*, pending the refitting of the *Trafalgar* for a new commission. His health was still unsatisfactory and he arranged to spend a few weeks' leave at Taormina in Sicily with Clements Markham and his wife. After a fortnight he considered himself fit for the ascent of Monte Venere, which he thoroughly enjoyed, and on May 22nd he left for Malta.

THE VICTORIA DISASTER

O N May 24th Markham arrived at Malta. He went to stay with Vice-Admiral Tracey in the Dockyard, and on the following day his flag was hoisted on board the *Camperdown*, as his proper flag-ship, the *Trafalgar*, had not completed the refit which she was undergoing in the Dockyard.

Two days later, the whole Mediterranean Fleet left Malta for the annual summer cruise under Vice-Admiral Sir George Tryon, K.C.B., the Commander-in-Chief, whose flag was flying on board H.M.S. *Victoria*. By the middle of June they were off the coast of Syria, anchored in the Bay of Haifa, about seven miles south of Acre, and literally under the shadow of Mount Carmel. Markham confessed that he was not much impressed with his first view of the Holy Land:

It looked barren—a long sandy coast, with Carmel rising in the background, and a few olive trees, dates, figs, etc., growing at its foot, and a row of white houses along the shore....

Markham had the opportunity during their short stay of visiting the Convent of Elias on Mount Carmel, and from Beyrout, which was reached on June 17th, he made an excursion to Baalbec and Damascus, accompanied by three brother officers.

On Thursday, June 22nd, the Fleet weighed and left Beyrout at 10 a.m. for Tripoli (Syria), about forty miles to the northward. It proceeded at a speed of about eight-and-a-half knots, formed in single column line abreast, and, when within about five miles of the anchorage off Tripoli, Sir George Tryon made the signal, at 2.20 p.m., for the Fleet to "Form Columns of Divisions in line ahead,

disposed abeam to port, Columns to be six cables apart."[1]
This brought the Fleet into the following formation:

2ND DIVISION	1ST DIVISION
PORT	STARBOARD
Camperdown	*Victoria*
Captain Charles Johnstone	Captain Hon. Maurice A.Bourke
Flag-ship of Rear-Admiral	Flag-ship of Vice-Admiral Sir
A. H. Markham	George Tryon, K.C.B.
Edinburgh	*Nile*
Captain John W. Bracken-bury, C.B., C.M.G.	Captain Gerard H. V. Noel
Sans Pareil	*Dreadnought*
Captain Arthur K. Wilson, V.C., C.B., A.D.C.	Captain Arthur W. Moore, C.M.G.
Edgar	*Inflexible*
Captain W. A. Dyke Acland	Captain Frederick S. Van der Meulen
Amphion	*Collingwood*
Captain John R. E. Pattisson	Captain Albert B. Jenkins
	Phaeton
	Captain Reginald Custance

With the light Cruisers *Barham* and *Fearless* in attendance.

The Fleet was then standing to the northward with the
land on the starboard beam, Sir George Tryon's intention
being to anchor the Fleet in the open roadstead off Tripoli
in such a way that, while the relative positions of the two
Columns to each other and to the land would be unchanged,
the ships in the Column would be in the reverse order, that
is to say, anchored in two lines running northwards
from the respective flag-ships *Victoria* and *Camperdown*.
To accomplish this object Sir George Tryon decided to
steam past Tripoli, and then to reverse the direction of the
Fleet by altering course 16 points (180°), the ships in each
Column turning in succession, so that the Fleet would
approach the roadstead of Tripoli from the northward in
the formation in which they would anchor. There were
four different manœuvres by which the direction of the
Fleet might have been reversed:

[1] A cable's length is equal to 100 fathoms or 200 yards.

(1) By the Fleet altering course 16 points *to Starboard*, Leaders together and the rest in succession.

(2) By the Fleet altering course 16 points *to Port*, Leaders together and the rest in succession.

(3) By the Fleet altering course 16 points *Outwards*, Leaders together and the rest in succession.

(4) By the Fleet altering course 16 points *Inwards*, Leaders together and the rest in succession.

Each of the first three manœuvres can be ordered by a single signal, but the fourth manœuvre is obviously a dangerous one if there is not sufficient room between the Columns, and probably for this reason no signal had been provided for it in the Signal Book. It was however open for an officer commanding a Fleet or Squadron to turn his Columns inwards by making a separate signal to each Column, and this Sir George Tryon did by hoisting the following signals simultaneously at about 3.24 p.m.:

Second Division alter course in succession 16 points *to Starboard*.

First Division alter course in succession 16 points *to Port*.

It must here be explained that in a Signal Code the individual flags and pendants each represent a letter, number, or a special signification, which, when hoisted singly, convey some special meaning, usually of an urgent nature. Generally, flag signals are made by hoisting combinations or groups of two or more flags or pendants, and these groups have special meanings attached to them in the signal books. The method of answering flag signals made by a Senior Officer is for the vessel or vessels addressed to hoist the answering pendant "at the dip" (about three-quarters up) directly the signal is seen, and "close up" when its purport is understood. When, however, a Fleet or Squadron is at sea, the ships astern of the Admiral experience difficulty in seeing and reading his signals owing to the masts and smoke of intervening ships, and the Admiral has a similar difficulty in seeing whether they have hoisted their answering pendants. The leader of the second Column, who has an uninterrupted view of the ships astern of the

Admiral, therefore repeats the Admiral's signal "at the dip," so that they may see it, and, when all their answering pendants are close up, he hoists the signal which he is repeating close up so as to inform the Admiral that the ships astern of him have all answered. If, however, the leader of the second Column[1] does not himself understand the Admiral's signal he does not hoist the signal which he is repeating close up until he is satisfied as to its purport.

It follows that, if there is an unusual delay in hoisting the signal "close up" on board the leading ship of the second Column, the Admiral will not know whether the delay is caused by one of the ships astern of him not hoisting the answering pendant close up or whether the leader of the second Column has some reason of his own for not hoisting the signal "close up." The Admiral has of course a direct view of all the ships in the second Column, and no repeating of signals is necessary between him and them. The repeated signal of the leader of the second Column and the answering pendants of all the other ships in the Fleet are kept flying close up until the Admiral hauls down his signal, which he does when he wishes the manœuvre to begin.

It must also be explained that it is necessary in manœuvring a Fleet that all ships should turn on arcs of equal diameter so as to retain their relative positions to each other. As a Fleet usually includes ships of different design and consequently different capabilities as regards turning, it would happen that, if they all gave extreme helm-angle when turning, some would turn on smaller arcs than others, and throw the Fleet more or less into confusion. Consequently, it is always arranged that the ships, when manœuvring, shall only give sufficient helm-angle to enable them to turn on the arc of the worst-turning ship. In the case of the Mediterranean Fleet, Sir George Tryon fixed the manœuvring arc on which his ships should turn as that of a circle having a diameter of 850 yards.

---

[1] When there are more than two columns a similar system of repeating is adopted.

It was therefore apparent that with the Columns only 1200 yards apart it was impossible for the ships to turn towards each other without danger unless they turned well inside the established arc by giving extreme helm-angle, and, in the case of some ships, by reversing the inside propeller as well.

When Admiral Markham saw Sir George Tryon's signals directing both Columns to turn inwards, leaders together, the remainder in succession, he at once appreciated the danger, and he said to his Flag-Lieutenant (Lieutenant Bradshaw), "It is impossible, as it is an impracticable manœuvre," and he ordered him to keep the signal that he was repeating "at the dip," as an indication that it was not understood. He then walked forward towards the fore bridge, and met Captain Johnstone (who was in command of the *Camperdown*) coming to him for directions. He said to him, "It is all right. Don't do anything. I have not answered the signal." Admiral Markham then returned to the after bridge, and directed the Flag-Lieutenant to keep the signal "at the dip" and to make the following signal by semaphore to the Commander-in-Chief:

"Am I to understand that it is your wish for the Columns to turn as indicated by signal now flying?"

Before this order could be carried out, he received a semaphored message from the Commander-in-Chief saying, "What are you waiting for?" to which he directed the reply to be sent, "I did not quite understand the signal." It then occurred to Admiral Markham that he wished him to turn 16 points as indicated by signal and that it was Sir George Tryon's intention to lead his Column round outside the Second Division. Having the fullest confidence in the great ability of the Commander-in-Chief to manœuvre the Fleet without danger, he ordered the signal to be hoisted "close up" as an indication that it was understood.

On the signal being hauled down, the *Victoria* and *Camperdown* put their helms over and commenced to turn towards each other. Admiral Markham watched the situation carefully and seeing that the *Victoria* continued to turn in, he ordered the Captain of the *Camperdown* to go full speed astern with the starboard propeller in order to decrease her circle of turning, and shortly afterwards, seeing that a collision was inevitable, he ordered full speed astern with both engines, but, before the speed of the ship had been materially checked, the stem of the *Camperdown* struck the *Victoria* on her starboard bow and crashed into the ship almost to her centre line. It was quite two minutes before the *Camperdown* was able, although going full speed astern with both engines, to get clear of the *Victoria*. The *Victoria* rapidly settled down by the head, and in a very few minutes she heeled over to starboard and, turning bottom upwards, disappeared. The boats from the other ships of the Fleet were promptly lowered and sent to the spot. Fortunately the sea was smooth, with only a light breeze blowing, and they succeeded in saving 29 officers and 262 men, but Sir George Tryon, 21 officers and 336 men were lost. Admiral Markham remained with the rest of the Fleet in the vicinity of the catastrophe until 5.30 p.m., when, being a little anxious about the safety of the *Camperdown*, which, in consequence of the damage she had sustained in the collision, was considerably down by the head, he reformed the Fleet and steamed into the anchorage, leaving the *Amphion, Barham* and *Fearless* to remain out till dark on the scene of the disaster.

To Markham the shock was terrible. In his private diary he recorded his sorrow at the loss of "our gallant and ever-to-be-lamented Chief," and the next day ordered Sir George Tryon's flag to be hoisted at half-mast on board the *Sans Pareil*, and the colours of all ships to be also flown at half-mast; he also ordered a solemn funeral service to be held on board each ship at 6.45 p.m. Shortly before sunset the *Sans Pareil* fired a salute of 17 minute guns, at the conclusion of which the Guards on board each vessel presented arms, the bands played an Admiral's salute, followed by a few bars from the "Dead March." At sunset Sir George Tryon's flag was finally hauled down.

Markham was much touched by the many telegrams of

sympathy which reached him during the next few days from the Admiralty, the Household Cavalry, the Brigade of Guards, Admiral Tracey at Malta, the Ambassador at Constantinople, the British Minister at Athens, and many others.

Captain The Hon. Maurice Bourke and the survivors of the *Victoria* sailed for Malta on Monday, June 26th, on board the *Edgar* and *Phaeton*, and on June 29th, the temporary repairs to the *Camperdown* having been completed, Admiral Markham shifted his flag to the *Nile*, and the *Camperdown* left for Malta escorted by the *Inflexible*.

On July 5th Markham, who had remained at Tripoli while the coast was being searched unsuccessfully for bodies and wreckage, sailed with the remainder of the Fleet, consisting of the *Nile* (flying his flag), *Dreadnought*, *Edinburgh*, *Sans Pareil* and *Collingwood* for Suda Bay, Crete. On July 14th Markham shifted his flag to the *Sans Pareil* and proceeded in her to Malta accompanied by the *Nile*, in accordance with telegraphic instructions received the previous day from Admiral Sir Michael Culme-Seymour, who had arrived at Malta from England to take up the Command of the Mediterranean Station in succession to Sir George Tryon.

On July 18th Markham arrived at Malta at 9 a.m., and found that the Court Martial to enquire into the loss of the *Victoria* was being held on board the *Hibernia*, having assembled on the previous day. The Court consisted of Admiral Sir Michael Culme-Seymour, Bart. (President), Vice-Admiral Richard Tracey, Superintendent of Malta Dockyard, and seven Captains. Markham pointed out to the President the disadvantage in which he was placed in being called as a witness at the Court Martial; actually he would be on his trial as the chief survivor of the disaster, but as a witness he would not be able to hear evidence, to cross-examine, or to call witnesses on his own behalf.

In his diary Markham writes on the July 19th:

I was the first witness examined to-day, and am by no means happy at the result of the examination....My position was a peculiarly painful one, for it was difficult for me to justify the course I took without, in a measure, implying culpability to Sir George Tryon.

The Court sat for ten days and on the 27th July delivered its finding, which included the following:

> ...it is with the deepest sorrow and regret that the Court further finds that this collision was due to an order given by the then Commander-in-Chief, the late Vice-Admiral Sir George Tryon, to the two Divisions in which the Fleet was formed to turn sixteen points inwards, leaders first, the others in succession, the columns at that time being only six cables apart.

> *   *   *   *   *   *

> The Court strongly feels that although it is much to be regretted that Rear-Admiral Albert Hastings Markham did not carry out his first intention of semaphoring to the Commander-in-Chief his doubt as to the signal, it would be fatal to the best interests of the Service to say he was to blame for carrying out the directions of his Commander-in-Chief present in person.

The Court, which was composed of nine distinguished officers, had given careful consideration to the matter and had expressly acquitted Admiral Markham from blame, and it was therefore to the intense surprise of the Navy that an Admiralty Minute was issued, three months later, reviewing the finding of the Court Martial. The Admiralty Minute[1] contained the following paragraph:

> Their Lordships concur in the feeling expressed by the Court that it is much to be regretted that Rear-Admiral A. H. Markham did not carry out his first intention of semaphoring to the Commander-in-Chief his doubt as to the signal; but they deem it necessary to point out that the Rear-Admiral's belief that the Commander-in-Chief would circle round him was not justified by the proper interpretation of the signal.

To Markham this Minute, which he first read on November 9th in the English newspapers whilst cruising in the Levant, brought much sorrow. He records in his diary that he was

---

[1] The Minutes of the proceedings of the Court Martial were published as a Blue Book (C. 7178), 1893, and the Admiralty Minute and the report of the Director of Naval Construction were also published (C. 7208), 1893.

much surprised and distressed to learn of this unjust Minute, and that he could not understand how such an unfair and illogical Minute could have been written.

The blame that was placed on Markham by the Admiralty was unjust, and their Lordships seem to have ignored the many considerations which, in common fairness, should have been taken into account. The Admiralty Minute condemned Markham by saying "the Rear-Admiral's belief that the Commander-in-Chief would circle round him was not justified by the proper interpretation of the signal." These words may have been literally correct in their narrowest sense, but they ignored some of the circumstances of the case—in particular, Sir George Tryon's dominant personality, his long experience and outstanding reputation as a tactician, and his constant custom of manœuvring his Fleet in a way which was not contemplated by the Admiralty Signal Books. These facts were touched upon in the evidence given by several of the important witnesses at the Court Martial, and must have been known to the Naval Lords who framed the Minute.

In using the phrase "the proper interpretation of the signal" the Lords of the Admiralty were technically perhaps within their rights in speaking of *one* signal, since after-events shewed that it was intended as a single signal by Sir George Tryon, who hauled down the two signals which composed it together. Markham was, however, perfectly justified in considering it to be two signals, which would probably be hauled down separately; since, if taken as a single signal, it directed a manœuvre which was obviously impossible, and which could not be considered as within the contemplation of the experienced tactician in command.

Until the two signals were actually hauled down, there were three alternatives in Sir George Tryon's hands. He might have first hauled down the signal to the Second Division which would have started that Division turning in succession, and have brought it within 350 yards of the line of the First Division but safely inside it, and then, by hauling down the signal to the First Division a little

M   16

later, the *Victoria* would have commenced to turn well
beyond the *Camperdown* and the ships of the Second
Division which would be following her in succession.
It is true that to keep clear of the Second Division the
First Division would have had to turn on the arc of a larger
circle than the fixed one of a diameter of 850 yards, but it
was open to the Commander-in-Chief to lead his Division
as he liked.

A second alternative would have been first to haul down
the signal to the First Division and turn that Division
inside the Second Division, the latter being turned later.

The third alternative was that which was actually
adopted, namely, to haul both signals down together. Even
then it was in the hands of Sir George Tryon to vary the
manœuvre ordered by leading his Division outside the
Second Division, whereas Admiral Markham was bound to
obey the signal made to his Division.

Then again, when the *Victoria* and *Camperdown* in the
course of their turn were pointing towards each other, and
it began to be apparent that a collision was imminent, the
"Rule of the Road" required the ships thus meeting to pass
on the port side of each other in order to avoid a collision,
and that would have also meant the *Victoria* keeping
outside and the *Camperdown* continuing her turn.

Admiral Markham had therefore no alternative, in all the
circumstances, but to continue his turn; but he endeavoured
to make it as small as possible by directing Captain Johnstone to put the helm hard over, and go full speed astern
with the starboard propeller.

Further, Sir George Tryon's imperious personality could
not have been absent from Admiral Markham's mind when
reading his semaphored message, "What are you waiting
for?" especially as it was accompanied by the showing of
the *Camperdown's* pendants—a signal well understood in a
Fleet to be somewhat in the nature of a reprimand, and to
call the attention of the Fleet to the fact that the ship
whose pendants are shewn is delaying the manœuvre, or
is inattentive. These two signals must therefore have

seemed to imply that of course the Commander-in-Chief knew what he was about, and that his orders must be promptly obeyed. Moreover, Markham's high sense of duty and discipline must have made him very anxious to set a good example to the Fleet by prompt attention to the Commander-in-Chief's signals.

From the finding of the Court Martial that "it would be fatal to the best interests of the Service to say he (Admiral Markham) was to blame for carrying out the directions of his Commander-in-Chief present in person," it is clear that the members of the Court must also have had in their minds the personality of Sir George Tryon; and the Lords of the Admiralty, by blaming Markham in their Minute, acted in a way which, in the opinion of the officers who sat on the Court Martial, "would be fatal to the best interests of the Service."

In his diary on the day following the disaster Markham wrote, from the statements of Captain Bourke and Staff-Commander Hawkins Smith of the *Victoria*, and that of Sir George Tryon's Flag-Lieutenant (Lord Gillford):

It appears that the danger attending the evolution of turning the Columns in, at a distance apart of only six cables, was pointed out to the Commander-in-Chief, and although he did not contradict the fact that it was dangerous, he persisted in attempting to execute it! Had I therefore protested by signal against the prudence of executing such a manœuvre (an act that might be regarded as subversive of discipline) it would have had no effect, the Commander-in-Chief having fully made up his mind as to its execution.

As regards Sir George Tryon's intentions, it can only be supposed that in planning the manœuvre in his mind, he confused the radius of the ships' turning circle, namely, two cables, with the diameter (four cables) and somehow pictured to himself a ship as starting her turn from the centre of the circle instead of from a point on its circumference. This seems very likely from the fact that if the two Columns had each turned in a distance of two cables it would have left them still two cables apart, which was the distance Sir George intended them to be on anchoring.

In describing at the Court Martial what took place on board the *Victoria*, Staff-Commander Hawkins Smith said that when he was taking instructions from Sir George Tryon as to the courses to be steered by the Fleet when approaching the anchorage, Sir George stated that he intended to form the Fleet in Columns of two Divisions six cables apart, and reverse the course by turning inwards. The Staff-Commander replied that it would require at least eight cables, and Sir George answered, "Yes, it shall be eight cables."

Later, Sir George made the signal for six cables, and, when the Staff-Commander saw the signal flying, he spoke to the Flag-Lieutenant (Lord Gillford) about it and asked him to see the Commander-in-Chief and make sure. Lord Gillford went below and reported this to Sir George Tryon who replied that he wished the Columns to be six cables apart. Captain Bourke, who was present at the time, also reminded the Admiral that he had said it was to be eight cables, and after Lord Gillford had left he again reminded the Admiral that their turning circle was 800 yards, to which he then replied, rather shortly, something to the effect "That's all right, leave it at six cables." Captain Bourke then went on deck.

In his evidence Captain Bourke added that he had some idea in his head that the Commander-in-Chief had some way out of it. His impression was that something was going to happen: "I had confidence in the Commander-in-Chief, and nobody ever questioned him." Later, in the course of his defence, Captain Bourke said:

Sir George Tryon had a master mind. He loved argument, but was a strict disciplinarian. He always used to say he hated people who agreed with him; but that again was different from arguing against a direct order. With this and the fact that I was serving under an Admiral whose experience was far-reaching, and whose vast knowledge of the subject of manœuvre was admitted by all, I seem to have left his cabin not clear in my mind what was to happen, but confident somehow that the Commander-in-Chief himself must be clear as to his intentions.

From all this it is clear that Sir George Tryon was determined to carry out the manœuvre in his own way, and Lord Gillford, on being asked by the Court whether he heard the Commander-in-Chief at any time after the collision make any remark as to whom he blamed for having caused it, replied, "The Admiral said, 'It was all my fault.'" Staff-Commander Hawkins Smith in his evidence stated that Sir George said to him, "It is entirely my doing, entirely my fault."

The loss of the *Victoria* caused Markham acute and lasting sorrow, to which was added the grief of having participated in so great a naval calamity; but as to his own action and responsibility with regard to the collision he held himself blameless, and to the end maintained that his conscience was clear. Though his naval reputation suffered in consequence of the view taken by the Admiralty, he bore the burden of implied and unmerited censure with a simple dignity which was the admiration of all who knew him.

Markham remained at Malta for some time after the close of the Court Martial, waiting for the *Trafalgar* to be ready. He records numerous letters from naval officers in England, which reached him during those days, all approving his conduct, especially letters from Admiral of the Fleet Sir Edmund Commerell and Captain Lord Charles Beresford, saying that they would have done exactly as he did. Admiral Sir Richard Vesey Hamilton, who had been First Sea Lord of the Admiralty until a short time before, wrote expressing the strongest approval of everything Markham had done, but advised him not to write any statement to the Admiralty in defence of his action.

On August 15th, much to Markham's relief, he sailed from Malta in the *Trafalgar*, in company with the rest of the Mediterranean Fleet under the command of Sir Michael Culme-Seymour. The Fleet cruised in the Levant and visited several Greek ports, and in October they were at Corfu, where Markham parted company with the Commander-in-Chief and returned to the Levant with his Division, consisting of the *Trafalgar, Collingwood, Hood, Camperdown* and *Barham.*

His diary continues to give a full account of his daily experiences. He records the cruises of his Squadron to the various ports and islands in the Levant, visits to the various Governors and many private friends, as well as numerous shooting expeditions and excursions to places of historical interest. At the Piraeus he had very happy relations with the King and Queen of Greece, and was frequently invited to the Palace; on December 29th their Majesties and the Royal Family came off to the *Trafalgar* to lunch with him, and remained on board until half-past six for the dance given by the officers on the upper deck.

On December 31st Markham notes with satisfaction the passing of the year 1893. It had brought him much pain, sorrow, and distress.

MARRIAGE—THE NORE COMMAND—LAST YEARS

AT the beginning of February, 1894, Markham left the Levant for Malta, there to await his successor, on the expiration of his appointment. Before leaving, he went round the Squadron to bid goodbye to the Captains and officers, and many went off to the *Trafalgar* to write their names in his book. He was much touched by the terms in which they spoke of his departure, and at the universally-expressed wish that they might again serve under his orders. When, accompanied by the *Camperdown*, the *Trafalgar* steamed out of Smyrna harbour, the ships' companies of the *Nile, Anson,* and *Amphion* gave him three cheers, the guards presented arms, the bands played "Auld Lang Syne," and the *Anson* saluted his flag with eleven guns.

Markham's saddened life was now cheered by the acquaintance of the lady who afterwards became his wife. One of Markham's young officers, by name Gervers, was seriously ill; Markham telegraphed for his father, who brought with him his wife and daughter. The patient, who had been moved to the Admiral's own port cabin, happily recovered; and Markham fell in love with his sister, Theodora. When his appointment terminated, it was agreed that they should all travel to England together.

On April 3rd they left Malta in the steamship *Paraguay.* Markham was told that all the officers of the *Trafalgar* and *Camperdown* had intended pulling him out to the vessel in a long procession of boats, but the stormy weather prevented this; indeed there was a doubt as to whether the steamer would be able to sail at all. Some of the officers, in spite of the weather, came to see Markham off, and as the *Paraguay* steamed out passing close to the *Camperdown,*

everyone on board assembled on the upper deck to clap
him as he went by, while the band struck up "Auld Lang
Syne."

Markham's engagement to Miss Gervers took place a
short time after their return, and they were married in
the following October. Amongst the wedding presents none
pleased Markham more than a beautiful silver ship as a
centre-piece, which came from his old steward in the
Vernon.

Eight months after their marriage Markham and his wife
were the guests of Mr Cayzer, owner of the Clan Line of
steamers, who was taking a large party in the *Clan Matheson*
to the opening of the North Sea Canal by the German Emperor. At Copenhagen Admiral and Mrs Markham with some
of the party were invited by Sir Donald Currie to meet
the King and Queen of Denmark on board the *Tantallon
Castle*, also bound for Kiel. Their Majesties were accompanied
by the Crown Prince and Princess, and Prince Waldemar.
The Crown Prince well remembered Markham's previous
visit to Copenhagen, when he was in command of the
Training Squadron, and both he and Prince Waldemar were
very cordial towards him and his wife.

At Kiel the crowd was enormous and, when Markham
went on shore to secure a permit for their steam launch
to pass between the lines, no wheeled vehicle was to be
obtained, and he could get no one to attend to him. Later,
fortunately, he met a German Admiral whom he happened
to know, with the result that he secured not only the necessary permission to pass between the lines of men-of-war,
but also a capital berth for their launch near the entrance
to the canal. While, of course, all the ships were dressed
with flags, it was very gratifying to see the White Ensign
flying from the masthead of each, in commemoration of the
Accession of Queen Victoria, it being June 20th. At noon,
a royal salute was fired by all in her honour, and then the
English flags were hauled down and the German substituted.
At 3 o'clock the appearance of the *Hohenzollern*, the
Emperor's standard at her main, was the signal for another

salute of 21 guns, and the Kaiser's passage through the canal proclaimed it open. The *Hohenzollern* was followed, in about half an hour, by the *Kaiser Adler*, having on board the King of Saxony and other German notabilities. It was not until 7 o'clock that the whole procession of ships had passed through. A large number of ships of various nationalities were present, seventy-five vessels in all, exclusive of torpedo-boats. After Germany, England's was the strongest Squadron. It was doubtless the most imposing Fleet that had ever assembled in any harbour.

In the winter Markham and his wife paid a visit to Malta, where they spent Christmas. They met a large number of naval and other friends and on Christmas Day Mrs Markham was invited to visit the *Trafalgar* and go round the men's messes. She was much touched to see on every one of the plum-puddings a picture of her husband by way of decoration.

In 1897 Markham's mother died at the age of eighty-seven. Throughout his life Markham had made a practice of writing to her every week, and keeping her in touch with all his interests. In the same year Markham attained the rank of Vice-Admiral, and when the South African war broke out, in 1899, he at once offered to serve in any capacity; much to his disappointment no opportunity was given him to serve.

Some years after his marriage a little daughter came to gladden the home. Though he had married comparatively late, Markham was essentially made for home life. His daughter, Joy Mary (to whom King George, then Prince of Wales, stood as godfather), was the apple of his eye, and he was never quite happy when he was parted either from his wife or daughter, even for a short time.

His interest in polar research was, of course, unabated. He was roused to enthusiasm by Dr Nansen's success and was treasurer of the fund for presenting him with a collection of books on Arctic subjects. Nansen gave Markham a copy of his book, *Eskimo Life*, and a warm feeling existed between the two Arctic explorers.

In August, 1901, Markham received a charming letter from
Lord Selborne, then First Lord of the Admiralty, offering
him the command of the Nore, to take effect on November
1st, and intimating that the appointment would be for two
years for certain, although he was within twelve months of
reaching the Admiral's list, and the Nore is considered as
essentially a Vice-Admiral's command. It was with keen
satisfaction that Markham once more saw his flag flying.

The question of Antarctic research had now become very
prominent and Markham naturally took a deep interest
in it. He was on the Antarctic Sub-Committee, formed
in 1899, and he and his cousin, Sir Clements Markham,
warmly advocated the leadership of Scott, whom Markham
considered far and away the best man for the post. The
Morning, the Antarctic relief ship, put into Sheerness on
her arrival from Norway, in December, 1901, and there
underwent a thorough cleaning.

In January, 1902, Markham was obliged to undergo
special treatment in a nursing home in London. For a
short time his condition was critical, but, once out of danger,
he made a rapid recovery and was able to resume his duties
at Sheerness by the end of the month. At various times
Sheerness was enlivened by the visits of foreign warships.
Amongst those which arrived for the celebration of the
coronation of King Edward VII were three Japanese
warships, which were for some weeks berthed in the
harbour under the command of Admiral Ijuin, Markham's
former midshipman in the *Triumph*. When congratulated
by his old Chief on his rapid promotion, he replied, "Had
it not been for you, sir, I should never have been an
Admiral." Prince Komatsu, a cousin of the Emperor,
also visited Chatham at this time. He afterwards telegraphed to his sovereign submitting Markham's name as
the recipient of a high Japanese Order. This Markham was
permitted to accept, and the Order of the Rising Sun was
conferred upon him.

In January, 1903, he attained the rank of full Admiral,
and in the following November he was made a Knight

Commander of the Bath. Though he fully appreciated this distinction, he always said that he considered it a far greater honour to be an Admiral in the British Navy.

In January, 1904, the appointment at the Nore terminated, and he received an official letter from the Admiralty expressing the satisfaction of their Lordships at the manner in which he had conducted the important duties of his command. In addition, Lord Walter Kerr wrote him a private letter: "Everything has gone well and efficiently, which is due to the constant and close attention of the Commander-in-Chief." Sir Albert and Lady Markham bade farewell to Sheerness amid many regrets on both sides. Their interest and labours had not been confined to the naval community, but had extended to the townspeople as well, and they had always been ready to help forward all the philanthropic efforts of the neighbourhood.

In 1906 Markham retired from the Navy, having reached the age limit. This severance from the Service he loved so well was a great trial to him; he still felt himself full of life and vigour and longed to be actively employed. He lived for the most part in London, latterly at 19, Queen's Gate Place, and was on the Board of Directors of several Companies, besides serving on various Committees.

In 1907 he took his wife and daughter for a trip to Canada and the United States, partly with a view to introducing them to his family in Wisconsin, and persuaded his elder brother and his wife to return with them on a six months' visit to England.

From 1886 Markham had been a keen Freemason. Freemasonry appealed to him as a beneficent factor in modern civilisation, and, in 1893, he was appointed by the Prince of Wales to be District Grand Master for Malta. In March, 1896, he was a Founder and the first Master of the Navy Lodge in London, and to the time of his death frequently attended the meetings of Grand Lodge.

On the outbreak of the European war, in August, 1914, Markham at once offered himself to the Admiralty, intimating that he was ready to waive his rank and serve in any capacity. But the call was for younger men, and the offer, though it received formal thanks, was not accepted. Markham, however, found an outlet for his energy in the treasurership of the Mine Sweepers' Fund, and in this cause he worked hard—too hard for his uncertain health—until a week before his death. When the first Canadian contingent was to arrive in England, Markham was invited to meet them at Plymouth, and from that day forward his house was always open to officers from Canada and Australia. Later, Lady Markham and other ladies started a Canadian Officers' Club in Prince's Gardens, called "The Rendezvous." The house was lent by Mrs Hamilton Fellows and Markham took the deepest interest in this undertaking.

The tragic death of his cousin, Sir Clements, was a great grief to Albert Markham. They had been devoted friends for many years and had always shared each other's interests. No one more suitable than Albert could have been chosen as his cousin's biographer, and he devoted himself to the task with characteristic thoroughness. It was his last literary work, and, in spite of the fact that it was undertaken when he was over seventy-four years of age, probably his best.

On October 23rd, 1918, Markham was at work as usual in connection with the Mine Sweepers' Fund. Almost immediately afterwards he was taken ill, and on the following Monday, October 28th, he passed peacefully away.

The funeral took place on November 1st. The first part of the Service was held at Brompton Parish Church, where he had attended as a boy, and twenty Admirals were present, including Viscount Jellicoe, Sir Edward Seymour, and Sir William May; also Sir Lewis Beaumont and Sir George Egerton, who, with Sir William May, had served with Markham in the Arctic Expedition of 1875. He was buried in Kensal Green Cemetery.

One portrait of Admiral Markham was presented by Lady Markham to Admiralty House, Chatham; another, painted by George Henry, A.R.A., was presented to the

Royal Geographical Society, and hangs in the map room, facing that of Sir Clements Markham.

Albert Markham was a man of many interests. He was a member of the Council of the Royal Geographical and Hakluyt Societies, of the Royal United Services Institution, and of the Navy Records Society. He had a ready pen and a gift of easy expression, and the record of his literary work together with a list of the new species discovered by him will be found in the Appendices.

His life was divided into two distinct parts by the *Victoria* disaster. Those who knew him only after that event knew a grave and at times silent man, lacking the boyish light-heartedness characteristic of his earlier years. "I always felt," wrote Viscount Jellicoe, "that I had in him a true friend, and his friendship was indeed worth having. His was a fine character and he never shewed that better than in the days which brought him so much sadness."

An intrepid explorer not unworthy of the tradition of Raleigh and Hudson, Markham displayed through a long and active life the quiet virtues of the Christian gentleman.

Appendix A

DESCRIPTION OF NEW SPECIES OF BIRDS FOUND
BY SIR ALBERT MARKHAM

Waved Albatross.

Diomedea irrorata sp. n.

Supra dorso medio et alis extus fuliginoso-fuscis, dorso antico
et uropygio albis nigro transverse variegatis: capite et cervice
tota albis, hac supra flavo lavata; subtus abdomine toto griseo-
fusco, albo praecipue in pectore et crisso, minutissime irrorato;
alis intus quoque albo et fusco variegatis; cauda fusca ad basin
alba; rostro flavido, mandibulae apice corneo, pedibus corylinis.
Long. toto 350; alae 20·5; caudae 5·5, rostri a rictu 6·2, tarsi 3·8,
dig. med. 5·1.

♂. Callao Bay, Peru, December 1881.

The Albatross described above seems quite distinct from any
hitherto known. It appears to come next to *D. melanophrys*,
having the bill similarly constructed (cf. Coues, *Proc. Acad. Phil.*
1866, pp. 186, 187), but the bill is much longer and the bird
larger in all its dimensions, except the tail, which is shorter
and more rounded. In coloration, too, there is great difference,
the upper back and rump being variegated with dusky and white
instead of pure white and the abdomen wholly dusky with
minute white freckles.

(Copy of original description by Osbert Salvin, M.A., F.R.S.,
in *Proc. Zool. Soc. London*, 1888, p. 430.)

Markham's Forked-tailed Petrel.

Cymochorea markhami sp. n.

Omnino fuliginosa fere unicolor, capite toto paulo plumbes-
centiore, tectricibus alarum dilutioribus, cauda profunde furcata,
rostro et pedibus nigerrimis. Long. toto 9·0, alae 6·9, caudae

rectr. med. 2·6, rectr. lat. 3·8, tarsi 1·0, dig. med. 1·1, rostri a rictu 1·0.

♀. Coast of Peru, lat. 19° 40′ S., long. 75° W., December 1881.

Obs. C. melaniae, Bp., apud Coues, certe similis, sed capite plumbescente, tarsis brevioribus forsan diversa.

This species is certainly very closely allied to *C. melania* of Bonaparte as described by Dr Coues (*Proc. Acad. Phil.* 1864, p. 76), but the head of that species is described as being darker on the sides and the region of the eyes as well as the upper parts generally. This can hardly be said to be the case in the present bird, the whole head and throat being rather paler than the body and with a plumbeous rather than a sooty tint.

As in *C. leucorrhoa* the wing-coverts are lighter than any part of the wing; but this species is obviously distinct, having a white rump, as is also the case with Mr Ridgway's *C. cryptoleucura*.

Captain Markham's collection contains two specimens of this species, which I propose to call after him. Both are marked as females. No species of this genus has been previously noted in these seas, *C. melania* being from the coast of Mexico.

(Copy of original description by Osbert Salvin in *Proc. Zool. Soc. London*, 1883, p. 430.)

Appendix B

BIBLIOGRAPHY OF SIR ALBERT MARKHAM'S WRITINGS

1873. *The Cruise of the "Rosario" amongst the New Hebrides and Santa Cruz Islands.* Exposing the recent atrocities connected with the kidnapping of natives in the South Seas. London, 1873.

1874. *A Whaling Cruise to Baffin's Bay and the Gulf of Boothia.* And an account of the rescue of the crew of the "Polaris." With an introduction by Rear-Admiral Sherard Osborn. London, 1874.

1878. *The Great Frozen Sea.* A personal narrative of the voyage of the "Alert" during the Arctic Expedition of 1875–6. London, 1878.

1879. *Northward Ho!* Including a narrative of Captain Phipps's expedition by a midshipman [Thomas Floyd]. London, 1879.

1880. *The Voyages and Works of John Davis, the Navigator.* Ed., with an Introduction and Notes, by Albert Hastings Markham. London, printed for the Hakluyt Society [No. 59], 1880.

1881. *A Polar Reconnaissance.* Being the Voyage of the "Isbjörn" to Novaya Zemlya in 1879. London, 1881.

1891. *Life of Sir John Franklin and the North-West Passage.* (The World's Great Explorers.) London, 1891

1917. *The Life of Sir Clements R. Markham.* London, 1917.

INDEX

M

C A M B R I D G E
Printed by W. LEWIS, M.A.
at the University Press

For EU product safety concerns, contact us at Calle de José Abascal, 56–1°,
28003 Madrid, Spain or eugpsr@cambridge.org.